The Hemmings Motor News Book of

PACKARDS

ISBN 0-917808-58-4

Library of Congress Card Number: 00-107815

One of a series of Hemmings Motor News Collector-Car Books. Other books in the series include:
The Hemmings Motor News Book of Cadillacs; The Hemmings Motor News Book of Chrysler Performance Cars; The Hemmings Motor News Book of Corvettes; The Hemmings Motor News Book of Hudsons; The Hemmings Motor News Book of Mustangs; The Hemmings Motor News Book of Pontiacs; The Hemmings Motor News Book of Postwar Fords; The Hemmings Motor News Book of Studebakers.

Hemmings Motor News
Collector Car Publications and Marketplaces
1-800-CAR-HERE (227-4373)
www.hemmings.com

The Hemmings Motor News Book of
PACKARDS

Editor-In-Chief
Terry Ehrich

Editor
Richard A. Lentinello

Designer
Nancy Bianco

Cover photo by Roy Query

This book compiles driveReports which have appeared in *Hemmings Motor News's Special Interest Autos* magazine (SIA) over the past 30 years. The editors at *Hemmings Motor News* express their gratitude to the following writers, photographers, and artists who made this book possible through their many fine contributions to *Special Interest Autos* magazine:

Robert Ackerson   Vince Manocchi
Arch Brown   Roy Query
Fred K. Fox   Michael G.H. Scott
George Hamlin   Jim Tanji
Tim Howley   Russell von Sauers
Bud Juneau   Bill Williams
John F. Katz   Josiah Work
Michael Lamm

We are also grateful to David Brownell and Michael Lamm, the editors under whose guidance these driveReports were written and published. We thank the Detroit Public Library, Gerald Farber, Image International, Jim Shulman, Cal Soest, and the Richard Teague Collection, who have graciously contributed photographs to *Special Interest Autos* magazine and this book.

CONTENTS

Special Interest Autos (SIA) magazine's back issues are referred to in this book by issue number. If in stock, copies may be purchased directly from Hemmings Motor News at 800-227-4373, ext. 550 or at www.hemmings.com/gifts.

LAST OF THE CLASSIC SIXES

drive report

PACKARD'S FIFTH SERIES

Originally published in Special Interest Autos #86, Mar.-Apr. 1985

by Arch Brown
photos by Vince Manocchi

YOU can actually peg the very day on which Packard moved into the preeminent sales position in the luxury car field. It was January 2, 1925. For on that day the company cut the price of its six-cylinder Second Series sedan from $3,375 to $2,585, with corresponding reductions posted for most other body styles. The new price structure pegged the Packard $610 lower than Cadillac, $1,310 below the new Pierce-Arrow Series 80, and a fat $2,215 under the least expensive Lincoln sedan.

The response was predictable. Packard production, which had already increased substantially with the introduction of the Single Six, back in 1920, shot dramatically ahead once again. Deliveries ran four months behind orders, and registrations of new Packards in 1925 were 68 percent ahead of the previous year, as thousands of motorists found themselves able, for the first time, to afford a Packard.

The original Single Six had been a very plain, even homely automobile, and its modest 54 horsepower certainly didn't create any wrinkles in the pavement. But it was a high-quality machine, powered by a notably smooth seven-bearing engine. Packard had referred to it as the First Series, which seems rather illogical since the company had been building cars since 1899!

Nor was it Packard's first six. As far back as 1911 there had been six-cylinder Packards, though from 1916 until the debut of the Single Six on September 1, 1920, the company had concentrated exclusively upon the production of a powerful, luxurious and very expensive 12-cylinder car called the Twin Six.

The Single Six, supplementing rather than supplanting the larger car, took Packard into a new market, that of the well-to-do "owner-driver" — as distinguished from the largely chauffeur-driven clientele that favored the Twin Six. By thus broadening the company's market the smaller car had been responsible for a sharp increase in Packard sales.

By the close of 1923 the First Series Six had been superseded by the Second Series, an improved and vastly more stylish variation on the same basic theme. Engine displacement remained at 241.6 cubic inches, however, and the horsepower was still rated at 54.

But in the meanwhile Colonel Jesse Vincent, Packard's vice president of engineering, had busied himself with the development of a new straight-eight, considered a radical configuration in

those days. Introduced in June 1923, the new Single Eight shared the 3-3/8 by 5-inch cylinder dimensions of the Single Six. Superior in a number of respects to the Twin Six, it was also much cheaper to produce; and within a few months the 12-cylinder car was dropped.

And here is where Packard's series designations become thoroughly confusing. For the Single Eight was referred to as a First Series car, while six months following its introduction the Second Series Single Six appeared. Thus Packard found itself in the peculiar position of producing, concurrently, the First Series Single Eight and the Second

Series Single Six — an insane practice in retrospect, and one that was continued until 1928.

Never mind; Packard went serenely about its business. The company in those days eschewed annual model changes. Whenever mechanical or styling modifications warranted such action, a new series was announced. Thus the lifetime of a given series might be as short as 11 months or as long as several years — always with the designation of the eight-cylinder car out of synch with that of the six! It was all rather bewildering if anyone stopped to think about it, but the typical Packard owner could scarcely care less, He was

Packard: Table of Prices and Weights
Fifth Series Six and Fourth Series Eight

	Price	Shipping weight
Series 526: 6-cylinder, 126-inch wheelbase		
Runabout, 4-passenger	$2,275	3,620 pounds
Phaeton, 5-passenger	$2,275	3,665 pounds
Sedan, 5-passenger	$2,285	4,000 pounds
Coupe, 2-4 passenger	$2,350	3,950 pounds
Convertible coupe, 4-passenger	$2,425	3,875 pounds
Series 533: 6-cylinder, 133-inch wheelbase		
Runabout, 4-passenger	$2,385	3,700 pounds
Phaeton, 5-passenger	$2,385	3,745 pounds
Touring, 7-passenger	$2,485	3,865 pounds
Coupe, 4-passenger	$2,685	4,000 pounds
Club sedan, 5-passenger	$2,685	4,085 pounds
Sedan, 7-passenger	$2,685	4,145 pounds
Limousine, 7-passenger	$2,785	4,205 pounds
Series 443: 8 Cylinder, 143-inch wheelbase		
Runabout, 4-passenger	$3,975	4,350 pounds
Phaeton, 5-passenger	$3,975	4,370 pounds
Touring, 7-passenger	$4,050	4,410 pounds
Coupe, 4-passenger	$4,950	4,635 pounds
Club sedan, 5-passenger	$4,950	4,710 pounds
Sedan, 7-passenger	$5,150	4,820 pounds
Limousine, 7 passenger	$5,250	4,860 pounds

Source: *Motor Age*, May 31, 1928

Above: Period accessories on driveReport car include sidemount mirrors and spotlights. Above right: driveReport car rides on 10-1/2-foot wheelbase, and that's the smallest wheelbase Packard offered in 1928! Below: Packard customers could also choose disc wheels instead of the wire or wooden variety. Bottom right: Plenty of room to store bottles of bathtub gin in the big door pockets.

PACKARD

driving a Packard; that was enough!

Exactly a month following the spectacular price reduction on the Second Series, the Third Series was announced. Styling was little changed, but a number of important mechanical modifications were made. The engine was bored to 3-1/2 inches, for starts, raising its displacement to 288.6 cubic inches and its horsepower to 61. The latter figure, by the way, was remarkably low. Pierce-Arrow, using the same cylinder dimensions in its Series 80 cars, rated its engine at 70 horsepower, and the Stutz Speedway Six — again employing a 3-1/2 by 5-inch bore and stroke — developed an impressive 80 horsepower!

Other modifications included increased bearing surfaces, and Bendix three-shoe internal four-wheel brakes replaced the earlier binders, which had employed external bands on the front wheels. The suspension was improved; connecting rods were drilled to provide lubrication to the wrist pins; and the Bijur chassis lubrication system, activated by a plunger on the dashboard, provided oil to 32 critical points. The frame of the Third Series car was heavier. Disc wheels replaced the earlier artillery type as standard equipment, and bumpers, a set of tools and a spare tire were furnished at no extra charge.

No previous Packard had ever approached the popularity of the Third Series Six, and it remained in production for 18 months.

A number of mechanical improvements characterized its Fourth Series successor, whose 11-month production run commenced on August 2, 1926. The

Packard Versus the Competition

	Packard 526	LaSalle 303	Pierce-Arrow 81
Price, f.o.b. factory (phaeton)	$2,275	$2,975	$3,100
Price, f.o.b. factory (convertible)	$2,425	$2,550	$3,350
Shipping weight (phaeton)	3,665 pounds	4,170 pounds	3,365 pounds
Shipping weight (convertible)	3,875 pounds	3,890 pounds	3,455 pounds
Wheelbase	126 inches	125 inches	130 inches
Engine	6-cylinder	V-8	6-cylinder
Bore and stroke	3½ x 5	3⅛ x 4.9375	3½ x 5
Displacement (cubic inches)	288.6	303.0	288.6
Hp @ rpm	82/3,200	30/3,000	75/3,000
Compression ratio	4.80:1	4.80:1	4.65:1
Valve configuration	L-head	L-head	L-head
Main bearings	7	3	7
Clutch	Double plate	Double plate	Single plate
Diameter	9¾ inches	9½ inches	11⅞ inches
Transmission	3-speed	3-speed	3-speed
Steering	Worm & sector	Worm & sector	Roller & sector
Rear axle	Semi-floating	¾ floating	Semi-floating
Final drive	Hypoid	Spiral bevel	Spiral bevel
Ratio	4.67:1	4.91:1	4.45:1
Brakes	Mechanical	Mechanical	Mechanical
Brake lining area (square inches)	308¾	280	240
Horsepower/c.i.d.	.284	.264	.260
Pounds/horsepower	44.7	52.1	44.9
Pounds/c.i.d.	12.7	13.8	11.7

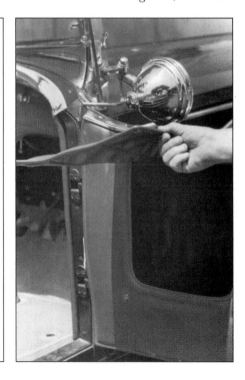

Left: *Radiator stoneguard is another factory accessory popular with restorers.* **Below:** *1928 was last year for drum-style headlamps on Packards.*

The Quintessential Packard Dealer: Earle C. Anthony

courtesy Cal Soest

It would be interesting to know how the townspeople reacted, that morning in 1897. For gliding silently along one of the town's main thoroughfares — at the breakneck speed of six miles an hour — was the very first horseless carriage ever to appear on the streets of Los Angeles!

There weren't many automobiles in those days, anywhere in the country. It was only four years, after all, since the Duryea brothers had run their first car. But things were beginning to stir in what was fated to become the country's most important industry. The Stanley brothers produced their first steamer that year, while Ransom E. Olds was busily putting together the Olds Motor Works. And out in Kokomo, Elwood Haynes and the Apperson brothers had already been building cars for three years!

The machine that was making its way around the streets of Los Angeles was a primitive affair, powered by a half-horsepower electric motor. its driver was the young man who had built it, a 17-year-old senior at Los Angeles High School. And although it eventually shattered itself on a yawning chuckhole when the youngster came careening down Beaudry Street hill, the little runabout represented an auspicious beginning for what would become a distinguished career in the transportation industry — and in several other fields of endeavor as well.

For the teenager was Earle C. Anthony, one of the most versatile individuals the automobile business has ever seen — and certainly one of the most imaginative! Consider just a few of his accomplishments:

• As an undergraduate at the University of California, just a few years after that wild ride down Beaudry Hill, "E.C.," as he was known to his friends, founded *The Pelican*, the delightfully risqué campus humor magazine that would entertain several generations of students at the Berkeley campus — and alternately titillate and irritate their elders.

• Armed with engineering degrees from both Cal and Cornell, Anthony — at the age of 24 —established a dealership in Los Angeles, handling Northern, Thomas Flyer, and

National Electric automobiles. A year later, in 1905, he obtained the coveted Packard franchise, and as long as Packard cars were produced, Earle C. Anthony continued to feature them. Not that he was exclusive about it; along the way, at various times, the Anthony agency sold Knox, Pope-Toledo, Stevens-Duryea, Scripps-Booth, Dort, Sheridan, Grant, Chalmers, Durant, Reo — and even Buick and Cadillac cars! And when hard times diminished the demand for Packards in the early 1930s, Anthony took on Hudson and Terraplane.

• When a city ordinance required that gasoline be sold only at "garages," Earle C. Anthony put a canopy over his curbside pumps, and the modern service station was born. Ultimately he had 250 such units, and when the chain was sold it became the nucleus of Standard Stations, Incorporated.

• In 1908, not yet out of his twenties, he founded the Los Angeles Motor Car Dealers Association, one of the earliest organizations of its kind in the world.

• In 1913, using stretched Packard touring cars, Anthony formed the El Dorado Motor Stage Lines, to carry passengers between Los Angeles and Bakersfield over the infamous "grapevine" route. In time this operation became known as the Pickwick Stage, one of the components of today's Greyhound Lines.

• An inveterate tinkerer, "E.C." became interested in radio, and in 1921 he founded station KFI, Los Angeles. Five years later that station was credited with performing the first successful remote control broadcast in radio history! And in 1929 he organized another station, KECA, devoted exclusively to the classical music he loved.

• On a trip to France, Earle C. Anthony became enchanted with neon lights, then unknown in the United States. Upon his return he had yet another surprise for his fellow Los Angelenos, for on the corner of Seventh and Flower Streets he erected a sign on which was emblazoned the name PACKARD. It was the first neon sign ever seen in this country.

• Sensing that traffic in and out of San Francisco would inevitably outstrip the capacity of the familiar ferryboats, Anthony — who had dealerships in both San Francisco and Oakland — mobilized the area's automobile distributors to push the campaign for a bridge across the bay. It took ten years of dedicated effort, but in 1936 that bridge became a reality.

• Along the way he built some of the most magnificent automobile showrooms ever constructed. Palaces they were, designed by the famed California architect Bernard Maybeck.

• A man of many hobbies, "E.C." became interested in photography. And when he was unable to buy a motion picture camera in the early days, he designed and built his own!

• His love of music included, in addition to the classics, the traditional melodies of Hawaii. He wrote the lyrics to a number of Hawaiian-style songs, some of which — "Coral Isle," for instance — achieved widespread popularity.

Probably no other automobile distributor has ever made an impact on his community and his state to compare with that of Earle C. Anthony, the quintessential Packard dealer. It must have been a great sorrow to him that he outlived the car with which he was so long and so intimately identified. For by the time Anthony died, on August 6, 1961, the Packard lived only in the memories of those of us who love fine automobiles.

Above: Packard phaeton and roadsters sported a raked windshield while closed cars and convertibles used a vertical-style windshield. *Right:* Three-lens taillamp was used on both sixes and eights.

PACKARD

hypoid differential was adopted, for instance. And a high-turbulence cylinder head with increased compression combined with improvements in manifolding and carburetion to boost the horsepower from 61 to 81! Production was increased slightly, but the factory still ran several weeks behind customer orders. Profits, meanwhile, rolled in at a record rate. Packard was riding high.

Had any other manufacturer introduced two new lines of cars on July 1, 1927, they would surely have been billed as 1928 models. But of course that wasn't Packard's way of going about such matters. The new cars were titled simply the Fourth Series Eight and the Fifth Series Six. Like the Second, Third and Fourth Series — and even the First Series during the latter part of its long production run — the Fifth Series was available on either of two wheelbases, 126 and 133 inches, with a total of 12 body styles available.

To compound whatever confusion there may have been in the matter of model nomenclature, on January 3,

Driving Impressions

With the top up, the convertible looks as snug as a steel-top coupe.

Years ago, when the movies wanted to portray the sound of an expensive automobile, it was the Packard transmission whose melodic whine was heard on the soundtrack. And so, although we had little opportunity in those earlier times to drive a Packard car, there was a wave of instant nostalgia when we slid behind the wheel of Clarence Blixt's Packard convertible and began to run it through the gears!

The clutch is as smooth as butter, and gearshift action is relatively easy — but a little tricky. Very precise timing, as well as double-clutching, is required if clashing the gears is to be avoided. Rapid shifts are, to say the very least, inadvisable!

Acceleration, for a heavy car with a relatively small engine, is really pretty good. Not that you'll chirp the tires with this car, but it gets off the line sufficiently quickly to keep up with the general stream of traffic.

Steering, as might be expected of such a heavy machine, is rather heavy. Still, this characteristic is noticeable chiefly when

the car is being parallel-parked. And the brakes, while they require a good deal of pedal pressure, are quite satisfactory, even for driving in heavy traffic.

The ride is marvelously smooth for a car of this vintage. With Clarence at the wheel we had no trouble taking legible notes on a clipboard held in our lap. Even railroad tracks are handled with aplomb. The seat is especially comfortable, though its fixed

Not nearly as sporty as a roadster with top down, but riders get just as much fresh air.

position doesn't provide quite as much leg room as we'd like.

On our drive through the San Joaquin Valley, south of the Blixt home in Escalon, there was no opportunity to test the Packard's hill-climbing proclivities. But Clarence reports that it takes the Interstate 80 climb over Donner Summit with consummate ease! Traveling down the flat valley highways we found 50 miles an hour to be an easy cruising speed, with lots of reserve on tap. The car rolls a bit on hard cornering, but it goes where it's pointed.

This is a nicely equipped automobile,

with a number of features that are both unusual and appealing. For instance, a remote control latch for the rumble seat is hidden inside the locking package compartment located behind the front seat. There's a back-up light among the three pods in the taillamp assembly, a most unusual feature in 1928. And the battery case is found at the rear of the right front fender, a much more convenient location than the customary placement in those days, under the front seat.

The dashboard is well equipped. In addition to the usual instruments — speedometer/odometer, oil pressure and ampere gauges, a hydrostatic fuel-level indicator — there's a fine Waltham clock and a handy map light. A cigar lighter reels out on a long cord; that's how it was done in the twenties. And the once-ubiquitous Boyce Moto-Meter was enjoying its last ride atop the Packard radiator cap. With the coming of the Sixth Series, Packard would join most of the rest of the industry in providing a temperature gauge on the dash panel.

The reader will have gathered that we like this car, and indeed we do. But it shares with a great many other automobiles of its day one irritating inconvenience. The opening between the seat and the door frame is too small for any but the daintiest of pedal extremities. There is simply no graceful way to get into — or especially out of — this car, if you happen to have big feet!

But that's a problem that a person can live with. And certainly one could live with a fine car like the Fifth Series Packard. With pleasure!

1928, Packard introduced a second Fourth Series Single Eight. They called it the "Custom," the previous car having been known as the "Deluxe." Exactly why this revised model wasn't dubbed the Fifth Series Eight is not clear, for it incorporated some fairly substantial changes. The most obvious was the use of chrome-plated brightwork, replacing the previous nickel finish. Other styling modifications were of a minor nature, but there were some significant mechanical improvements: twin-coil ignition, for instance, and an improved cylinder lubrication system. Unfortunately, at the same time the magnificent hard maple steering wheel was replaced with the ordinary hard rubber type.

But of course Packard's production was concentrated chiefly upon its six-cylinder car. Output of the Fourth Series Single Eight was deliberately held to 500 units per month, a figure exceeded 6-1/2 times over by production of the Fifth Series sixes.

And what a handsome car this moderately priced Packard was! Smoother of line than the Fourth Series, it featured a short, cadet-type sun visor in place of the long roof overhang of the previous car. Smaller wheels — 20 inches instead of 23 — gave it a lower, more graceful profile. The open models — phaeton and roadster — presented a sleek, modern appearance with their sloping windshields and sweeping lines. The closed cars, including the convertible, clung to the traditional "vertical" styling, but their classic beauty nevertheless ranked them among the best-looking cars on the road!

With the mid-1927 introduction of the LaSalle, Cadillac had commenced to close the sales gap. Still, Packard's 1928 sales were comfortably ahead of Cadillac and LaSalle combined. In part the explanation doubtless had to do with price, for in 1928 a Packard sedan could be had for a couple of hundred dollars less than a LaSalle — a difference of something like nine percent of the purchase price. And of course the Packard name had a magic that couldn't be matched by the upstart from Cadillac Division!

But the men of Packard were realists. They knew that the day of the six-cylinder luxury car was about over, and Colonel Vincent and his staff were busying themselves with the development of a new, smaller "eight." Billed as the Sixth Series Standard Eight, it replaced the Fifth Series on August 1, 1928, and it paced Packard to greater sales than ever before.

For our driveReport we used two Fifth Series Packards. The phaeton that is our principal photographic subject was built in 1927, while the convertible coupe from which our driving impres-

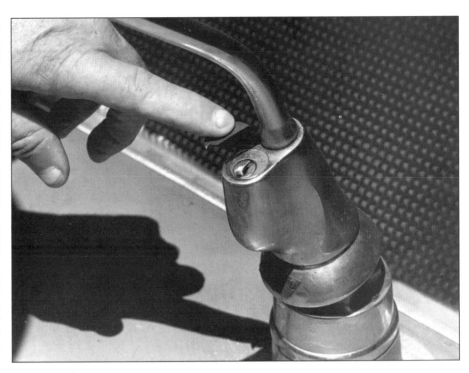

Above: Transmission lock served as early anti-theft device. *Left:* Levers control light switch and throttle. *Below left:* Original dealer's selling plate is mounted on dash. *Below:* Packard boasts symmetrical, understated instrument panel. *Bottom:* Driving position is comfortable; steering wheel is a bit high for shorter drivers.

specifications

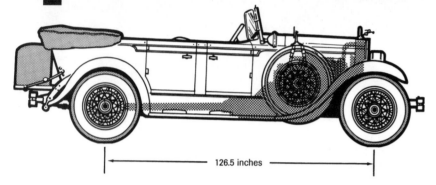

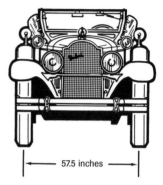

126.5 inches

57.5 inches

Packard 526 (Fifth Series)

Price	Phaeton: $2,275; Convertible: $2,425 f.o.b. factory with standard equipment
Standard equipment	Front and rear bumpers, shock absorbers, automatic windshield wipers, spare tire lock, cigar lighter, Waltham clock, Bijur automatic lubrication system

ENGINE

Type	6-cylinder cast en bloc
Bore and stroke	3½ inches x 5 inches
Displacement	288.6 cubic inches
Max bhp @ rpm	82 @ 3,200
Max torque @ rpm	n/a
Compression ratio	4.80:1
Valve config.	L-head
Main bearings	7
Induction system	Single updraft carburetor, vacuum feed
Lubrication system	Pressure to mains, rods, camshaft, wristpins, timing case
Exhaust system	Single
Electrical system	6-volt

CLUTCH

Type	Double plate
Diameter	11 inches
Actuation	Mechanical, foot pedal

TRANSMISSION

Type	3-speed selective, floor-mounted lever
Ratios: 1st	3.35:1
2nd	1.75:1
3rd	1.00:1
Reverse	4.18:1

DIFFERENTIAL

Type	Hypoid
Ratio	4.33:1
Drive axles	Semi-floating

STEERING

Type	Worm and sector
Turns, lock to lock	3
Ratio	n/a
Turning radius	23 feet

BRAKES

Type	Internal 4-wheel mechanical
Drum diameter	14 inches
Total braking area	308.75 square inches

CHASSIS & BODY

Frame	8-inch channel iron with tubular cross members
Body construction	Composite, steel over hardwood framing
Body styles	Phaeton and convertible coupe

SUSPENSION

Front	38-inch x 2-inch semi-elliptic leaf springs, solid axle
Rear	56-inch x 2¼-inch semi-elliptic leaf springs, solid axle
Tires	32 x 6.00
Wheels	Disc (optional wires on phaeton)

WEIGHTS AND MEASURES

Wheelbase	126½ inches
Overall length	189 inches (including bumpers)
Overall height	78 inches
Overall width	68½ inches
Front tread	57½ inches
Rear tread	57½ inches
Ground clearance	8.21875 inches
Shipping weights	3,665 (phaeton); 3,875 (convertible)

CAPACITIES

Crankcase	7 quarts
Cooling system	21 quarts
Fuel tank	22 gallons

Packard Market Penetration:

1925	0.8 percent
1926	0.9 percent
1927	1.2 percent
1928	1.4 percent

Was there ever a more distinctive, attractive radiator design on any American car than Packard's in the twenties and thirties?

PACKARD

sions were recorded left the factory in 1928. In comparing these cars to their competitors, however, we are treating both as 1928 models, since the production run of the Fifth Series coincided roughly with the 1928 model year as defined by most other manufacturers.

Little is known of the early history of Charles "Cy" Painter's handsome phaeton, except that the metal plate affixed to the dash reveals it to have been sold by a San Jose, California, Packard dealer. Cy bought the car in 1971 from a collector in Campbell, California, a San Jose suburb. It had been partially restored and was in excellent mechanical condition at that time, except that a

hopelessly plugged up radiator created chronic problems of overheating. Painter promptly re-cored the radiator, transforming the Packard from a headache into an excellent tour and — especially — parade car.

Other than correcting the radiator problem, it has only been necessary for Cy Painter to dress the car up a bit. It wasn't even necessary to do anything about the paint, which is dark green with black fenders, set off by yellow pinstriping and yellow wheels. Some of the brightwork had to be replated, however, and Cy added a stone guard and a pair of side mirrors. He has a set of the standard disc wheels, but in Cy's view the phaeton looks better with the optional wires. Also in Painter's possession is the accessory rear-compartment wind-shield, but this was omitted for Vince Manocchi's photo session on the grounds that it detracts

10

a little from the car's sporting appearance.

It's a magnificent automobile — roomy, comfortable, and beautifully finished. First cabin, all the way! We were especially fascinated by the three small, locking cabinets, fitted into the back of the front seat. This car was built, of course, at the height of the Prohibition Era, the time of hip flasks and bathtub gin, and one can't help speculating on the purpose for which those three little cabinets may have been intended!

Clarence Blixt's convertible was retained by its original owner for no more than a year before being traded back to the Chicago dealership from which it had been purchased, in exchange for a Sixth Series car. It was then bought by Forrest Jackson, a mechanic at the agency, and it remained in Jackson's possession until 1948.

At that point Jackson, who had long since moved west, sold the car to a Riverside, California, collector named Clinton Reynolds. Reynolds was not one for restoring his cars, and at the time of his death in 1963 the Packard showed all too clearly the ravages of 15 years spent in open storage. But at least it had been saved from the wreckers! At the estate sale the convertible was purchased by Roger Abbott, who devoted his spare time over the next several years to its restoration. Eventually, Abbott turned the Packard over to a Santa Ana, California, restoration shop for painting and the finishing touches.

At this point Clarence Blixt, an Escalon, California, Packard lover, entered the picture. The final re-assembly of the convertible had been repeatedly postponed due to Roger Abbott's other commitments, and in 1969 he finally decided to offer it for sale. With Bill Lauer of Packards International acting as the intermediary, the purchase was arranged,

Above: Top-down visibility is superb. With top and curtains installed it's terrible. Below left: Sturdy six first appeared in 1920. Below right: Scads of stowage room behind the front seat, too.

and Blixt spent two weeks of his vacation putting the Packard back together again before bringing it home to Escalon, 350 miles to the north.

For several seasons the blue convertible was a familiar sight on the con-cours circuit, picking up two first-place trophies at Silverado (1970 and 1972) and a number of other awards. But in recent years Clarence and Elizabeth Blixt have enjoyed using this lovely automobile, the oldest of their five fine Packards. taking it on tours to places as far distant as Lake Tahoe. Writing in the *Packards International* publication some years ago. Clarence commented, "Although I am a white-knuckled driver when operating this fine automobile, I deeply appreciate its good and faithful performance."

And that, at least in part, is what a Packard is all about! ☙

Acknowledgements and Bibliography
Richard Burns Carson, The Olympian Cars; *Jerry Heasley,* The Production Figure Book for US Cars; *Beverly Rae Kimes (ed.),* Great Cars and Grand Marques; *Motor Age (various Issues); G. Marshall Naul,* The Specification Book for US Cars, 1920-1929; *New York Times, August 8, 1961; Packards International publication, Summer 1973 and Summer 1976; Ralph Stein,* The American Automobile; *Robert E. Turnquist,* The Packard Story.

Our thanks to Ralph Dunwoodle, Sun Valley, Nevada; Harold Gibson, Pasadena, California; Dan Luckenbill, archivist, University of California at Los Angeles; Carol Mauck, secretary, Packards International, Santa Ana, California: John Padmos, DDS, Modesto, California; Telford Work, Pacific Palisades, California. Special thanks to Clarence Blixt, Escalon, California; Charles "Cy" Painter, Laguna Beach, California.

How Good Is It, Really?

We've had occasion, in the recent past, to drive — in addition to the Fifth Series Packard — both of its major competitors. So comparisons are inevitable.

All three cars — Packard, LaSalle, and Pierce-Arrow (you'll find the latter in *SIA* #83) — are very nice, thoroughly competent automobiles. Within the context of their time, they're comfortable, easy to drive, dependable, and more than adequate in their performance.

It's not easy to make a fair comparison when the cars aren't being driven consecutively on the same day, so we'll withhold any comment with respect to acceleration, hill-climbing ability and the like. But each car has a strong suit that stands out in our memory:

• The gearshift action of the LaSalle is clearly the best of the lot. Cadillac Division really knew how that game was played, for the transmission is very easy to shift without clashing.

• The Pierce-Arrow, on the other hand, is finished and trimmed a little better than either of its rivals — as befits the car that was, initially, the most expensive of the trio. A case in point is the beautiful hardwood steering wheel, which makes the hard rubber numbers on the other cars look cheap by comparison.

• But it was the Packard that was the stellar value of the group, especially in the phaeton body style. For although there was no compromise of Packard's traditional quality, the Series 526 phaeton was priced, in 1928, $700 below the corresponding model from LaSalle and $825 below the Pierce-Arrow!

In the purchase of an automobile you always pay for what you get. Whether you always get what you pay for may be quite another matter, of course. But in the case of the Fifth Series Packard, the buyers did indeed get a lot of car, a lot of quality, a lot of luxury, and a lot of value for their money!

With trunk on the back, this "little" Packard measures over 20 feet long.

1930 PACKARD 734 SPEEDSTER

AMERICA'S FIRST MUSCLE CAR?

VIEWED from overhead, a taper-tailed roadster slashes diagonally across the page. "The thrill of soaring power unleashed at a toe-touch is his who drives the Speedster," sang the elegant italic text. "[But] due to its instant response, caution must be exercised in using the Speedster's greatest power only under the most favorable highway conditions."

The old brochure beckons from another time, balancing its heady promise of performance with a quaint plea for caution. Yet the automobile it advertises anticipated a more modern trend by at least three decades. To build the 734 Speedster, Packard souped up the big straight eight from the 740/745 series cars and stuffed it into a mid-size 733 chassis. The 734 was a muscle car, pure and simple.

Fewer than two dozen exist today, and of those, the pineapple-yellow example on these pages has led a more interesting existence than most. Originally purchased in New York and shipped to

by John F. Katz
photos by the author

Hawaii, it spent more than a quarter-century in the islands before making its way inexorably eastward, finally settling at the home of Billy and Helen Vaccaro in northern New Jersey.

Packard's famed chief engineer Col. Jesse Vincent himself hatched the Speedster concept. Sometime after opening the Packard Proving Grounds in Utica, he built an experimental model using a Fourth Series chassis and a fish-tail racing body. Col. Charles Lindbergh topped 100 mph in this car while visiting the Proving Grounds in 1928.

Meanwhile, Packard engineers prepared a line of production Speedsters for 1929. That year, Packard replaced its six-cylinder cars with two new "Standard Eight" models: the 626 (for

Sixth Series, 126-inch wheelbase) and 633 (same chassis stretched to 133 inches), both powered by a 90-bhp, 319.2-cubic-inch straight eight. To create the "626 Speedster," however, the engineers took the 384.8-cubic-inch power plant from Packard's 640 "Deluxe Eight" and 645 "Custom Eight" models, boosted its output from 105 to 130 bhp with a high-lift camshaft and a high-compression head, and installed it in the relatively light 626 chassis. Despite the "Speedster" designation, Packard offered sedan and phaeton versions as well as a rumble-seat roadster. With a 3.31:1 rear, open models could pass the magic 100 mph mark.

The 626 Speedster succeeded technically, but not aesthetically. Built on a chassis length normally reserved for sedans and coupes, the phaeton lacked room, and the roadster looked more stubby than speedy. Packard stretched its shortest chassis by an inch and a half for 1930, renaming it 726. But the 1930 734 Speedster would ride on the

Driving Impressons

Surprisingly. Billy Vaccaro's Packard Speedster has never been restored. Guy Slaughter remembered seeing an Eighth-Series mechanical fuel pump on the car in 1952, which someone subsequently replaced with a modem electrical unit. Billy said that some wiring had been replaced as well, but there's no sign that the car has ever been apart It's the very best kind of original-condition automobile: a bit worn in spots but sufficiently sound for driving.

Despite the small, square doors — and with the canvas top up — I can still squeeze into the driver's seat more easily than I can in most vintage speedsters. The seats themselves feel firm and reasonably comfortable, and sit higher off the floor than I expected. They don't adjust, but everything fits my five-foot, nine-inch frame just fine. And the staggered seating arrangement really does provide some extra elbow room.

A key at the far right of the dashboard switches on the ignition and the fuel pump, then a toe-tap on the starter brings the old engine rumbling to life. I had expected Packard's characteristic ghostly silence, but instead the Speedster plays a symphony of happy straight-eight sounds. This is, after all, a sporting machine.

First gear — the "low-low" gear, Billy calls it — is a creeper, "strictly for getting you out of trouble." The shift pattern reflects this; instead of being ahead to the left, opposite second, first is *back* and to the left, *alongside* second, and separated from it by a rather strong spring. Reverse lies ahead and to the left, exactly where a traditional three-speed would put it. A person could drive this car for months and never find more than three forward gears.

Swung down into second (which is "first" for most purposes), the long gear lever cozies up to my thigh. The clutch travels a long way up from the floorboard, but the throttle requires very little effort, and the old Packard launches itself off the line with smoothness and authority. Then it's down with the clutch, ahead with the shifter...and the clash of straight-cut gears reminds me how I've come to take the blessings of synchromesh for granted. We've nearly coasted to a stop before I coax the lever into third — but the big straight-eight has little difficulty moving off from rest in that gear, either.

This time I remember to shift *very slowly*, and the gear lever glides into fourth with a wondrously clean and sensuously mechanical clunk-thunk. The flapping canvas above and the chugga-chugga of the engine drown out the gear noise as we accelerate. The engine's high gear flexibility and terrific throttle response would do credit to a modern car.

With a wheelbase 16 inches longer than that of a new Lincoln Town Car, the 734 doesn't maneuver well around tight, 90-degree corners. Out on the open road, however, the Packard is surprisingly nimble. It leans into turns and tries to understeer, but a gentle squeeze on the throttle settles it nicely into a more neutral attitude. Years of wear have reduced on-center steering feel, but once in a turn the steering feeds back all the needed information, with absolutely none of the kicking, shimmying, or other bad habits that can afflict cars of that era.

We found only one road that unsettled the Packard: an undulating, heavily crowned two-lane that sent its nose lolling rhythmically from side to side. Otherwise, it rode flat, smooth, and quiet. The brakes are surprisingly strong, requiring a bit of effort by modern standards but fairly little for their own time. On a long, straight road, or on one with wide, sweeping curves, the Speedster could cover ground pretty quickly.

Back in my office, listening to a tape I'd made in the Packard, I realized that something was missing. I rewound the tape and listened again. Where were all the squeaks, the rattles, the loose banging sounds that one almost expects in an old, original-condition car?

After 60 years of driving, Billy Vaccaro's Packard still feels and sounds as solid as if it had just left the factory. I can't think of a higher tribute to an automobile than that.

1930 PACKARD

*Top: Long, sweeping lines are typical of Packards from this era. **Above:** Graceful C.M. Hall headlamps and sidelamps subtly echo Packard radiator shape.*

The 1930 Packards Compared

Model	726	733	740	745	734
Base price	$2,375	$2,425	$3,190	$4,585	$5,200
Wheelbase, in.	127.5	134.5	140.5	145.5	134.5
Displacement, cu. in.	319.2	319.2	384.8	384.8	384.8
Horsepower	90	90	106	106	145*
Weight, lb.**	4,265	4,325	4,560	4,805	4,580
Tire size	6.00x20	6.50x20	7.00x19	7.00x19	6.50x19

*125 with 4.85:1 head
**with lightest available sedan body

longer, 133-1/2-inch 733 chassis.

The engineers retained the 6.0:1 head from the 626 Speedster (the standard 4.85:1 head remained as an option), but developed new, separate intake and exhaust manifolds, the latter cooled by fins cast and then machined into its upper surface. They enlarged the exhaust valves to 1 5/8 inches (the same size as the intakes) and provided a muffler cut-out for even freer breathing at speed. And while the Speedster engine still borrowed its bore and stroke dimensions from the senior Packards, the Speedster block casting itself was unique, featuring larger, angled ports. Initially, the company announced axle ratios of 3.31 and 4.66, but apparently replaced the latter with a more realistic 4.07 when production began.

Packard relocated some of the 733's frame members to accommodate the larger engine, and specified the Deluxe Eight/Custom Eight (designated 740/745 for 1930) rear axle as well as the larger cars' 16x2-inch forged brake drums — with cooling fins unique to the Speedster. The 734 also borrowed its headlamps, running lights, fenders, and bumpers from the 740/745, leading some writers to erroneously conclude that the Speedsters were built on shortened Deluxe Eight frames.

Packard's own custom shop built most of the bodies, which measured about three inches lower and narrower

Left: *Access to the taper tail is limited.* **Below:** *Triple lens taillamp also has radiator shape as part of design.* **Bottom:** *Fuel filler hides in valley on left side.*

than those of other 1930 Packards. Still, the longer wheelbase allowed for a roomier sedan and phaeton, a handsome four-passenger Victoria, and — the most popular Speedster of them all — a stunning, boat-tailed, stagger-seat roadster that Packard humbly called a "Runabout." (Later in the year, the company revived the rumble-seat Roadster, but probably built no more than seven.)

Samuel Northrup Castle chose the Runabout style when he bought his new Speedster in New York. We can only presume that one of Castle's many business interests had brought him to the East Coast. He lived most of his life in Honolulu, where he had been born in 1880. An old newspaper clipping cites his parents as "builders of early Hawaii," and Castle himself became one of the leading construction engineers and industrialists in the islands. His first cousin, William R. Castle, served as Undersecretary of State under President Hoover. Castle once told fellow Packard enthusiast Guy Slaughter that he had known Jesse Vincent personally.

After he died in 1959, Castle's obituaries portrayed him as a bright-minded old man dressed in plus-fours, cruising the islands in his vintage cars. A black Model A Duesenberg and the 734 Speedster were his favorites. Apparently, he kept his entire fleet in an open carport at his home in the Manoa Valley section of Honolulu.

Castle had suffered a stroke around 1956, and although he continued to attend the board meetings of at least six different corporations, his infirmity may have convinced him to sell some of his cars. Kamehameha schoolteacher Jay Hyde bought the 734 Speedster in

---

Road & Track Tests The New Packard.... Road & Track?

The last real Packards had rolled off the line two summers before, leaving the proud old nameplate uncomfortably pinned to an awkwardly fish-mouthed Studebaker. Still, *Road & Track* published a road test of the "new" Packard 734 Speedster — in March 1958.

The article was one of a series of "Classic Tests" that the magazine ran in those days. Written in the present tense — as if the editors had forsaken their MG's for time machines — the Packard 734 test was even datelined "July, 1930." It was accompanied by *Road & Track*'s standard specification and performance chart filled in for a 734 Phaeton with a "4.00" (presumably the 4.07) axle. The figures presented, according to an editor's note, represented "an accurate synthesis of material published during the time the car was produced."

Acceleration, seconds
0-30 mph 5.8

0-40 mph 9.4
0-50 mph...12.3
0-60 mph...17.2
0-70 mph...23.2
0-80 mph...29.3
standing-start 1/4-mile 20.5

Performance
Top speed ....92.5 mph
Fuel consumption ....1014 mpg
Coefficient of drag...........................0.65

The magazine cited no specific sources, but the numbers do look reasonable. The accompanying text praised the Packard as "a remarkably easy machine to drive... extremely smooth and quiet at all times... It rides beautifully and seems singularly free from the all too common troubles of front-end shake, shimmy, and tramp."

After driving a 734 Speedster ourselves we can attest that that much. at least, is true.

illustrations by Russell von Sauers, The Graphic Automobile Studio
© copyright 1991, Special Interest Autos

specifications

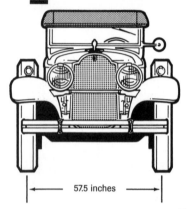

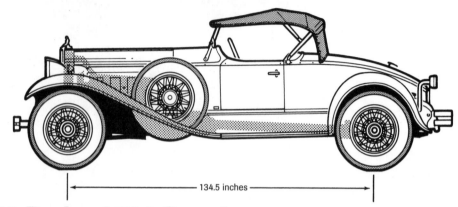

57.5 inches

134.5 inches

1930 Packard 734 Speedster

Base price $5,200
Options on dR car: Radiator stone guard, "Adonis" radiator ornament

ENGINE
Type	Straight 8
Bore & stroke	3½"x5"
Displacement	348.8 cu. in.
Compression ratio	6.00:1
Bhp (gross) @ rpm	145 @ 3,400
Torque @ rpm	290 @ 1,600*
Taxable hp	39.2
Valve gear	L-head
Valve lifters	Solid with roller tappets
Main bearings	9
Carburetor	1 Detroit Lubricator 2-bbl
Fuel system	Originally Stewart vacuum tank with crankshaft-driven booster pump; now has electric fuel pump
Lubrication system	Pressure
Exhaust system	Single
Electrical system	6 volt

TRANSMISSION
Type	4-speed manual
Ratios: 1st	3.14:1
2nd	1.84:1
3rd	1.38:1
4th	1.00:1
Clutch	10" long double disc

DIFFERENTIAL
Type	Hypoid
Ratio	3.31:1

STEERING
Type	Worm & sector
Turns lock-to-lock	n.a.
Ratio	15:1
Turning circle	48 feet

BRAKES
Type	Four-wheel mechanical, finned drums
Size	16.0x2.0"
Swept area	402.1 square inches

CONSTRUCTION
Type	Body-on-frame
Body	Steel over wood frame
Frame	Steel channel
Body style	2-seat boattail roadster

SUSPENSION
Front	Beam axle, semi-elliptic springs
Rear	Live axle, semi-elliptic springs
Shock absorbers	Houdaille hydraulic
Wheels	19-inch wire with lock rings
Tires	Martin 19x6.50

WEIGHTS AND MEASURES
Wheelbase	134.5"

Overall length	n.a.
Overall width	n.a.
Overall height	n.a.
Front track	57.5"
Rear track	59.0"
Ground clearance	7.9"
Dry weight	4,295 lb.
Curb weight (with water and gas)	4,520 lb.

CAPACITIES
Crankcase	10 quarts
Transmission	2 quarts
Rear axle	3.5 quarts
Steering gear	1.1 pints
Chassis lubricator tank	1 quart
Cooling system	6.5 gallons
Fuel tank	25 gallons

CALCULATED DATA
Bhp/c.i.d.	0.38
Lb./bhp	31.2
Lb./c.i.d.	11.7
P.S.I. (brakes)	11.2

PRODUCTION
Total 1930 734 Speedster	118**
"Speedster Runabout" only	39**

*estimated by *Road & Track*, March 1958
**estimated by Packard enthusiast R. Bruce Grinager

All 734 series cars were of quite limited production and had extra attention devoted to their styling and construction beyond Packard's usual lofty standards.

1930 PACKARD

1957. An avid Packard collector who used a '35 sedan as a daily driver, Hyde had learned of Castle's Packard through Slaughter. Years later, in a letter to current owner Vaccaro, Hyde recalled Castle's sadness as he parted with the car he had driven for 27 years. "He had tears in his eyes," he wrote, "[and] wouldn't let our three little kids near it!!"

After he brought it home, however, Hyde let his entire family enjoy the Speedster. "Our son would ride in front of his mother in the front," he continued, "and the two girls would be facing aft in the trunk." But he returned to his native Oregon shortly afterward, taking the Speedster with him, and then sold it to dealer Leo Gephart in the mid-seventies. It passed through several other owners before Vaccaro, then living on Staten Island, acquired it in 1985.

Billy believes that the leafy-green hue of the fenders is pretty close to original, but a peek inside the doorjambs reveals that the body was once the color of pea soup. Castle had painted it an unimaginative tan by the time Hyde bought it from him in 1957. Although the current paintwork, applied sometime in the seventies, is cracking in spots, Billy "sort of likes" the color combination. "I think I might [restore it]," he mused. "I'm mentally planning it.... It's too nice not to. But then it's too nice to restore."

Packard stopped building 734 Speedsters at the end of April 1930. Earlier that month Packard President Alvan Macauley had fed brave words to the

Right: Detroit Lubricator carburetor was standard. Far right: There's better than average leg room. Below: Stomp on this button for the cutout. Below right: Lovely up front, dramatic in the back. Bottom: Lots of stowage space in the doors.

1930 PACKARD

press about weathering "irregularities of the market" — while he laid off around 2,000 employees, cut remaining salaries, and reduced the factory work week from six days to five. A fast and flashy speedster just didn't suit the times.

The company hadn't advertised the 734 anyway. and built very few. Through statistical analysis of surviving body and chassis numbers, Speedster owner R. Bruce Grinager has estimated a total production of only 113 units — plus maybe five more custom-bodied cars. We've found higher estimates, but none over 150. Eleven of the boattail Runabouts survive, along with five phaetons, two sedans, two rumbleseat roadsters, two custom-bodied specials, and a lone Victoria.

Still, the Speedster left a legacy. Packard applied the 734 block, with its larger, free-breathing ports, to the entire Packard line in 1931, raising the rated horsepower of the Standard Eight to 100 and that of the Deluxe Eight to 120. Then, in 1932, stylist Ed Macauley (Alvan's son) assembled a new Speedster prototype using a surplus 734 boattail body. Still sporting full running boards; small, square doors; and large, round wheel openings, this beautiful automobile nonetheless anticipated the 12-cylinder 1106 Speedster of 1934. ◈

Acknowledgements and Bibliography
Richard Burns Carson, The Olympian Cars; *Athel F. Denham, "Packard Offers Speedster Series With Shorter Wheelbase,"* Automotive Industries, *January 25,1930; Beverly Rae Kimes and Henry Austin Clark, Jr.,* Standard Catalog of American Cars 1805-1942; *Beverly Rae Kimes and Richard Langworth (editors),* Packard: A History of the Motor Car and the Company; *Ed Martin, "1930 Packard 734 Speedster Sedan: The Find of a Lifetime."* Car Collector and Car Classics, *August 1987; Smith Hempstone Oliver, "Packard 734 Speedster."* Road & Track, *March 1958; "Packard Brings Out the Speedster Line,"* Motor, *February 1930; "Packard Offers Speedster in Four Body Styles,"* Motor World Wholesale, *February 1930; "Classic Packard 734 Phaeton,"* Road & Track, *March 1958.*
Thanks to Kim M. Miller of the AACA Library and Research Center; R. Bruce Grinager; and of course Billy and Helen Vaccaro.

Packard 734 Production

Unfortunately, no production records exist for the 734 Speedster. Fortunately. however, Packard gave the 734 its own sequence of chassis numbers. And each of the five Speedster body styles had its own sequence of body numbers as well.

R. Bruce Grinager, who owns a 734 Phaeton with chassis number 184026 and body number 1, has matched up all the known body and chassis numbers and then filled in the gaps with some logical speculation. For example, the highest known Roadster body number is 7, and it was mounted on the highest known chassis number, which is 184115 — so it's a good bet that Packard made only 7 of the rumble-seat models. On the other hand, Runabout body number 31 was bolted down to chassis number 184100. So there were at least 31 runabouts, and probably a few more on the chassis between 184100 and 184115. Using this method, Grinager has constructed the following table, which he believes to be accurate to +/- five percent:

Body style/style number	Number built	Number surviving
Runabout/442 (boattail)	39	11
Sedan/443	19	2
Phaeton/445	32	19
Victoria/447	16	1
Roadster/452 (rumble seat)	7	2
Custom bodies	5	2
Total	118	23

James Ward Packard

"After sharing a few of his ideas for improvement with Alexander Winton regarding his motor carriage, Winton barked back at James: 'If you're so damned smart, why don't you build your own car?'"

PACKARD. The name alone conjures up images of wealth, sophistication and class. And it should. These were the cars driven by movie stars, entrepreneurs, presidents, and other dignitaries. From its very inception, the men who built Packard were adamant on producing high-quality automobiles. In this never-ending quest for perfection, some of the most extravagant vehicles ever to be built were those offered from Packard. While the company founder, James Ward Packard, was already a wealthy businessman, he still believed that customers deserved not only a quality product for their money, but also a strong support base to assist in servicing and repairing the automobiles. By offering the Packard to the retail market, which began simply enough as a project to fix the shortcomings of an automobile he himself purchased, James Packard built one of the most renowned motor vehicle companies ever created in the past 100 years.

James W. Packard was born on November 5, 1863, in Warren, Ohio. His father, Warren, was a successful and self-made hardware and lumber mogul, owning many retail stores in Ohio and Pennsylvania. When James and his older brother William were old enough, they became interested in their father's business. While both were hard-working and served their father well, William's interests were in sales and accounting, and James was fascinated with mechanical and electrical engineering.

Always a firm believer in education, James attended Lehigh University. While studying engineering, he concocted many electrical devices, including an electromagnetic door lock for his dorm room, a wall-mounted alarm clock that he controlled at his bedside, and even an alarm system.

After graduating in 1884 with a mechanical engineering degree, James was employed by the Sawyer-Mann Electric Company—an early pioneer in light-bulb manufacturing. Within six years he had more than 40 patents and eventually became the plant manager. Although young James found great success at Sawyer-Mann, he decided to leave the large New York City-based firm and return to Warren, Ohio.

There he and William started the Packard Electric Company and the New York and Ohio Company in 1890 to make their own electrical components. While the company was very successful, James was still fascinated by all things mechanical, including the then new "motor wagons."

After an impressive demonstration of a Winton automobile, James decided he needed one of his own. He bought the car and drove it from the Winton shop in Cleveland more than 75 miles back to Warren. Much to James's dismay, the car had many mechanical shortcomings and proved to be unreliable. At first, James fixed the car. But as problems became larger he found himself back at the Winton shops for heavier repairs. During these visits, he developed a good working friendship with two of the company's employees, shop foreman William Hatcher and head engineer George Weiss.

Every time James showed up at the Winton shops he always had a few ideas on how owner Alexander Winton could improve his vehicles. One time James caught Alexander on a bad day and, after sharing a few of his ideas for improvement, the shop owner barked back at James: "If you're so damned smart, why don't you build your own car?" James left the shop that day, thought about Alexander's challenge, and decided to do just that—build

his own cars. Not only did he take his advice but he also took Hatcher and Weiss for his staff.

In 1899, the men had successfully built their first automobile, the one-cylinder, 4-passenger Model A, in a small wing of the New York and Ohio Electric plant. It was followed by four more cars. The following year they decided to show their cars at the New York Auto Show. Response to their automobile was tremendous. Their keen sense of high quality parts drew the most attention, resulting in the sale of more than 40 vehicles.

Winton on how not to run an automobile manufacturing company, James insisted on a strong customer service base just in case a vehicle had a problem. He also insisted that with every sale, a Packard representative would instruct the owner on how to operate the new vehicle. Along with the strong customer service policy, improving mechanical innovations was a continuous progression. By 1901, Packards had a floor-mounted accelerator, automatic spark control, and a spring-operated clutch cam to absorb vibrations from the flywheel during actuation.

Being strongly disposed toward high quality, Packard rigorously tested all components before they were installed on a car. In many cases, parts that were procured from outside vendors were rejected to the point that automobile production was slowed down. Some vendors even refused to supply parts to the obsessed car builder.

In 1902, the company was incorporated as the Packard Motor Car Co. The following year Packard had outgrown its shop complex and relocated to Detroit. However, James Packard, the soft-spoken and somewhat elusive president, still lived in Warren, Ohio, although he made regular trips to the Detroit factory to conduct business.

James served as the company president until 1909, but remained the chairman of the board until 1915. To show appreciation to his alma mater, James donated $1,000,000 to Lehigh University. Although he never sold any of his treasured company stock, he actually gave much of it away shortly before his death in 1928.

James Ward Packard's yearning for all things mechanical was the reason Packard became one of the most successful automotive companies in the prewar era; it was an empire that was worth millions by the mid-1920s. His insistence on quality control and durable components became a Packard hallmark, characteristics that are still revered in these timeless classics today. ஒ

THE LIGHT 8 has always been something of a closet Packard. Packard dumped it—or at least dumped the name — after less than a year, and the CCCA never has accepted the Light 8 as a classic.

Yet the 1932 Light 8's only sin so far as we can tell was that it was inexpensive. Not cheap, but inexpensive by Packard standards. Its rivals in price that year included the Stutz 6, Reo Royale, Buick 90, Hupp 8, and Studebaker President.

The Light 8 became, in fact, the second Packard since 1901 offered at less than $2000. The sedan started out at $1750 at its Jan. 1932 introduction, but Light 8 prices rose to just under $2000 a few months later. Being basically a smaller, lighter edition of the Standard 8 (engines and transmissions were identical, and the Light 8 weighed some 600 pounds less), it out-accelerated the Standard 8 and probably outran it on the top end. The Light 8's workmanship, quality of materials, and general appointments were wholly on a par with any senior Packard.

The idea behind the Light 8 sounded reasonable enough, but unfortunately it didn't work. The idea, as explained by Jack Triplett, one of today's authorities on the Light 8, involved what current economists call price discrimination. Price discrimination means that a company tries to sell the same basic product in two different markets at two different prices—a higher and a lower price. Car makers do this all the time. For example, consider the 1974 Continental Mark IV. It's really the same basic car as the 1974 Ford Thunderbird, but with a Lincoln engine and Continental appointments. In effect, successful price discrimination means you sell the higher-priced version (Continental) to the carriage trade and the regular version (T-Bird) to housewives. If you're successful, as Ford has been and Packard was not, you make money both ways.

Packard tried price discrimination with the Light 8, but they couldn't fool enough people. Instead of increasing Packard's overall sales, the Light 8 merely stole sales away from the bigger 8s—the Standard 8s and DeLuxe 8s. Who, after all, wanted to pay another $500-$900 for the same basic car?

Before Cadillac captured the luxcar market in 1936, Packard remained the leader in that field, both in sales volume and name. Packard outsold Cadillac every year from 1924 through 1934 by an average of two to one. (This excludes La Salle sales—also after 1935 and the introduction of the Packard 120, Packard's sales lead increased substantially over Cadillac, but this spelled the end of Packard's senior-car dominance.) During this same period, Packard outsold Lincoln by more than five to one and Pierce-Arrow by six to one.

That makes it sound like Packard had a great thing going, but in terms of sheer numbers, luxcar sales dropped nearly dead during the Depression. In 1934, one of the industry's worst years, Packard registrations fell to 6552 from a 1929 high of 44,634 (see chart, p. 22). More dramatically, Packard's stock nosedived from 163 a share on the New York exchange in early 1929 to *less than two points* in 1933. Granted, there had been a 5:1 split late in 1929, but even so.... Packard's gross receipts likewise fell from a nice $25 million profit in 1929 to losses averaging about $6 million a year throughout the Depression.

Packard management grasped frantically at any straw during those terrible times. One straw was the Light 8, another was the V-12, which bowed the same year (1932). If the Light 8 had caught on as Packard management reasonably hoped, it could have saved the day. But saving the day would have meant dealers moving two or three times as many Light 8s as they did (only about 6750 found buyers during 1932). One big problem with the Light 8 was that it brought in only about half as many profit dollars per car as the senior Packards. Thus each sale the Light 8 stole away from the seniors meant a double loss. The company's net drubbing for 1932 totalled $6.8 million.

But Packard had worries on both ends of the price spectrum here, not just on the Light 8 side. With the Depression cylinder race on, Packard had to add pistons to keep up—and more pointedly to keep control of the luxcar market. Cadillac and Marmon had launched V-16s; Pierce-Arrow, Auburn, Cad, Franklin, and Lincoln released or were about to release new V-12s. So Packard also had to come up with a V-something. They'd dropped their earlier Twin 6 (V-12) in 1923, and Cornelius Van Ranst, the Cord L-29

drive report

chief engineer, had built an experimental V-12 for Packard with front-wheel drive in 1930. The V-12 engine for this car was put into production with minor modifications for 1932. All of which meant that Packard had to sink considerable capital into these two 1932 products—sums that neither car repaid. (As an aside. Packard also toyed with an in-line 12 which, if nothing else, shows what lengths auto makers went to during the cylinder race.)

Packard hadn't been caught totally unprepared for the Depression, and the company reacted more swiftly than most. Engineering vice president Col. Jesse Vincent had been designing smaller, lighter, less expensive Packards for several years before the stock market crash. In 1927, for instance, he'd laid out an "economy" Packard on a 117-inch wheelbase. And Packard president Alvan Macauley announced in 1929, before the crash, a possible $28-million expansion into the lower price field. Macauley was called Packard's "flywheel rather than its spark plug." His

bywords were system and stability, and he was known by presidents of other motor car companies as "the only gentleman in the automobile business." Macauley oversaw all important decisions, including engineering decisions, personally. He was shy and soft-spoken: traits that lent weight to his words. "He has every praiseworthy executive quality except a salesman's gusto," wrote *Fortune* magazine in 1937, "and he compensates for that by not discouraging (though he may wince at) the gusto of some of his subordinates."

It was to Mr. Macauley's credit that nine out of 10 Packard owners remained Packard owners, that all the company's important executives plus 64% of its factory foremen and 12.5% of its workmen had been with the company 10 years or longer. That's the sort of stability Macauley valued. So it's not hard to understand why the Depression and its upheavals put extraordinary pressures on Macauley and his staff and why they became desperate with falling sales.

At Mr. Macauley's right hand sat Col. Jesse G. Vincent, executive and engineer extraordinaire, one of the industry's all-time greats. Col. Vincent had followed Mr. Macauley into Packard from the Burroughs Adding Machine Co. in 1912. Col. Vincent, who loved fast cars and fast boats, helped create the 1915 Packard Twin 6. He also drew up the original blueprints for the first Liberty aircraft engine with the cooperation of Mr. Hall of Hall-Scott. And he oversaw many of those myriad firsts that Packard patented over the years.

Vincent always remained an enthusiast and a sort of very sophisticated hot rodder. He hired, among others, Indy drivers Ralph de Palma and Tommy Milton. De Palma eventually became a Packard dealer in Ft. Wayne, Ind., and Milton served for many years as Packard's chief service engineer. And while de Palma's Twin 6s never won major races, they turned so many fast laps at Indy and Sheepshead Bay that every school kid associated Packard with speed.

Col. Vincent himself made Packard the fastest name in speedboat engines. In 1922, the colonel won the Gold Cup with a Packard Liberty V-12 cut in two—an in-line 6—and Packard engines won most of the Gold Cups up to WW-II. Gar Wood's entire series of Miss Americas used Liberty or Packard engines.

All this is by way of showing that while Packard engineering seemed conservative on the surface, the man behind it wasn't by nature. He rarely rejected radical ideas until he'd tried them. Under Vincent worked a host of young, rising-star engineers: Forest R. McFarland was in Packard's research department, and by 1944 had become chief research engineer. Clyde Paton came to Packard in 1930 from Studebaker; he eventually became Packard's chief engineer and later fathered the Aero Willys. Cornelius Van Ranst, fresh from Indy triumphs and the Cord L-29, worked as a Packard consultant until 1935, not just on fwd and the V-12 but later on some rear-engined prototypes and a V-8 engine, all of which were rejected in favor of a conventional Packard 120.

Col. Vincent probably oversaw development of the Light 8 himself, because apparently neither McFarland, Paton, or Van Ranst had much (or anything) to do with it. Vincent's habit was to let each experimental group work by itself in sort of a pod system.

The Light 8's development started with a new chassis, the drafting apparently beginning

THE LIGHT 8 FOOLED NO ONE THAT YEAR. IT DREW SALES AWAY FROM THE SENIOR PACKARDS BY OFFERING AS MUCH QUALITY PLUS THE BIG 8 POWERPLANT AT A MUCH LOWER PRICE.

By Michael Lamm, *Editor*

Packard Light 8

sometime during 1930. Since the Light 8 used the Standard 8 engine and trans, the main job was to design a new frame and body. Front and rear axles were part of the new chassis. The Light 8's frame carried a hefty X-member plus a sturdy K-member up front. Previous Packards had used X-member frames, but this marked the first time Packard had a K-member. This new frame turned out to be lighter, yet stronger than previous Packards'. Wheelbase was set at 127.75 inches, only two inches shorter than the 1932 Standard 8's, so this really wasn't a small car by traditional standards.

As for styling, the Light 8 became something of a predictor of future Packard styling. Packard's other 1932 production bodies, even the new V-12-engined cars, clung to lines and silhouettes that Packard had carried for several years. Nothing new among the seniors. But along came the Light 8 with an entirely fresh, much less conservative approach—a low little windshield swept back at a rakish tilt, very classic tablespoon front fenders in the L-29 vein, plus the Light 8's most distinctive focal point, its shovel-nose grille. This car stood in the vanguard of 1932 design.

At that time Werner Gubitz acted as what we'd now call Packard's chief stylist. His office, though, was merely an arm of Engineering, and Gubitz reported to Col. Vincent. Most likely Gubitz created the Light 8's actual lines. He passed away a few years ago, so we might never know for sure, but the assumption seems safe. At any rate, the shovel-nose grille might have been a little too advanced by Packard standards, and it lasted that one year only. Gubitz covered the front frame horns with a moon-shaped skirt that blended together from the two front fenders—a bold move toward the "integrated look" that such cars as the 1932 Graham Blue Streak, the Aerodynamic Hupp, and a few others would pioneer.

Fortune observed correctly: "The designer of any Packard has a head start on designers of any other car because the Packard 'life lines'—its yoke-shaped radiator and bonnet—give him fixed

Light 8s were offered in 1932 only in four body styles—coupe (shown), roadster, victoria, and 4-door. Shipments began in March, making this a mid-year model. Prices started at $1,750 f.o.b.

starting points that he cannot and does not have to question."

We had the pleasure of driving and riding in the Light 8 coupe owned by Fraser Reay of San Francisco. Mr. Reay is this car's third owner, the second owner, John Perez, having given the coupe to him as part of Mr. Perez's estate. The Light 8's odometer now shows 21,813 miles, and the car's condition is nothing short of flawless.

The Light 8 series, along with all other 1932 Packards, came with two items of standard equipment that we were anxious to try out. The first was an automatic vacuum clutch, and the second was Ride Control—adjustable shock absorbers.

We found the vacuum clutch fun to use but not really very practical. Its on/off control is a red button beside the headlight switch on the steering hub. Push up to cut in the vacuum assist or down to disengage it. You can engage or disengage at any time and any speed.

With vacuum, when you pull to a stop, you needn't shove down the clutch pedal, naturally. Then when you're ready to roll again, simply feed gas. But in this particular car (and not, we

Luxcar Depression Registrations			
	Packard	Cadillac	Lincoln	Pierce-Arrow
1929	44,634	14,936	6,151	8,386
1939	28,318	12,078	4,356	6,795
1931	16,256	11,136	3,466	4,522
1932	11,058	6,269	3,179	2,692
1933	9,081	3,903	5,422	2,152
1934	6,552	4,889	3,024	1,740

Source: R.L. Polk registration figures.

Ventilators in cowl and both kick panels are augmented by windshield that opens outward.

Donut chaser hood ornament was one of several. Others included boy-on-a-slide and cormorant.

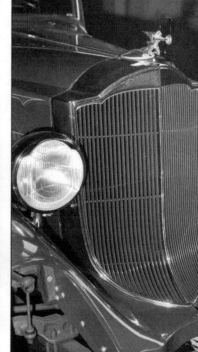

Shovelnose grille is unique to Light 8. Frame's front K-member likely dictated this styling.

Light 8 used Senior 8's 110-bhp engine and trans. Being lighter, car out-performed its bigger kin.

Packard's yoke graces parkers and headlamps.

Ride Control (above) adjusts shock absorbers for firm or soft ride. Firm counters potholes. Vacuum clutch button (below) stands at right in steering hub. Vacuum clutch causes freewheeling on deceleration—a feature that negates value.

Twin gloveboxes supplement door map pockets.

Besides lacquered disc wheels, factory offered chromed discs and chromed or unchromed wires.

Rear glass rolls down so rumbleseaters can talk. There's a narrow bin (not visible) behind seat.

With key and starter at opposite sides of dash, Startix comes in handy. It cost $13 additional.

understand, in all Packards), you have to get the engine up to a fairly high rpm before the clutch engages automatically—around 1200. Now if the engine normally idles at 500 rpm, you usually engage the clutch at, say, 700 rpm. So 1200 rpm makes for too brisk a takeoff. There's hardly any slippage at those revs. Also, there's a lag as you gingerly edge the gas pedal to the needed 1200 rpm.

Now you can also approach the vacuum clutch another way. You can simply tromp the gas pedal, in which event the clutch takes hold right now and with a fair whump. It's almost like revving the engine and dumping the clutch in drag racing, and we suspect the drivetrain wouldn't entertain too much of that. On gravel, it's almost impossible not to spin the rear tires while using the automatic clutch.

We understand that the vacuum engagement can be adjusted so the clutch takes hold at a lower rpm, say at around the normal 700. In that case, clutchless driving should be much more comfortable and we'd withdraw one objection to this device.

There's another, though, and this is perhaps more serious: it's simply that with the vacuum feature "on," you're automatically in free-wheel-ing, because every time you ease off the gas, the clutch disengages. Freewheeling was a popular selling gimmick in 1932, but it remains, to our mind, one of Detroit's more sinister inventions. You lose all engine braking with any type of free-wheeling. This in turn puts undue strain on a car's brakes, particularly coming down hills. So as far as we're concerned, Packard's vacuum clutch—along with similar vacuum clutches from other automakers (most of them supplied by Bendix)—gets thumbs down in terms of desirability.

Now we come to Ride Control. We noticed when we climbed into Mr. Reay's car that the Ride Control knob was pulled all the way out—to the softest setting. As we drove along, and especially on rough surfaces, we began to play with the knob. There are four click-settings, soft being all the way out and firm being all the way in. There was no occasion that we could feel when the firm (jiggly) setting became more comfortable than soft. And we drove at many speeds over paved and unpaved surfaces of all sorts. The firm setting is supposed to counter bottoming on especially rough roads, but we couldn't find any roads rough enough to bottom even the softest setting.

Ride Control's softest setting isn't mushy by any mean—it feels about like a modern

Golfbag door (standard) reveals rumbleseat foot rail. Aluminum step plates (center) make tail light vulnerable to heavy feet. Rumble uses leather.

"Next to Ford, Packard is perhaps the most valuable *name* in the industry. For a generation its luxurious cars have never carried lesser folk than rich invalids to their airings, diplomats to embassies, gangsters to funerals, stars to the studios, war lords through Chinese dust, heroes through ticker tape, heiresses across Long Island and Grosse Pointe...."—**Fortune** Magazine,

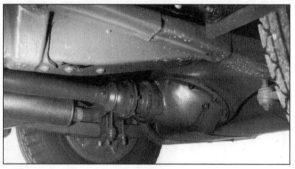

So-called "angleset" rear axle drops driveshaft an inch lower and gives an entirely flat floor.

The Light 8 siphoned sales away from bigger Packards, thus the designation was dropped for 1933.

Packard Light 8

car with heavy-duty suspension. The firm setting turns this into something approaching a Jeep or one of the new Japanese mini-pickups, unloaded. It's very easy to feel the difference between these two extreme settings.

For those of you who wonder, Ride Control shock absorbers were supplied to Packard (and to other automakers) by Delco-Remy. These were lever shocks, and in each one there was a bypass in a sleeve valve that had two little holes, one smaller than the other. With the control knob pushed all the way in (firm), the sleeve valve moved to a position where the hydraulic bypass was cut off entirely. Pulled out one notch, the sleeve moved to expose half of the smaller hole. One more notch and the sleeve opened the smaller hole completely. At the third notch, the entire smaller hole and half the larger one opened. And all the way out opened both holes. As the holes opened, of course, hydraulic fluid could pass more and more freely from chamber to chamber inside the shock body. The sleeve valve was controlled directly from the driver's seat by rods that ran from the dashboard knob to each of the four shock absorbers.

In scanning our driving-impression notes, we recall these reactions. The ignition key seems a long reach—it's all the way across the instrument panel, where it certainly needn't be. The starter button itself stands on the left side of the steering column, about three feet our side of the key. It's a small thing, but it seems like a lot of wasted motion.

The 3-speed transmission (Packard had used 4-speeds in the senior 8s of 1930, '31, and early 1932), shifts like absolute butter—so smoothly that the lever seemed to be guiding our hand rather than the other way around. This gearbox, along with a truly effective vacuum clutch (without freewheeling), would come awfully close to an automatic transmission.

Steering feels moderately heavy, but not overly so. Brakes take only a light touch and bring the car down with great authority (they

Light 8's chassis was all new, as was the body. Hefty frame had K-member up front plus central X-member. Massive 8-cylinder engine rests well behind front axle for better weight distribution.

specifications

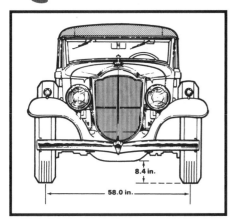

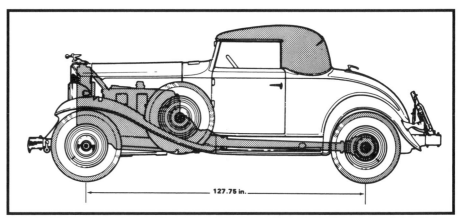

1932 Packard Light 8, Model 900 coupe

Price when new . . . . . . $1795 f.o.b. Detroit (1932).

Options . . . . Custom equipment (twin sidemounts, luggage rack, full rear bumper, fender parking lamps), clock, hood ornament.

ENGINE

Type . . . . L-head, in-line 8, water-cooled, cast-iron block, aluminum crankcase, 9 main bearings, pressure & splash lubrication.
Bore & stroke . . . . . . 3.1875 x 5.00 in.
Displacement . . . . . . 319.2 cid.
Max. bhp @ rpm . . . . 110 @ 3200.
Max. torque @ rpm . . N.a.
Compression ratio . . 6.0:1 (6.52 opt.).
Induction system . . . . Single 1-bbl. updraft carb, mechanical fuel pump.
Exhaust system . . . . Cast-iron manifold, single muffler.
Electrical system . . . . 6-volt battery/coil.

CLUTCH

Type . . . . Single dry plate, woven asbestos lining.
Diameter . . . . N.a.
Actuation . . . . Mechanical foot pedal or automatic, by vacuum.

TRANSMISSION

Type . . . . 3-speed manual, floor lever, synchro 2-3.
Ratios: 1st . . . . . . 2.46:1.
2nd . . . . . . 1.30:1.
3rd . . . . . . 1.00:1.
Reverse . . 2.84:1.

DIFFERENTIAL

Type . . . . Hypoid, "angleset."
Ratio . . . . 4.35:1.
Drive axles . . . . Semi-floating.

STEERING

Type . . . . Worm & sector.
Turn lock to lock . . . . 4.0.
Ratio . . . . 17:1.
Turn circle . . . . 43.0 ft.

BRAKES

Type . . . . 4-wheel mechanical drums, internal expanding.
Drum diameter . . . . . 15.0 in.
Total lining area . . . . 212.0 sq. in.

CHASSIS & BODY

Frame . . . . U-section steel, front K-member, central X-member.
Body construction . . Composite wood & steel.
Body style . . . . 2-door, 2/4-passenger rumbleseat coupe.

SUSPENSION

Front . . . . I-beam axle, semi-elliptic longitudinal leaf springs, adjustable lever shock absorbers.
Rear . . . . Solid axle, semi-elliptic longitudinal leaf springs, adjustable lever shock absorbers.

Tires . . . . 6.50 x 17, 6-ply tube type whitewalls.
Wheels . . . . Cast steel discs, demountable drop-center rims.

WEIGHTS & MEASURES

Wheelbase . . . . 127.75 in.
Overall length . . . . . . 195.375 in.
Overall height . . . . . . 64.625 in.
Overall width . . . . . . 71.875 in.
Front tread . . . . 58.0 in.
Rear tread . . . . 59.0 in.
Ground clearance . . . . 8.375 in.
Curb weight . . . . 3990 lb.

CAPACITIES

Crankcase . . . . 8 qt.
Cooling system . . . . . 19 qt.
Fuel tank . . . . 20 gal.

FUEL CONSUMPTION

Best . . . . 13-16 mpg.
Average . . . . 12-14 mpg.

PERFORMANCE (from **The Autocar** test of 1933 Packard 8 sedan, 7/21/33):

0-50 mph . . . . 15.6 sec.
0-60 mph . . . . 23.0 sec.
Top speed (av.) . . . . . 88 mph.

---

ought to with 15-inch drums). Visibility leaves something to be desired—it's plainly hard to see out in most directions. Up front there's the midget windshield plus the long hood; out back there's a fairly small window, and the rear quarters are absolutely blind. But so were many 3-window coupes in that day. This one looks more like a convertible and, in fact, was built on what's basically the convertible body. The canvas-padded steel top looks and feels as though it ought to fold.

The British magazine THE AUTOCAR tested a 1933 Packard 8 sedan in July of that year. The 1933 Packard 8 became the Light 8's lineal descendant, so it's fair to paraphrase some of that test here.

During timed runs at Brooklands, THE AUTOCAR found this Packard's top speed to be 88 mph. That was with a 5:1 compression ratio (THE AUTOCAR'S particular Packard was assembled in Canada specifically for export). In this country, the Light 8's normal c.r. was 6:1, with a 6.52:1 optional at no extra cost. With either of these, the car ought to do better than 88 mph. THE AUTOCAR found high-gear-only acceleration amazingly quick, as did we.

There's some whine from low and second. but all in all it's a very quiet car. And it's agile and flexible in traffic, easily keeping up with today's cars. We didn't corner fast (we found no opportunity and didn't feel it fair to create one), but we'd guess there's plenty of easily controlled understeer. That's speculation, and we might be wrong, because the engine does stand well back behind the front axle.

Packard got off to a late start with the Light 8. They announced it in Jan. 1932 but didn't begin shipping until March. Victorias (called coupe-sedans) didn't get into dealer showrooms until April. And then prices shot up that summer, so even buyers who'd been waiting became twice discouraged.

The Light 8 might have scared off some Packard snobs, so for the 10th series. Packard dropped the Light 8 designation and, in effect, renamed this model simply the "8." (Packard didn't go along with yearly model changes but rather announced a new series whenever it be-came reasonable. The Light 8 belonged to the 9th series, which roughly amounted to 1932 models. The

10th series began in 1933.) The '33 8 spanned the same wheelbase and equalled the same car, but gone were the Light 8's shovelnose grille and tablespoon fenders. In quick deference to popular demand, Packard added valences to all 1933 front and rear fenders. The 8 went back to a completely vertical grille, same as other Packards had, and the 1933 8's dash panel was also changed. Prices again went up, but mechanically the 1933 8 was essentially still the 1932 Light 8.

So the Light 8's name, plus its low price and shovelnose grille, made it a one-year run. Why the CCCA recognizes the 1933 8 as a classic and not the 1932 Light 8 (same car) is one of those head-nodders. The AACA does consider the Light 8 a classic. Mox nix, though, because either way it's still one of the better Packards, and as everyone knows, they were all good. ☙

Our thanks to Jack Triplett, Adelphi, MD.; Burt Weaver, Dwight Heinmuller, and George Hamlin, of the Packard Club, Box 2808, Oakland, CA 94618; Forest McFarland, Flint, MI; Raymond H. Dietrich, Albuquerque, NM; and Fraser S. Reay, San Francisco.

Style and Substance

drive report

1935 Packard Eight

Driving Impressions

YOU open the broad, rear-hinged door, climb behind the big wheel, and are ensconced in a cozy though uncramped cockpit on a leather seat squarely between firm and supple that'd do a judge's study justice. Turn the key and, despite a months-long slumber, the added electric fuel pump whirs softly. Pressing the starter button invokes a short growl from the gear-reduction starter half the size of a winch motor. The velvety 320-cubic-inch in-line eight fires immediately, the 97.5-pound, nine-main-bearinged, counterbalanced crankshaft and roller cam valve train delivering a smooth, rapid idle reeking of lightly leashed power. Though the valves are purposely set a trace loose to ensure performance at speed and to prevent their scorching (a wise auld mechanic's touch with such hoary dead-lifter mills), the Packard emits a whispering idle, as low as 350 rpm. There's no vibration anywhere; no unseemly intrusion to distract or irritate working executive or exuberant

by Michael G.H. Scott
photos by the author

playboy en route to business or pleasure.

The 12-inch clutch is a light, easy joy, belying a manhole-sized flywheel. The ready torque and 4.69:1 axle launch you from the garage with the eagerness of a mahogany-decked GarWood or Hacker-craft burbling from a private slip. (Many of those floating brethren to this coupe-roadster were also used to commute to lower Manhattan and other water-bound financial arenas.) Smitten with the understated luxury and grand style of it all, you almost don't notice how quickly the car gathers speed, and flick the tall, gracefully crooked gearshift up and over into second. It snicks with astonishing ease and a surprisingly short throw; far less movement than many column shifts to come. The "cane shift," as Packard called it, falls readily to hand, as close or closer than the "Handishifts" to appear in just a few years.

The convertible rushes ahead with unruffled authority. This is a civilized if sporty carriage, so despite the "coupe-roadster" appellation there are both roll-up windows and crank-out vent panes. A gentle click into high, where you leave the long lever unless you come to a serious hill or full stop.

There's no side sway, the big car taking winding two-lane back roads with a sure-footed moxie recalling many a smaller, outright sports car. Packard knew a few things about spring rates and suspension tuning, and even this beam front axle that'd support a loaded UPS truck allows deft handling and instant but always gentle feedback. Like the seat, the big coupe-roadster's ride is poised just between firm and supple. Weight and wheelbase alone cannot deliver such a taut glide through town and country. There's real all-pervading quality afoot, constantly reassuring driver and passengers alike, through the controls, through the seat.

Below the dash to the left of the steering wheel is the Ride Control knob,

Originally published in Special Interest Autos #166, Jul.-Aug. 1998

which adjusts the shocks for firm flight over rough or undulating trails, or a compliant acquiescence over boulevard. Ride Control was introduced in 1932, when even the wealthy had lost their sense of humor, since Packard received complaints over the dash-mounted instruction plaque: In-Hard Out-Soft.

The big Bendix vacuum-boosted mechanical brakes haul the car down quickly, smoothly, the rods, shaft, levers and cables so well engineered that unless you knew better, you'd swear this car had hydraulic binders; they're really that good. A long-time '35 Cadillac driver admitted that its vacuum-boosted Huck mechanicals, little more than scaled up from unboosted Chevy installations, left much to be desired. I can't recall the feeling of the front hydraulic/rear mechanical brakes retained by Rolls-Royce/Bentley until the Silver Cloud/S-Series debuted late in '55, but surely few yesteryear systems can compare. Pierce-Arrow kept Bendix mechanicals until the bitter end in '38, part of their advertised "world's safest car" package. Packard's junior car, the One Twenty, debuted with Bendix hydraulic brakes in '35, adopted by the seniors from '37 on.

The torque subtly crescendos to horsepower, and with turbine ease the Packard laps up the road, accompanied only by the deep thrum of the exhaust. Remarkably, despite a five-inch stroke and 4.69:1 rear cog (4.36, 5.07 optional; 4.06 available only in the Super 8 and Twelve), even at an actual 65 and 70 there's no sense of strain or unhappiness, only a sublime note between a hum and a well-muffled roar. This is all the more impressive as the 130 horsepower peaks at just 3,200 rpm and there's 29 square feet of frontal area — that imposing grille and all — limiting top speed to an honest 84. A '36 Cord,

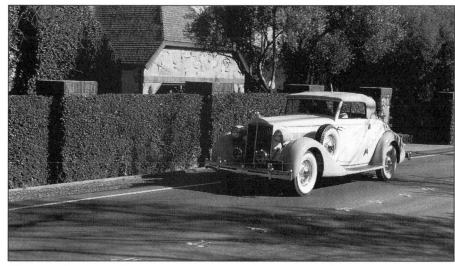

Above: *Packard Eight drives and handles beautifully; smooth, balanced, sure-footed, with power to spare.* **Below left:** *Door hinges fit for a bank vault are typical of Packard's quality construction.* **Below right:** *The "lady with a donut" mascot points the way.* **Bottom:** *Accessory Trippe lights accent the dignified grille.*

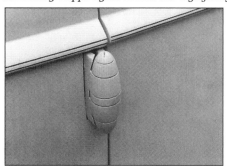

with less horsepower but only 23 square feet of frontal area and a 2.75:1 overall fourth gear, gave an *Autocar*-attested 89-92. For comparison, a period Dodge and Lagonda share 27 square feet, bucking the wind, topping out at around 80 and 97, respectively. Packard's hallmark grille was raked a bit more for '35, in keeping with the company's gradual address of streamlining.

Underpinning and contributing to the

car's tightness and quality ride is the new, stiffer frame with extended X-member. As you barrel along, all points of the steering and suspension—even the clutch throw-out bearing—are oiled by 20W nondetergent from the vacuum-operated Bijur automatic chassis lubricator, a feature shared with other fine cars such as Auburn, Bentley, Cord L-29, Daimler, Duesenberg, Graham-Paige, Horch, Lancia, Rolls-Royce, Rover, Stutz and Willys-Knight. Bijur lubricating systems are still used in factory equipment. Paul Saunders, tech support at the Bijur Lubricating Corp., 50 Kocher Drive, Bennington, Vermont 05201-1994, just across town from *Hemmings Motor News/Special Interest Autos*, will help owners of Bijur-equipped cars with parts and service; 1-800-631-0168; fax 1-802-442-1998.

But Bijur chassis lubrication joined mechanical brakes and the solid front axle in Packard Valhalla after 1936, the i.f.s. of 1937 demanding a grease gun. The 120 junior car debuted with Packard's unique Safe-T-Flex i.f.s. in '35, which spread to the seniors two years later, and to Rolls-Royce, Bentley, Daimler and, as a rear suspension, to Lagonda after the war. R-R dropped it from the '56-on Silver Cloud in favor of a standard GM-ish i.f.s. for the same reason Packard omitted it from the '41 Clipper; the lowered floor pan left no

1935 Packard

room for Safe-T-Flex's long torque arms.

As you roll merrily along in this majestic coupe-roadster you reflect what a change five or six years brought. A senior forties Packard shares with this handsome Model 1201 nine main bearings and a car-wide preponderance of fine-threaded bolts. Detroit production job or not, Packard, like Rolls-Royce and Bugatti, believed in "stitching" a car together. But the Packard of the forties would be a more sedate, businesslike affair; quality of an increasingly self-conscious moderne era, a Lockheed Electra to this Beech Staggerwing.

But it's still 1935 as you rush along in this paragon of refinement, smoothness, and East Grand style, secure in the very real knowledge that there is no finer car in the whole world than your Packard Eight coupe-roadster, unless it's a Super Eight or Twelve.

You open the Eight's throttle enough to whoosh past a struggling Essex, and follow the winged goddess home, patterns of canopying shade trees fleeting over the sleek pods of the headlamps, along the length of hood, dancing over the canvas top, down the rumbleseat lid and upfolded luggage rack.

Jim Lawrence bought this car, still ambulatory if tired, on December 5, 1971, but has yet to discover who first took delivery of serial number 388 324 over 63 years ago at Earle C. Anthony's dealership on Van Ness Avenue, then as now San Francisco's auto row. California's Packard distributor, Anthony had also owned, since 1905 at age 25, the Los Angeles Packard agency. Anthony began another Packard tradition by photographing denizens of the growing movie colony alongside Packards, contributing to the proliferation of Packards on the silver screen and wearing his stamp throughout the Golden State.

Above: Sidemounts add a touch of opulence to the front end. *Below left:* Thoughtful arm-pad/scuff protector for rumble seat passengers. *Right:* No classic roadster is correct without a separate door for the golf bags.

Anthony claimed to have opened the first gas station, which he may or may not have done, and was responsible for first using that Parisian novelty, neon light, for domestic advertising. During the twenties, Anthony anticipated the rise of radio, building the powerful and still thriving LA station KFI, over which he advertised Packards. While California's Cadillac distributor, Don Lee, is

perhaps best remembered for having given a young Harley Earl his start, customizing Cads for gregarious film celebrities, Anthony seems to have been the state's live wire.

"A real estate appraiser friend told me about an old Packard in a garage," recounts Jim, long something of a legend himself in A-C-D and CCCA circles for managing to make his and other 1936-37

	Twelfth Series Packards			1935 Packard
	Eight	**Super Eight**	**Twelve**	**One-Twenty**
Price*	$2,385	$2,990	$3,820	$1,060
Wheelbase*	127.375 inches	132.25 inches	139.25 inches	120 inches
Weight*	4,815 pounds	5,080 pounds	5,695 pounds	3,510 pounds
Cylinders	8	8	12	8
Displacement, cubic inches	320	384.8	473	257.2
Compression	6.5	6.3	6.4	6.5
Horsepower/rpm	130/3,200	150/3,200	175/3,200	110/3,850
Torque ft. lb./rpm	260/1,600	300-310/1,600 (est.)	365/12,00	203/2,000
Wheels	Wire	Wire	Wire	Disc
Tires	7.00x17	7.00x17	7.00x17	disc/7.00x16
Ply	6 ply	6 ply	6 ply	4
Axle ratio	4.36, 4.69 std., 5.07	4.06, 4.41 std. 4.69, 5.07	4.06, 4.41 std., 4.69, 5.07	4.36 std., 4.54
Steering, lock-to-lock	5	5	5	4.5
Turning circle	44 Feet, 8 inches	45 feet	49 feet	39 feet

*base four-door sedan on shortest wheelbase f.o.b. Detroit

Packard's open car styling possessed just the right deft combination of formal and sporty, plus an enviable consistency in their design through the thirties.

Cords run as well as they look. "I'd had some old Chryslers (a '26 Model 70 roadster and '37 Royal sedan), and really wanted a '33–'34 Packard with those lean front fenders; so I wasn't fired up when I opened the door and saw this '35 Eight with the damaged grille and front bumper laying on the floor. But Lillie [Jim's wife] saw the same car advertised in the local paper under 'home furnishings,' of all things, for only $1,500. She fell in love with it, and I ran back to give the owner a deposit. No one answered the door but a large-sounding dog. I slipped the check under the door with a note, hoping the dog wouldn't eat the check.

"I'm sitting home later and the phone rings. 'I got your check,' the guy says. 'Does that mean you want the car? There's someone else over here looking at it right now.' I ran back, gave him the rest of the money, and used our tow truck to take it home. Lillie was waiting for me, clutching the hood ornament."

Having built Ford-based roadsters as a teen, serving as a machinist's mate in the Navy at the end of World War II, riding bikes including a '40 Triumph Speed Twin then and a '48 Ariel Square Four today ("I mostly admire it now; my luck might've run out."), Jim worked as a mechanic and salesman in his father's Chrysler-Plymouth dealership, fine honing a natural mechanical bent as strong as Werner Gubitz's artistic flair. This skill came in handy as Jim performed most of the Packard's frame-off restoration himself. Cords, apparently, are rigorous training for anything. Twelve years after he began, in 1988 Jim completed the magnificent survivor.

"The engine needed most of the drivetrain work; the transmission and rear end showed no wear. Lillie picked out the colors, '79-to-date Mercedes ivory over '79 Lincoln Continental beige, which I didn't think would work. But everyone who sees the car admires the combination."

A word for purists. Two-toning was certainly available for 1935 senior Packards, and if the exact hues aren't among those offered at East Grand Boulevard that year, the soft, muted colors are still very much in the mood and dignity of the coupe-roadster, which is more than can be said for so much of the lipstick concours color going around like a nasty flu. surely a Mercedes shade can't be all bad for a Packard, the company winding up with both more defense work and the US Mercedes-Benz distribution rights under a last-ditch management contract proposed by aero giant Curtiss-Wright in May 1956, interested in Packard mainly as a tax write-off against huge defense profits.

Jim clearly loves this car, but compared with the lower, more compact Cords he owns ('36 Westchester, '37 Phaeton), his "modern" '41 Cadillac convertible, and even his modern-looking (if not in fact) '41 Lincoln Continental club coupe, the Packard seems dated and "high hat. But then I drive it and feel all that quality and... if I sold it I'd miss it. And Lillie'd kill me."

If Jim ever does sell or trade it — perhaps for a 1940-42 160 convertible — whoever gets it will have the last laugh. But regardless who buys or sells, you can toss out all the officious "price guides," since these blue chip ragtops don't appear often. Your best bet is to follow *Hemmings*, then the Packard Club, and CCCA bulletins. And promise you'll give it a good home.

Alvan Macauley, Packard's president from 1916–39, chairman until 1948, and president of the Automobile Manufacturers Association from 1928–45, was often called "the only gentleman in the automobile business." So it seems fitting that the straight-shooting owner of Walnut Creek, California's Lawrence Volvo, whose father was a respected Buick and Chrysler dealer since 1921, should own this resplendent example of "the car built by gentlemen for gentlemen."

specifications

illustrations by Russell von Sauers, The Graphic Automobile Studio

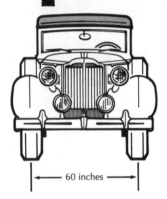

← 60 inches →

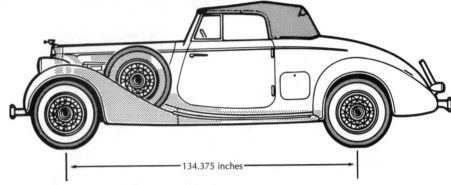

← 134.375 inches →

1935 Packard Eight, Model 1201

Price	$2,945 approx. as equipped, f.o.b. Detroit
Standard equipment	Front and rear bumpers, twin taillamps, twin horns, safety glass throughout, extra wheel (spare tire extra).
Options on dR car	DeLuxe equipment consisting of sixth wheel, wells in fenders, side wheel brackets and trunk rack; Mascot of Speed (flying lady) hood ornament, driving lights, whitewall tires, radio.

ENGINE

Type	8-cylinder in-line L-head, separate cast-iron block and aluminum crankcase; cast-iron head
Firing order	1-6-2-5-8-3-7-4
Bore x stroke	3.1875 inches x 5 inches
Displacement	319.2 cubic inches (5.23 liters)
Warm idle speed	350 rpm
Horsepower @ rpm	130 @ 3,200
Torque @ rpm	260 @ 1,600
Valve lifters	Mechanical, roller cam
Valve face angle	45 degrees intake and exhaust
Main bearings	9 (2.625-inch diameter)
Fuel system	Packard Stromberg EE-23 two-barrel downdraft, automatic choke; mechanical fuel pump
Lubrication system	Full pressure, gear-driven pump, 35 pounds @ 25 mph
Cooling system	Centrifugal, belt drive, 4-blade fan, 155-degree thermostat controlling grille shutters
Exhaust system	Single, 2.25-inch pipe; muffler 4.25-inch diameter, 45 inches long
Ignition	Delco-remy dual-point, fixed points fire 1-2-8-7
Electrical system	6-volt positive ground
Chassis lubrication	Bijur automatic vacuum

TRANSMISSION

Type	Packard 3-speed, 2nd and 3rd synchronized
Ratios: 1st	2.458:1
2nd	1.525:1
3rd	1.00:1
Reverse	2.878:1

CLUTCH

Type	Long semi-centrifugal single dry plate
Diameter	12 inches
Actuation	Mechanical, foot pedal

DIFFERENTIAL

Type	Packard, angle-set, semi-floating, hypoid
Ratio	4.69
Drive	Hotchkiss, propulsion through rear springs

STEERING

Type	Packard worm and roller
Turns lock-to-lock	5
Ratio	18.6
Turning diameter	46 feet 8 inches

BRAKES

Type	Vacuum-boosted Bendix mechanical, internal-expanding (w/4-wheel parking brake)
Drum diameter	14 inches
Effective area	240.125 square inches

CHASSIS & BODY

Frame	Taper double-drop box-type front side rail, 8 inches deep; 5 cross members and X-member
Body	Packard, steel panels

SUSPENSION

Front	Packard solid axle, 42-inch-longitudinal semi-elliptical leaf springs
Rear	Solid axle, 60.5-inch longitudinal semi-elliptical leaf springs
Shock absorbers	Hydraulic 2-way adjustable from front compartment; static control valve
Tires	7.00 x 17, 6 ply
Wheels	Wire

WEIGHTS AND MEASURES

Wheelbase	134.375 inches
Overall length	212.5625 inches
Overall width	74 inches
Overall height	70.75 inches
Front track	60 inches
Rear track	61 inches
Min. road clearance	8.75 inches (to engine oil sump)
Weight	4,725 pounds

CAPACITIES

Crankcase	8 quarts
Transmission	4.5 pints
Differential	6 pints
Cooling system	20 quarts
Fuel tank	25 gallons

CALCULATED DATA

Horsepower per c.i.d.	.407
Weight per hp	36.35 pounds
Weight per c.i.d.	14.8 pounds

PERFORMANCE

Top speed	84.6 mph (Autocar)
0-60 mph	25 seconds (starting in 3rd) (Autocar)

*Facing Page, left: Packard Eight's air cleaner/silencer leads to Packard Stromberg EE-23 dual downdraft carb. **Right:** Simple, rugged Packard Eight is, like the entire car, a paragon of refinement. **Above:** There's no mistaking it for anything but a senior series Packard, even though the Eight represented the "low priced" line of big Packards.*

1935 Packard

History and Background

Overshadowed by the mighty Twelve and Super Eight, aped by the new junior One Twenty, the Packard Eight nonetheless represented America's proudest automaker to people the world over. Along with its senior stablemates, the Twelve and Super Eight, as well as the new 120 introduced in January 1935, the Packard Eight continued the company's traditional, if evolutionary, styling, leaving trends to less illustrious marques. As customary at Packard, the big news was unseen refinement, and why the Detroit firm's products were renowned the world over as road cars.

Chief among these improvements were the new copper-lead, steel-backed precision connecting rod bearings, in place of the old babbitt-type shells, for all three senior lines as well as the new junior car. Though the 320-c.i.d. Packard Eight shared a five-inch stroke (3.1875 x 5) with the 385-c.i.d. Super Eight (3.5 x 5; same as the 1933-38 Pierce-Arrow and 1931-34 Chrysler Imperial straight eights), an assembly-line-stock Model 1201 Eight sedan

equipped with the new bearings ran wide open for 25,000 miles at the Packard Proving Grounds' 2.5-mile banked oval, then the fastest track in the world—this at a time when Rolls-Royce and Mercedes-Benz were warning owners to avoid continuous high speeds on Hitler's new Autobahn. Finned connecting rod bearing caps introduced for 1933 already contributed to better heat dissipation.

The Packard Eight was now offered on four wheelbases: 127 inches for the base $2,385 four-door sedan (same wheelbase as 1932's Light Eight and '33's entry-level Model 1001 Eight); $2,470–$5,240 and $2,630–$5,385 for an array of production and factory semi-custom bodies, akin to designer jeans or department store Ralph Lauren, on 134- and 139-inch wheelbases; and a pair of 160-inch commercial chassis.

The engine was first used in the 1928–29 Sixth Series Standard Eight, a small-bore version of the 385-c.i.d. straight eight shoehorned into the former volume Six, its firewall indented to accept the new, longer motor. Packard's practice of referring to its models as "series" started with the Olympian Models 48 and 38 Sixes of 1912–15, but began afresh with the new First Series "Single Eight" introduced June 1923, the industry's first straight eight by a

volume producer. Isotta-Fraschini's Tipo 8, introduced August 1919, was the first in-line eight-cylinder engine put into series production, followed by Duesenberg's limited-production Model A in October 1920. The Single Eight, so named to avoid possible confusion with Packard's fabled 1915–23 Twin-Six, replaced and outperformed that storied powerplant, itself the industry's first volume-production V-12.

One of the Packard Eight's greatest assets was the distinguished styling shared with its brethren, notably the radiator grille and long, chiseled hood. The ox-yoke-shaped "Packard" radiator with cusps flanking the curved top portion was lifted from the early French Mors, like Panhard et Levassor, a sophisticated Gallic auto. Former Mors plant superintendent, part-time racing driver Charles Schmidt, a Frenchman with over eight years' design experience in his native country, had joined Packard in 1902, recommended to company founder James Ward Packard by Henry Bourne Joy, investor/g.m./president of Packard Motor Car Co. and responsible both for abandoning J.W. Packard's single-cylinder dictum and moving the fledgling auto firm from Warren, Ohio, to the open-shop atmosphere of Detroit. The first overwhelmingly successful Packard was the 1904

1935 Packard
continued

four-cylinder Model L. It was Schmidt's design and its lines reflected the Mors, especially the front end. Although its prototype was built in Warren, the Model L is considered the first Detroit Packard. The red hexagon began on the wheel hubs of the 1906 four-cylinder "24" (Model S). Both radiator motif and hexagon would survive through the last Detroit Packards in 1956, even the for-lorn "Packardbakers" of 1958. And every designer who ever served Packard knew you might adapt and stylize these halcyon trademarks, but never drop them. This included Werner Hans August Gubitz, who oversaw Packard styling from the last year before the Wall Street crash, all through the thirties, into the forties. Gubitz is overshadowed by more flamboyant designers. Unfortunate, since his strengths were restraint, understatement, detail. Rather than to bow to trendy streamlined themes sweeping the industry, Gubitz shepherded Packard's trim, aristocratic look through a subtle, gradual sleekening.

Like previous models, the 1935 Twelfth Series' clean, elegant lines flowed from Packard's own design studio, overseen since 1928 by Gubitz. Born in Hamburg, Germany, July 29, 1899, Gubitz was as old as Packard Motor Car Company itself. Emigrating to the United States with his parents in 1905, a fascination with automobiles and a talent for graphic arts landed Gubitz a job in 1919 as a delineator at New York's Fleetwood studios (themselves absorbed by Fisher Body in 1925). He jumped ship for LeBaron in 1922, joining custom body designer J. Frank deCausse. Gubitz entered MIT two years later but dropped out in 1925 when his LeBaron mentor Ray Dietrich lured him to Detroit as an illustrator/ designer at Dietrich, Inc., now a division of Murray Corp. Gubitz left to join Peerless in Cleveland, then Ohio Body & Blower Co., working on Moon, Jordan and Gardner designs before leaving that moribund scene to open a restaurant. That proved unsuccessful, so in 1927 he rejoined Dietrich in Detroit, later that year settling at Packard, where his attention to detail, unerring taste, and respect for evolutionary gothic style heralded Packard up to and including the unified aero-look '41 Clipper, itself still subject to Gubitz's ministrations and ultimate censure as company styling chief.

The 1935 Twelfth Series Packards are testimony to Gubitz's genteel approach. He deftly took the elegant 1933-34 design to a timeless present, but not beyond. From Packard's December 31, 1934, Annual Report:

*Above: Factory trunk rack was a decorative necessity. **Below left:** Graceful steering wheel, woodgrained dashboard also projected quality image. **Right:** Upholstery could hardly have been more unadorned. **Facing page, top:** Long, graceful shifter and symmetrical instrument panel await the driver's command. **Below:** Rear styling is pleasant but plain.*

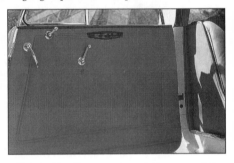

"Our new Twelfth Series cars priced $2,385 to $4,950 were announced during September 1934 and have met with cordial approval. With these cars the Company inaugurated a new style cycle, the fifth in the thirty years in which it has kept its identifying lines. Ordinarily, new styles are announced from year to year, only relatively minor changes in body design being necessary. But once in five years, or thereabouts, it is necessary to inaugurate a new style cycle, in order to maintain style leadership. It was decided under this principle that Twelfth Series cars should inaugurate a new style cycle in body designs while still retaining the essential features of traditional Packard appearance. Accordingly, all of the forty bodies for Twelfth Series cars were redesigned and modernized and gotten into production and necessarily at large expense for designing, tooling and preparation. Our owners who have purchased these new Twelfth Series cars praise them highly. We believe there is nothing so fine in appearance or in operation manufactured anywhere else in the world. An examination, or better yet, a trial trip in one of these cars by our stockholders will, we believe, confirm our high opinion of them. The increased attractiveness of our new Twelfth Series cars will, we think, be undoubtedly reflected in their increased popularity."

While the Depression still ravaged the nation and world, Packard maintained its domination of the fine car field ($2,000 and up). In 1933, Packard secured 38.4 percent of all fine car business; 42.7 in '34, and still better in '35. But that field was drying up like the dust bowl, and there were no longer enough customers to sustain even the leader, which led to the new 120 junior car. "We have an Episcopalian reputation, and we want to do business with the Methodists," quipped Vice-President Max Gilman's advertising manager as Packard recruited General Motors alumni savvy in the ways of cost engineering for the 120 program.

Pierce-Arrow remained devoted to the carriage trade and died a couple years later, despite a trickle of expensive house trailers (see *SIA* #145) and talk of a junior, likely Hayes-bodied car (see *SIA* #73) to join Lincoln's Fordish Zephyr; Cadillac's now Olds-based LaSalle and, for that matter, the entire downsized '36 Cadillac V-8 line; and Packard's 120, the sales leader, in the trenches. But Packard's overall stature and vitality are better appreciated when you consider that the company was able to facelift its traditional senior lines even as they toiled to introduce the new junior car premiering January 1935. Of Packard's total $7,290,549 operating costs itemized in the December 31,

1934, annual report, nearly half, $3,541,500, were "expenses incidental to the Model 120." Of non-120 costs, $1,559,975 were senior Twelfth Series tools (the 120 was never considered part of the proper Twelfth Series), the remaining costs were branch, $438,827, and factory, $1,750,247, losses due to low volume.

Packard's 1936 senior Fourteenth Series cars were (as building owners skip the thirteenth floor, so would Packard omit a "Thirteenth Series") largely unchanged but for another few degrees rake of the grille and chrome strips added to the headlight shells. The junior car's fortunes were turning the venerable firm's fiscal tide, as reported in "The Car of Enduring Identity, A Message to Packard Stockholders," dated June 27, 1936: "We are pleased to enclose your dividend check due July 1. On February 11, 1936, Packard paid a dividend of $1,000,000. On July 1, 1936, Packard is paying a dividend of 42,250,000. In the first six months of 1936 Packard's net earnings will be approximately the same as for the entire year of 1935, which were $3,315,622. This excellent showing is due mainly to the great popularity and increased sales of Packard cars. During the first six months of 1936, Packard's sales will have totaled about 34,000 cars, an increase of some 16,700 cars, or 97 percent over the corresponding period of 1935. In May 1936, the last month for which complete figures are available,

deliveries of Packard cars passed the previous all-time monthly record made in August 1929."

For all the postmortems and Monday-morning quarterbacking of what Packard "should've done," the reality is that the company was interested in hawking expensive automobiles like our '35 Eight coupe-roadster and its fellow seniors, with their higher profit margins, for so long as they possibly could. In 1933, Packard had 107,000 stockholders, and was the most widely held automotive stock after GM, with 360,000 (Ford was privately held). After the inexpensive and ubiquitous Ford, Packard was the most recognized automotive name in the world. Five of the Supreme Court justices owned Packards. Embassies at home and abroad hosted fleets of senior sedans and limousines.

You can gauge Packard's entrenchment in fine car practice by considering that during the 1936 model year, 2,500 of the company's assembly staff built 5,303 senior Eights, Super Eights and

Twelves while the remaining 2,600 workers in the second plant assembled 55,042 One Twenties. ❧

Acknowledgments and Bibliography

Blond, Stuart, editor, various issues of The Cormorant News Bulletin *(monthly of the Packard Club, 420 S. Ludlow St., Dayton, Ohio 45402); Holls, Dave and Lamm, Michael,* A Century of Automotive Style: 100 Years of American Car Design, *Stockton, California, Lamm-Morada, Inc., 1997; Kimes, Beverly Rae, editor., November 1990 issue of* Classic Car Club of America Bulletin *(monthly of the CCCA, 1645 Des Plaines River Rd, Suite 7, Des Plaines, IL 60018); Kimes, Beverly Rae, editor,* Packard, A History of the Motor Car and the Company, *Princeton, New Jersey; Princeton Publishing, Inc., 1978; Langworth, Richard M.,* Illustrated Packard Buyer's Guide, *Osceola, Wisconsin, Motorbooks International, 1991; Langworth, Richard M., editor, various issues of* The Packard Cormorant Magazine; *Packard Motor Car Company, Annual Report, Detroit, Michigan, Packard Motor Car Co., January 31, 1934; Packard Motor Car company,* The Car of Enduring Identity: A Message to Packard Stockholders, *Detroit, Michigan, Packard Motor Car Co., June 27, 1936; Scott, Michael G.H.,* Packard, The Complete Story, *New York, New York, Tab Books, Division of McGraw-Hill Companies, 1985, 1987.*

Special thanks to Jim and Lillie Lawrence, Lafayette, California. Additional thanks to Donald C. Figone, Santa Rosa, California, and Sheridan W. Hale, Walnut Creek, California.

1937 PACKARD SIX

PACKARD HAD a sensational year in 1937. Never before had it made so many cars—or so much money. Nor would it, ever again. It is true that by a narrow margin more new Packards were registered in 1949 than in 1937; but the overall sales couldn't quite reach the company's high-water mark. (The discrepancy between registrations and sales can be accounted for in part by the difference between the model year and the *calendar* year, and in part by the bustling export business that Packard enjoyed prior to World War II.)

It was the new Six that did the trick. Packard had invaded the medium-price field two years earlier with its sensational One-Twenty, a straight eight priced to compete with the mid-range Buicks. Some automotive historians have accused Packard of abandoning the luxury market, its traditional niche; but the truth is that by the mid-thirties there was hardly a luxury market left. Packard's new car registrations, which had numbered well over 44,000 in 1929,

by Arch Brown
photos by Vince Manocchi

had dropped to 6,500 five years later. That this dismal figure was still one-third ahead of Cadillac's total was cold comfort to the men out on East Grand Boulevard, for Cadillac had all the resources of General Motors behind it while Packard stood alone. So the One-Twenty was born of necessity, and there can be no doubt that it added at least a decade to the company's lifespan.

But the bulk of the sales of mid-priced cars in those days was still one notch, which is to say about $150, below the One-Twenty's price tag. Now, a hundred and fifty bucks may not sound like much in relation to automobile prices nowadays, but in the mid-thirties it represented a differential of something over 15 percent. Ergo, there was a whole market segment out there, dominated at the time by the Buick Special.

Packard took aim.

The new car was derived from the One-Twenty, sharing most of the latter's sheet metal and mechanical components. The wheelbase was chopped by five inches—the difference being entirely in the length of the hood—and a newly developed, six-cylinder engine was fitted. It was based on the One-Twenty's power plant and had larger

bore, same stroke, two less cylinders. Trim was a little less elaborate and a blended fabric was substituted for the One-Twenty's woolen upholstery, but basically the Six was the same car—just a bit smaller, lighter and less powerful. And a public accustomed to seeing Packard price tags averaging around $3,000 found itself looking at f.o.b. Detroit prices running as low as $795.

Seven hundred and ninety-five dollars for a Packard! Of course, there were skeptics. The new car was, after all, still priced a few bucks above the Buick, and its weight and wheelbase were more closely comparable to those of the $650 Pontiac. *Fortune* reported a sanitized version of the comment made by one cynical competitor: "The new virgin is always the busiest girl in the harem. For a while. Sooner or later she will have to take her chances with the rest of us."

Sour grapes, perhaps. Packard, whose sales had already overtaken those of Studebaker and Nash, passed Hudson in 1937 to become the sales leader among the independent automobile manufacturers. Quite a change from three years earlier, when even the hapless Hupmobile had outsold Pack-

Originally published in Special Interest Autos #67, Jan.-Feb. 1982

A PACKARD FOR $795

In terms of styling, the Six was pure Packard through and through, right down to its hubcaps with the famous red hexagon. Body shell was shared with One-Twenty series Packards, wheelbase was five inches shorter than small eights'.

ard, and Hudson had out-produced it nine times over!

In some respects the new, smaller Packard was an anachronism, but then, Packard had never pretended to lead the parade in terms of innovations. General Motors had introduced the seamless steel "turret" top in 1935, for instance, and by 1937 virtually everyone had copied it. Everyone, that is, but Packard; they stuck with the old-fashioned fabric insert. Chrysler, Nash, Studebaker and some of the others were offering the new Borg-Warner overdrive; Packard wouldn't get around to that one for a while.

No matter. The car had *class*. It looked like a Packard, it *rode* like a Packard, it *sounded* like a Packard. And it sold like ice cream on a hot July day, to the tune of 65,000 cars for 1937. Buick's Special might have its "turret" top and a valve-in-head straight eight engine, Chrysler's Royal could boast its overdrive and a fistful of other mechanical innovations, but neither of them had that indefinable quality, that mystique, that could only have come from a company which for over 30 years had catered to the moneyed classes. A British writer was moved to comment, "The general road performance of this Packard would be exceptional and praiseworthy if the car cost twice as much.... A greater compliment cannot be paid to this car than to say I wish it were a British one...."

Sad to relate, Packard's tenure as "sales king of the mountain" (at least among the independents) was a brief one. The recession of 1938 played hob

with everyone's sales, Packard's included, but at least the company managed to hang on to its first-place standing among the smaller manufacturers—for one more year. In 1939, however, the tide turned. Studebaker unveiled its sparkling, low-priced Champion (see *SIA* #35), while Nash offered a high-styled automobile whose tall, narrow grille could only have been inspired by the LaSalle. And Packard fell to third place. Two years later it ranked fourth, the "cellar" position among the larger independents, which it was fated to occupy for most of the company's remaining years.

Which brings us to the question that has been a topic for speculation among Packard lovers for many years: How come? Having climbed to the top, why

was Packard unable to stay there?

At least three factors merit consideration.

First, by 1941 Packard was more deeply involved in military work than any other automobile manufacturer. Turning out Rolls-Royce Merlin aircraft engines, as well as the great V-12 Packard Marines that powered the Navy's legendary PT boats, the engine plant was working double shifts. Obviously, this had a limiting effect upon the company's capacity for civilian production.

Second, Packard's 1941 models met with a less than enthusiastic public reception. The "massive" look was in, and Packard didn't have it. Four-hundred-eighty pounds lighter and nearly eight inches shorter than the

Comparison Table
1937 Business Coupes Priced from $715 to $795

Make:	Cyls.	C.I.D.	B.H.P.	Valve Config.	Compr. Ratio	Wheel-base	Axle Ratio	F.O.B. Price (1937)
Packard "115"	6	237.0	100	L	6.30:1	115"	4.38	$795
Buick "Special"	8	248.0	100	I	5.70:1	122"	4.40	$765
Chrysler "Royal"	6	228.1	93	L	6.50:1	116"	4.10	$715
Graham "Cavalier"	6	199.1	85	L	6.70:1	116"	4.45	$725
Hudson "74"	8	254.0	122	L	6.25:1	122"	4.11	$770
Nash "Ambassador"	6	234.8	93	I	5.67:1	121"	4.11	$755
Oldsmobile "L-37"	8	254.0	110	L	6.20:1	124"	4.37	$785

1937 PACKARD

Buick Special, the Packard Six was comparable in size and heft to the smallest Pontiac, priced $135—which is to say about 13 percent—lower than the Packard. Nor did its 100 horsepower compare favorably in the public's eyes with Buick's 115. And so, while the industry scored an impressive gain over 1940, sales of the Packard One-Ten (the official designation for the six-cylinder car) fell by some 45 percent.

Packard's troubles for 1941 might have been a good deal worse, had it not been for the mid-season introduction of the sensational, Briggs-bodied Clipper (see *SIA* #59). Essentially a re-bodied One-Twenty, the Clipper had—in spades—the two qualities that the conventional Packards lacked that year: It was high-styled, and its appearance was massive. And so, despite a price differential of $114 over the One-Twenty and $319 over the One-Ten, the Clipper immediately became Packard's best-selling car. Unfortunately, due to its late introduction, the Clipper's selling season was short. Overall Packard sales for 1941 were nearly six percent below those of 1940.

For the 1942 season there were both six-cylinder and eight-cylinder Clippers, and luxury Clippers on the One-Sixty and One-Eighty chassis as well. Except for the convertible and commercial models, the conventionally styled car was dropped altogether from the two Junior series; and its sales on the senior chassis were negligible. It has been said that the sale of the 1941-42 Packard body dies to the Soviet Union, which was effected during the war years (see *SIA* #55), took place under heavy pressure from President Franklin D. Roosevelt. That may be so. The evidence suggests, however, that Packard may well have been glad to be rid of a body style that had proved to be something of a pariah, particularly inasmuch as the Clipper had been such a smash hit.

And finally, there may have been an

Above: Interior is distinguished by banjo steering wheel, big, round speedo, cluster of rectangular instruments in center of dash. Right: By 1937, fabric top was a rather old-fashioned feature on Six. Below: Smallish oval rear window gives intimate feel to interior. Below right: Rear fenders were also shared with One-Twenty.

"Flying lady" radiator mascot was supposed to represent a combination of perfection in motion: speed, power, and grace. It was an extra-cost factory accessory popular on all series of Packards from 1924 until WW II.

Past the Point of No Return

For years, car buffs in general and Packard aficionados in particular have speculated on the possible fate of the Packard Motor Car Company, had it been a part of the 1954 merger that created American Motors. No end of theories have been advanced to explain why that didn't happen, and only recently has the inside story been told by the man who is in the best position to know the truth: George Romney. (See *SIA* #66.)

But perhaps we've been addressing the wrong question. It may be that what we really ought to be asking is, *Would 1954 have been too late to save Packard?*

The accompanying graph tells the story. Although Packard never again achieved the degree of success it had enjoyed in 1937, its share of the American automobile market continued through 1949 to hover around the two percent mark, a very respectable figure for an independent manufacturer. But after that, a brief rally in 1952 notwithstanding, it was downhill all the way. By 1954, the year Nash and Hudson joined forces to create American Motors, Packard held less than three-quarters of one percent of the market. It was a slump from which the grand old marque never recovered.

Would a merger with Nash and Hudson, and perhaps Studebaker, have helped at that point? Perhaps. At least it would have expanded Packard's dealer network. But Packard's body dies were obsolete; a complete retooling—at a cost that even the combined resources of Packard, Nash and Hudson could ill-afford at the time—would have been called for. (The alternative, of course, would have been to build Packards using the Nash body shell. One shudders at the thought!)

And consider this: While the American Motors merger saved its constituent companies, it failed to rescue either the Nash or the Hudson. Instead, it gave birth to the Rambler and the whole "compact car" movement. Would Packard have fared any better? Or would a compact Packard have been the result? The idea boggles the mind!

With the vision of hindsight, it is clear that Nash's far-sighted president, George Mason, had the right idea back in 1948: Merge the four great independents then, while among them they held nearly 13 percent of the market. To have done so would have created a corporation that almost certainly would have been a major force in the industry.

But perhaps by 1954 Packard, Nash and Hudson had all passed the point of no return.

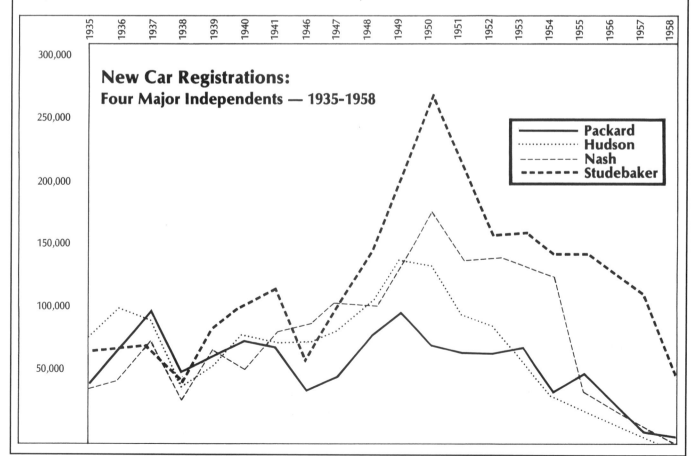

specifications

illustrations by Russell von Sauers, The Graphic Automobile Studio

© copyright 1981, Special Interest Autos

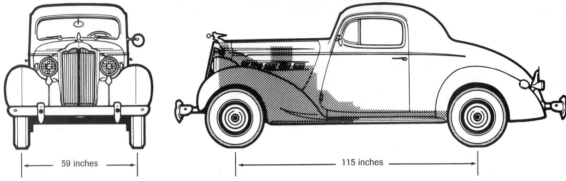

59 inches

115 inches

1937 Packard Six, Series 115C

Price:	$795 f.o.b. Detroit, Michigan.
Optional equipment on d/R car:	Radio, "banjo" steering wheel, "Flying Lady" radiator ornament, agate gearshift knob.

ENGINE:

Type:	6 cylinder in-line, L-head, 4 main bearings.
Bore x stroke:	3 7/16 inches x 4 1/4 inches.
Displacement:	237.0 cubic inches.
Max. bhp @ rpm:	100 @ 3600 (28.36 taxable).
Max. torque @ rpm:	200 @ 2000.
Compression ratio:	6.3:1 (6.75:1 optional).
Induction system:	Chandler-Groves AOC-2 single bbl (1 1/4 inch) downdraft carburetor; A.C. camshaft-driven fuel pump; automatic choke.
Electrical system:	Delco-Remy, 6-volt.
Engine rpms per mile:	3165.

CLUTCH:

Type:	Semi-centrifugal, single dry plate.
Diameter:	9 1/2 inches.
Actuation:	Mechanical, foot pedal.

TRANSMISSION:

Type:	Selective sliding gear, 3-speed; synchronized second and third gears.
Ratios: 1st:	2.43:1.
3rd:	1.00:1.
Reverse:	3.18:1.

DIFFERENTIAL:

Type:	Hypoid.
Ratio:	4.36:1.
Drive axles:	Semi-floating.

STEERING:

Type:	Worm and double-tooth roller, center point linkage.
Turns, lock to lock:	4 1/2.
Ratio:	18.4:1 gear, 21.96:1 overall.
Turning radius (minimum):	19 feet 2 inches.

BRAKES:

Type:	4-wheel hydraulic, internal expanding, 2-shoe.
Drum diameter:	11 inches.
Total lining area:	168 square inches.

CHASSIS & BODY:

Frame:	Welded I-beam, X-type.
Body construction:	Composite steel and wood.
Body style:	2-passenger business coupe.

SUSPENSION:

Front:	Independent coil springs (5.17" outside diameter).
Rear:	54-inches x 1 3/4-inches semi-elliptical leaf springs.
Tires:	6.50 x 16.
Wheels:	4.5 x 16 steel disc.

WEIGHTS & MEASURES:

Wheelbase:	115 inches.
Overall length:	192 3/32 inches.
Overall height:	67 1/4 inches.
Overall width:	72 inches.
Front tread:	59 inches.
Rear tread:	60 inches.
Ground clearance:	7 3/4 inches.
Shipping weight:	3215 pounds.

CAPACITIES:

Crankcase:	7 quarts.
Cooling system:	17 quarts.
Fuel tank:	17 gallons.

PERFORMANCE:

Top speed (av.):	78-80 mph.
Cruising speed:	60-65 mph.
Acceleration, 0-50:	14.4 seconds.
Standing quarter mile:	22 seconds.
Fuel consumption (est. highway, legal speeds):	18 mpg.

SOURCES:
Automotive Industries, November 21, 1936 and ruary 27, 1937.
The Motor, January 26, 1937.
1937 Packard Owners' Manual.
1937 Packard Six and 120 data book.

1937 PACKARD

element of truth in that anonymous competitor's observation about "the new virgin in the harem." By 1941 a Packard within the reach of the middle class was no longer a novelty, and perhaps the edge had been taken off the thrill of owning a Packard. The competition, of course, was brutal, not only from Buick and its corporate siblings, but also from Chrysler, Studebaker, Nash and Hudson.

It is interesting to speculate on the possible outcome of Packard's struggle, had not World War II intervened. By war's end the car-starved public was prepared to buy whatever kind of automobile it could get its hands on. The competition among the manufacturers had to do with a scramble for allocations of steel and other materiel, rather than a struggle for sales. It was an unfamiliar battle, and on the face of it, not one in which Packard was conspicuously successful.

Driving Impressions

Don Anderson has been fascinated by Packard cars ever since he was a kid growing up in Wyoming, back in the Depression years. There was in Don's town a pool-hall operator known, by reason of the flashy ring that he wore, as "Diamond Dick." And Diamond Dick was the only person in the community who was prosperous enough to drive a Packard. Young Anderson was impressed. Small wonder that he always wanted to be "The Man Who Owns One."

There was another Packard in Don's life, some years ago, one of the classic "senior" cars; but it was registered to Don's company, and when Don sold the business and retired, the car was part of the deal. Don hated to lose the

Packard; and three years ago his wife secretly bought the little coupe that is our driveReport car, presenting it to her husband as a Christmas gift

It is an original car, which spent its first 38 years in the hands of its initial owner. A plate on the firewall announces that the Packard was first delivered in Phoenix, Arizona, on April 3, 1937. The odometer reading, just over 63,000 miles, is valid, and it's the first time around. Upholstery is original and the car's finish is some 30 years old. Don plans a cosmetic restoration in the near future, but we found the car to be very presentable just as it stands.

It is authentic in every respect save one. Somebody—presumably its first owner, but possibly the "interim" possessor from whom Mrs. Anderson bought it—converted the Packard's headlamps to sealed beams. They do provide better light than the originals, but when the car is restored Don will reconvert the lamps back to factory stock,

Mechanically the car was very nearly

perfect when it came into Don's possession. The only repair to date has been the installation of a new clutch plate. After 44 years, the original had begun to slip. Incredibly, the pressure plate turned out to be as good as new, and was left in place.

The engine starts readily, by means of a button at center dash, and idles in near silence. (Don reports that even after two months of disuse the engine will fire on the first turn.) The clutch engages smoothly, requiring little pressure. Shifts are accomplished with ease, though the throws are long and the action could hardly be described as "crisp." Under way the Packard has a remarkably solid feel to it, and the ride belies its relatively modest size and weight. The men at Packard obviously knew what sound insulation was all about; even at speed the car is pleasantly silent.

Acceleration is good for a car of this vintage, and the low-end torque is impressive. Second-gear starts are accomplished without strain. We didn't

Right: Even the Six's sturdy flathead engine was derived from the One-Twenty; carried larger bore, same stroke, developed 100 bhp at 3,600 rpm. Below: Six's performance is more than adequate. Steering is a pleasure, hydraulic brakes are outstanding for their time.

George T. Christopher

It goes without saying that when the decision to build the One-Twenty was made, in 1933, the people at Packard didn't know any more about mass production methods than a hog knows about Sunday. From its inception, just before the turn of the century, the Packard Motor Car Company had catered to the "carriage" trade, their cars carefully handcrafted with little regard to cost.

The One-Twenty, they knew, would change all that; and indeed it did! By 1936, as Robert Turnquist has recorded, 51 percent of Packard's production work force was involved in turning out the new, cheaper car, which already accounted for over 90 percent of the company's unit volume. Or to put it another way, nearly nine times as many man-hours went into the manufacture of each "senior" Packard as were required to assemble a One-Twenty.

To bring about the necessary transformation, Packard lured George Christopher, an acknowledged expert in low-cost mass production, out of retirement. A 1911 graduate of the Rose Polytechnic Institute, Christopher had worked first for Westinghouse, then for Standard Wheel before joining GM's Delco-Remy division in 1918 as vice president in charge of manufacturing. In 1927 he became chief inspector at Oldsmobile, then vice president in charge of manufacturing at Pontiac in 1930, moving over to Buick in the same capacity two years later.

Christopher surrounded himself with a cadre of new recruits, each man hired for his expertise in some phase of mass production methods. Less than one year following his arrival at Packard, cars were rolling off the new One-Twenty production line. After that, adaptation to the building of the "Six," less than two years later, was a piece of cake. And it had all been done virtually without a glitch!

Christopher's contributions were recognized promptly enough by the high command at Packard. Hired initially as production manager for the One-Twenty project, within a matter of months George Christopher was appointed assistant vice president of manufacturing, and then—in 1935—vice president. By April 1942, Christopher was Packard's president and general manager. The Packard Motor Car Company had entered into a new era, symbolized by the man who had become its president.

1937 PACKARD

get into the hill country in our brief tour, but our guess—confirmed by Don Anderson—is that the little Packard must be a very creditable mountain climber. Steering, typically for a car of its vintage, is rather slow; but it's light and fairly precise. There is some tendency to lean in the turns, but not as much as some of Packard's competitors did back in 1937. Brakes, in typical Packard fashion, are excellent; and the two-tone trumpet horns must have been inspired by Packard's senior models.

There's lots of room in every dimension for two passengers; three would be a little tight, but not at all impossible.

The seats offer good support, and we conclude that it would be a comfortable car on a long trip. Side vision is a bit restricted due to the blind quarter panels, but we've seen a lot worse, and the rear view is circumscribed by the very small (but smartly styled) window. The dash layout is attractive. Rectangular gauges give the driver readings on the oil pressure (which holds at a steady 30 pounds), temperature (also steady at 180 degrees), fuel supply, and generator output.

Vent wings on the windows are crank-operated. One of the least impressive "signs of progress" in recent years has been, in our view, the elimination of this feature—which of course was introduced amid great fanfare nearly 50 years ago. We'd like to see the little panes return!

1937 Packard "Six," Model 115-C
Body Style Availability and Price Table

Body Style:	Passengers	Shipping Weight	Price 9/3/36	8/9/37
Business Coupe	2	3140 lbs.	$795	$960
Sport Coupe	2-4	3215 lbs.	840	1005
Convertible Coupe	2-4	3285 lbs.	910	1075
Touring Coupe	5	3235 lbs.	860	1025
Sedan	5	3265 lbs.	895	1060
Club Sedan	5	3275 lbs.	900	1065
Touring Sedan	5	3310 lbs.	910	1075
Station Wagon	8	N/A	---	1205

Source: Turnquist, Robert E., *The Packard Story.*

Below: *Plenty of room for luggage for two in the coupe's trunk. Additional storage space is available behind the seats and on parcel shelf.*

The coupe was intended as a business car, of course, and ample stowage is provided for the salesman's cases or luggage. There's a large package shelf behind the seat and an ample space beneath it accessible by tipping either side of the divided backrest. To the rear the deck opens up to reveal a sizable trunk, though its usefulness is impeded somewhat by the narrow deck lid and a plywood shelf above the spare tire.

Packard used a good deal of wood in the construction of their bodies in 1937, which helps account for the excellent sound insulation as well as the resounding "thunk" when the doors are closed. This type of construction has posed problems for many a restorer of vintage cars; but in this instance, thanks to the dry Arizona climate, the original wood is as good as new throughout the car.

The antenna for the radio is a simple wire screen, buried under the fabric insert in the Packard's top. We question its effectiveness, for the radio, which provides excellent tone quality, has a very limited range.

Your reporter was a senior in high school when Packard introduced its new Six. We were totally captivated by it then.

We still are today. ✑

Acknowledgements and Bibliography

Automotive Industries, *September 5, 1936; November 21, 1936; February 27,1937; Clarke, R.M., Packard Cars, 1920-42, Cobham, Surrey, England, Brooklands Books (no date given); Fortune, January 1937; Heasley, Jerry, The Production Figure Book for US Cars, Osceola, Wisconsin, Motorbooks International, 1977; Turnquist, Robert E., The Packard Story, New York, A.S. Barnes, 1965; 1937 Packard Owner's Manual.*

Our thanks to Chuck Holmes, Stockton, California; Bill Lauer, Santa Ana, California; Richard Langworth, Contoocook, New Hampshire; George Hamlin, Clarksville, Maryland; special thanks to Don Anderson, Tustin, California.

CLASSIC FASTBACK

by Josiah Work
photos by Bud Juneau

THE Packard Motor Car Company had created something of a sensation during April 1941, with the introduction of the original Packard Clipper (see *SIA* #59). Built on the chassis of the popular, medium-priced One-Twenty, it came in only one body type, that first year: a four-door sedan, featuring smooth, flowing fenders and concealed running boards. The grille, continuing Packard's traditional gothic theme, was tall, narrow and very impressive. Three inches lower and more than an inch wider than the One-Twenty, the Clipper represented one of the most thoroughly modern designs of its time, and certainly one of the most beautiful. And best of all, it was priced at $1,420, just $129 higher than the One-Twenty sedan.

Responsibility for styling this gorgeous automobile was claimed by Howard "Dutch" Darrin, who had been doing some lovely semi-custom convertible victorias for Packard. But while Darrin was unquestionably involved in

1947 PACKARD CUSTOM SUPER EIGHT

the design process, and may even have provided the inspiration for the Clipper, it was Packard stylist Werner Gubitz who was actually in charge of the program. And there is evidence that the design, as it finally emerged, was primarily the work of Howard Yaeger, a member of Gubitz's staff.

In an interview published in the Spring 1992 issue of *The Packard Cormorant*, Joel Prescott quotes William Reithard, another Packard designer, as saying this about Darrin: "In my opinion, Dutch was not a great designer. He did have a good feeling for form and a good sense of proportion, but he was not a careful detailer. He was a terrific salesman, though — a good front man. You know, when he and Thomas Hibbard were together over in Paris, Hibbard was responsible for the design work and Dutch was the salesman. Sometimes, he even *over*sold...."

In any case, credit for the Packard Clipper's styling has been debated for more than a generation, and will doubtless continue to be a matter of dispute

Above: Front-end styling is carryover from prewar Clipper with some '42 Chrysler touches thrown in as well. **Below:** Factory accessory mirror is gracefully designed to blend with curves of car.

1947 Packard Prices* and Weights

	Price	Weight	Production**
Clipper Six (120-inch w/b)			14,949
Sedan, 4-door	$1,937	3,520 lb.	
Club Sedan	$1,912	3,475 lb.	
Clipper Deluxe Eight (120-inch w/b)			28,855
Sedan, 4-door	$2,149	3,695 lb.	
Club Sedan	$2,124	3,650 lb.	
Super Clipper (127-inch w/b)			4,802
Sedan, 4-door	$2,772	4,025 lb.	
Club Sedan	$2,747	3,980 lb.	
Custom Super Clipper (127-inch w/b)			7,480
Sedan, 4-door	$3,449	4,090 lb.	
Club Sedan	$3,384	4,045 lb.	
Custom Super Clipper (148-inch w/b)			***
Limousine, 7-passenger	$4,668	4,920 lb.	
Sedan, 7-passenger	$4,504	4,890 lb.	

* Mid-year prices shown
** Production figures by body style are not available
*** Included with 127-inch w/b Custom Super Clippers

1947 Packard

for some time to come.

To power the Clipper, the compression ratio of Packard's 282-c.i.d. straight-eight was increased from 6.41:1 to 6.85:1, raising the horsepower from 120 to 125. This was a prudent move on Packard's part, in view of the fact that the Clipper outweighed the One-Twenty sedan by 215 pounds. Performance was satisfyingly brisk, especially when the car was fitted with the automatic overdrive, a $60 option that carried with it a numerically higher axle ratio.

By the time the Clipper made its debut, less than five months remained in the 1941 model year. Yet the new car's sales fell only 500 units short of the full season's total for the less expensive One-Twenty. Packard had come up with a bell-ringer! And a good thing, too, for even with this hefty assist from the Clipper, Packard's 1941 model year output came to just 72,855 cars, a decrease of nearly 26 percent compared to 1940. (By way of comparison, Buick was at the same time racking up a new sales record, with production running about one-third ahead of 1940.)

Capitalizing on the new model's popularity, Packard offered four series of Clippers for 1942 — Six, Eight, Super Eight and Custom Super Eight — each consisting of two body styles: the original four-door sedan and a new two-door fastback known as the Club Sedan. Only the convertibles, some stretched-wheelbase sedans and a few semi-customs retained the previous season's conventional styling.

For the Clipper's second season, only the senior cars — the Super Eight and Custom Super Eight series — retained the 127-inch wheelbase of the 1941 model. Both junior lines, the Clipper Eight (replacing the One-Twenty) and the Clipper Six (formerly the One-Ten) using a 120-inch chassis, the reduction appearing in the length of the hood.

The 1942 Clippers were instantly popular, and until Pearl Harbor caused Packard's assembly lines to close down on February 7, 1942, cars rolled out of the East Grand Boulevard factory at a rate 44 percent faster than the 1941 average. Had the company been able to sustain that pace for a full year, it would have enjoyed the second-best year in its history, surpassed only by 1937.

Parenthetically, much has been written deploring Packard's sale of the conventionally styled 1941 body dies to the Soviet Union, a move reportedly made in response to pressure from the White House. Obviously, this transaction led to the demise of the semi-custom Packards, the prestigious modifications undertaken in limited numbers by

*Above: Fastback styling gives the Packard a low, sleek, flowing appearance. **Below:** Hood can be lifted from either side, or removed altogether for heavy-duty repairs.*

LeBaron, Rollson, Darrin and others, for the Clipper body did not lend itself readily to custom work. But as the sales figures reveal, the bald truth is that the 1941 Packards, apart from the Clipper, were not well received by the public, and the company was probably well rid of the dies. Alongside the low, wide, sleek new cars from Buick and Cadillac, the conventional 1941 Packards had looked "dated" from the time of their introduction.

It would be fair to say that Packard entered the postwar market with at least one advantage over most of its competitors, for the Clipper styling, though five years old by that time, was still fresh and highly attractive, and far more contemporary than, say, 1946 models from Chrysler or Ford. The same four series were offered, again in the same two body types, together with a huge, 148-inch-wheelbase Clipper that took its place at the top of the Custom Super Eight line.

Like most other automakers, Packard was handicapped by a shortage of raw materials during the early postwar years. Sheet steel, in particular, was hard to come by. The company's production figures tell the story: During model year 1946, with customers literally standing in line, cash in hand, awaiting their opportunity to buy a new car, Packard built only 30,793 cars, less than one-third of the 1940 total. That figure rose to 51,086 for model year 1947 — a substantial improvement, but still well below even the recession year of 1938. In view of the almost unlimited potential market, it must have been a frustrating time for the men of Packard.

Management, however, was shrewd enough to make the best of available resources. During 1940 and '41 the costly (and profitable) One-Sixty and One-Eighty models had accounted for only 7.7 percent of Packard's total production. But taking advantage of the postwar "seller's market," the company increased production of the "senior" cars until they represented one-fourth of the Twenty-First Series (1946-47) total. (In fact, by 1947 the Custom Super Eights even outnumbered the Super Eights by a ratio of better than three-to-two, a situation unique in Packard's history.) The costliest models were late in reaching the market, however. According to Martin Cousineau, writing in *The Packard Cormorant,* "The first postwar Packard was assembled in October 1945, but it wasn't until June 1946 that the first Custom Super Clipper came down the line."

These fine automobiles were not markedly different from their prewar counterparts, their main distinction being a slightly modified grille. Both the Super Eight and the Custom Super Eight were powered by Packard's superb 356-cubic-inch, 165-horsepower straight-eight, a powerplant that had first appeared in 1940's Eighteenth Series. One would be hard-pressed to think of a smoother engine than this one, with a 105-pound crankshaft cradled in nine main bearings; and in combination with the optional overdrive it was capable of propelling the car to speeds of 100 miles

illustrations by Russell von Sauers, The Graphic Automobile Studio

specifications

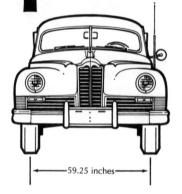
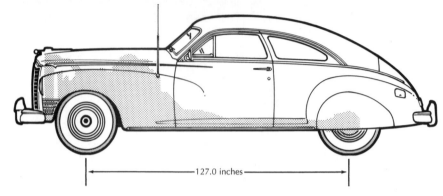

59.25 inches

127.0 inches

1947 Packard Custom Super Eight, Series 210

Original price	$3,140 ($3,384 at mid-year) f.o.b. factory, with standard equipment
Options on dR car	Overdrive, Electromatic clutch, radio, heater/defroster, white sidewall tires, wheel trim rings, deluxe hood ornament
Aftermarket access.	Fog lights, turn signals, locking gas cap

ENGINE

Type	L-head straight-eight
Bore x stroke	3.5 inches x 4.625 inches
Displacement	356.0 cubic inches
Compression ratio	6.85:1
Horsepower @ rpm	165 @ 3,600
Torque @ rpm	292 @ 2,000
Taxable horsepower	39.2
Valve lifters	Hydraulic
Main bearings	9
Fuel system	Carter WDO 531S 1.25-inch downdraft carburetor, camshaft pump
Lubrication system	Pressure
Cooling system	Centrifugal pump, driven by fan belt
Exhaust system	Single
Electrical system	6-volt battery/coil

TRANSMISSION

Type	3-speed selective with overdrive; synchronized 2nd and 3rd gears; column-mounted lever
Ratios: 1st	2.43:1
2nd	1.53:1
3rd	1.00:1
Reverse	3.16:1
Overdrive	0.75:1

CLUTCH

Type	Single dry plate
Diameter	11 inches
Actuation	Mechanical, foot pedal

REAR AXLE

Type	Hypoid
Ratio	4.09:1; engine to driving wheels ratio (in overdrive): 3.07:1
Drive axles	Semi-floating
Torque medium	Springs

STEERING

Type	Gemmer worm-and-roller
Turns lock-to-lock	5.25
Ratio	20.19:1
Turning diameter	46 feet

BRAKES

Type	4-wheel internal hydraulic,
Drum diameter	12 inches
Effective area	208.2 square inches

CHASSIS & BODY

Construction	Body-on-frame
Frame	Double drop taper pressed steel
Body type	2-door club sedan
Body construction	All steel

SUSPENSION

Front	Independent, coil springs, torsional stabilizer
Rear	Rigid axle, 54.375-inch x 2-inch semi-elliptic springs; torsional stabilizer
Shock absorbers, front	Two-way direct-acting
Shock absorbers, rear	Double-acting
Tires	7.00 x 15 4 ply
Wheels	Pressed steel disc

WEIGHTS AND MEASURES

Wheelbase	127 inches
Overall length	215.5 inches
Overall width	76.125 inches
Overall height	64 inches
Front track	59.25 inches
Rear track	60.69 inches
Min. road clearance	7.5 inches
Curb weight	4,025 pounds

CAPACITIES

Crankcase	7 quarts
Cooling system	20 quarts
Fuel tank	20 gallons
Transmission	2 pints
Overdrive	1.25 pints
Rear axle	6.75 pints

CALCULATED DATA

Horsepower per c.i.d.	.463
Weight per hp	24.4 pounds
Weight per c.i.d.	11.3 pounds
P.S.I. (brakes)	19.3

PERFORMANCE

Top speed	103-108 mph (est. average)
Acceleration: 0-60 mph	19 seconds (est. average)
Mpg	16-21 (est. average)

(From *The Packard Cormorant*, Spring 1992)

This page: Use of bright trim is very restrained throughout the car. Packard let the car's shape give the illusion of motion. *Facing page, left:* Front parking lamps are nearly hidden in grille. *Right:* Traditional Packard script adorns trunk lid.

1947 Packard

an hour or better. Thus, the senior 1946-47 Packards were almost certainly the fastest American production cars of their day. Silence was maintained by means of hydraulic tappets. A colleague of the writer's owned one of these great automobiles, a Custom Super Eight sedan, purchased second-hand in about 1950. So smoothly, swiftly and quietly did this car eat up the miles that its owners — who kept it for more than a decade — called it "The Magic Carpet."

The Twenty-First Series Custom Super Eights were expensive automobiles, costing $798 more than the Super Eights and, in club sedan guise, $938 more than the Cadillac Sixty-Two. Nor are differences between the Super Eight and Custom Super Eight models particularly obvious. Mechanically the two are identical, and of course they share the same styling. So at first glance one might find it difficult to justify their cost, vis-a-vis that of the Super Eights. Probably the most important distinction lies in the interior, where the Custom Super upholstery was done in rich broadcloth and leather, available in a choice of four colors: tan, maroon, navy and green, each with smart piping of light toned broadcloth. Door panels were of matching material, with leather kick panels, while floors were covered in "Mosstred" carpeting from New York's Shulton Looms. Individually wrapped coil springs were used in both seats and

backrests, while seat backs were padded with finest down. Imitation wood paneling, exquisitely done, added another touch of quality, and there was even a unique fore-to-aft stitched headliner.

Exterior differences were more subtle, yet they, too, added to the richness of these top-of-the-line cars. Handsome cloisonné hubcap medallions were provided and fender skirts were standard; and in a reversal of customary practice, identifying script, used on the doors of all three lesser series, was eliminated on the Custom Super Eights.

The option list was relatively short, at least in comparison to what we've become accustomed to in recent times. White sidewall tires, almost obligatory for concours purposes today, were virtually impossible to find during 1947, and were therefore not usually listed. Heater and radio were to be had, of course, the latter often found in combination with a roof-mounted antenna. Overdrive was popular, as well as an "Electromatic" clutch. Evidently intended as a response to Cadillac's popular HydraMatic trans-

mission, this device did not relieve the driver of the need for shifting gears, but at least gear changes could be made without using the clutch.

The Twenty-First Series Packard Custom Super Eights are accepted as full Classics, upon individual application, by the Classic Car Club of America. They have also been designated as Milestone Cars by the Milestone Car Society. The club sedans, of which only one 1946 model and fifteen 1947 examples are known to survive, are particularly desirable, and they change hands so rarely that it is almost impossible to estimate their value with any degree of accuracy.

Driving Impressions

Dr. Neal Gapoff, who is licensed as both a dentist and a chiropractor, had known about his Custom Super Eight club sedan for eight years. During that time he occasionally reminded its owner that he would be interested in buying the car, should it ever become available, and finally, early in 1993, a deal was struck.

1947

By 1947, with World War II well behind us, America was settling down to a more or less normal pace. The economy was booming, and although certain durable goods, notably automobiles, were still in short supply, on the whole life was sweet.

Among the highlights of the year were the following:

● Led by Christian Dior, the fashion world gave America's ladies the "New Look," featuring radically lowered hemlines. Needless to say, the sight of dresses that reached to the wearers' ankles had little appeal for the men.

● Margaret Truman, the president's daughter, made her singing debut with the Detroit Symphony Orchestra. Fortunately for the nation, she subsequently turned her attention to writing mystery novels.

● During the summer, "flying saucers" were observed, streaking across the sky in various parts of the country. The sightings provoked a rash of jokes, most of them unprintable.

● Middleweight boxer Rocky Graziano told a New York County grand jury that he had been offered $100,000 to "throw" a fight.

But of course, life had its serious side:

● For the first time since the onset of the Great Depression, Republicans controlled both houses of Congress.

● Secretary of State George C. Marshall, in a speech at Harvard University, announced a government plan — soon to be known informally as the Marshall Plan — for the economic and military rehabilitation of Europe and China.

● The last of Manhattan's streetcars were replaced by diesel-powered buses. This was supposed to represent progress.

● "Mother Nature" was seemingly on a rampage. During April a cyclone crossed the western part of Texas and Oklahoma, killing 134 persons and injuring 1,300. Then in September a hurricane took the lives of 100 persons in Florida, Louisiana, and Mississippi. The Missouri overflowed, inundating nearly a million acres of farmland, and two days after Christmas a 25.8-inch snowfall blanketed the eastern United States from Maine to Washington, halting airplane, railroad and bus service.

● A mine explosion in Centralia, Illinois, took the lives of 111 miners, prompting United Mine Workers president John L. Lewis to honor their memory by closing the

nation's soft coal mines for six days.

● An even worse explosion took place at Texas City, Texas, when a nitrate-laden French freighter exploded at the wharf. Property damage amounted to $50 million, and the death toll reached 512 persons.

And its bright side:

● Broadway brought us *Brigadoon*, a delightful fantasy with a fine score by Lerner and Loewe.

● At the movies we saw *Life With Father*, starring William Powell and Irene Dunne; and *Miracle on 34th Street*, with Maureen O'Hara.

● Books of the year included James Michener's *Tales of the South Pacific*, soon to inspire a musical that was a major hit both on Broadway and in the movies.

● The National League's New York Giants set a record of 221 home runs for the season, though it was the American League's Yankees that won the World Series.

● And Texas's "Babe" Didrickson Zaharias became the first American ever to win the British women's amateur golf championship.

Taken all in all it was, as Frank Sinatra would say, a Very Good Year.

1947 Packard

Above: For a big car, Packard handles quite nimbly. *Below:* Interior abounds with wood-grain and fine fabric. *Facing page, left:* Unusual tube directs air from fan to breather intake. *Top right:* Huge doors give easy access front and rear. *Right:* Fastback styling pinches trunk space. *Below:* Piping gives distinctive look to seats. *Bottom:* The old smoothie. Nine-main, 356-cube straight eight is unbeatable for velvet delivery of power.

1947 Packard versus Cadillac

	Packard Custom Super Eight	Cadillac Sixty Two
List price, club sedan	$3,140	$2,200
Shipping weight	4,000 lb.	4,080 lb.
Wheelbase	127″	129″
Overall length	215.5″	220.0″
Overall width	76.125″	80.75″
Overall height	64″	66.69″
Front track	59.25″	59″
Rear track	60.69″	63″
Ground clearance	7.5″	8.0″
Engine	Straight Eight	V-8
Displacement	356.0 cu. in.	346.0 cu. in.
Horsepower @ rpm	165/3,600	150/3,600
Torque @ rpm	292/2,000	274/1,600
Compression ratio	6.85:1	7.25:1
Valve configuration	L-head	L-head
Valve lifters	Hydraulic	Hydraulic
Main bearings	9	3
Crankshaft diameter	2.75″	2.5″
Steering	Worm/roller	Recirculating ball
Ratio	20.4:1	21.3:1
Turning diameter	46.0 feet	40.2 feet
Turns, lock-to-lock	5.25	3.94
Final drive ratio, standard	3.92	3.77
Car fitted w/overdrive	4.09	N/A
Overall, o/d engaged	3.07	N/A
Car fitted with HydraMatic	N/A	3.36
Braking area	208.2 sq. in.	208.0 sq. in.
Drum diameter	12″	12″
Tire size	7.00/15	7.00/15
Hp per c.i.d.	.463	.434
Weight per hp	24.2 lb.	27.2 lb.
Weight per c.i.d.	11.2 lb.	11.8 lb.
P.S.I. (brakes)	19.2	19.6

This particular car was delivered to its first owner by Stein Motors, of Milwaukee, Wisconsin, on July 3, 1947, making it a relatively late-production unit. The Packard had passed through the hands of two more owners and had found its way to California before Dr. Gapoff acquired it. Yet it remains a low mileage, largely unrestored car. (When we started our test drive, the odometer registered just 54,673 miles.)

The upholstery is original, and while it has faded slightly, it shows virtually no wear. The exterior was refinished in a rich blue shade by the third owner. Plating is original, and in remarkably good condition.

Dr. Gapoff does not show his cars; he drives them. To that end, upon acquiring the Packard he did a complete brake job; replaced the wheel bearings all around; rebuilt the carburetor, generator and starter; went through the transmission and overdrive; installed a new-old-stock voltage regulator; and replaced the lugs, points, condenser, wiring harness, timing chain, water pump and radiator. At the time of Bud Juneau's photo session, he was preparing to take the Packard to a Classic Car Caravan at Grand Junction, Colorado, an 850-mile tour during which, we have since learned, the car performed flawlessly.

It would be difficult to imagine a better car for use on such a journey, for the Packard cruises contentedly at speeds of 65 to 70 miles an hour. The ride is marvelously comfortable, leg room is ample, and the seating is downright luxurious; and although the suspension is comparatively soft, the car corners without heeling over excessively.

In driving a number of older Packards over the years, we've noted that they tend to steer lighter than most of their contemporaries. That is certainly the case with this Custom Super Eight, which handles with remarkable ease; although corkscrew turns require a fair amount of wheel-winding. Pedal pressures are correspondingly light, the clutch is smooth, the brakes are excellent, and gear changes are crisp, requiring little effort.

Given the heft of this machine — the shipping weight runs to two tons — performance is surprisingly nimble. With 292 foot pounds of torque on tap, it accelerates rapidly and "flattens" the hills; and it will idle along smoothly in top gear, then pick up speed without downshifting. The overdrive is a major asset, but the Electromatic clutch was not in working order when we drove the car. (This device, we are told, tends to be

troublesome.)

By the close of 1947, the Twenty-First Series Packards were gone, their place taken by the car that has become known as Packard's "pregnant elephant," a model which, oddly enough, was awarded the New York Fashion Academy's Gold Medal, as "Fashion Car of the Year." But in retrospect, it was no match for the Clippers of earlier times when it came to sophisticated good looks. And we're left to wonder what Packard's fate might have been, had the Clipper's styling theme been further developed instead of being then cast aside. ❑

Acknowledgments and Bibliography
Automotive Industries, *March 15, 1947;* Gunnell, John (ed.), Standard Catalog of American Cars, 1946-1975; *Langworth, Richard M.,* Encyclopedia of American Cars, 1940-1970; *Mahoney, Tom, "Packard: A Great Name Passes On,"* Automobile Quarterly, *Vol. I, No. 3;* The Packard Cormorant, *Spring 1992; Stein, Ralph,* The American Automobile; *Turnquist, Robert E.,* The Packard Story.
Our thanks to Bud Juneau, Brentwood, California; Bill Lauer, Durango, Colorado; Rob McAtee, Durango, Colorado. Special thanks to Dr. Neal Gapoff, Tiburon, California.

1948 Packard Station Sedan

by Bill Williams, *Associate Editor*

driveReport

Originally published in Special Interest Autos #17, Jun.-Jul. 1973

PACKARD CALLED it the Station Sedan because it used mostly sedan body stampings. Everything ahead of the rear doors, and even the doors themselves and the rear fenders, were interchangeable with the Packard 8 sedan. The Station Sedan's roof and rear panels were unique, but they mated with the standard sedan's floor and body sides.

The Packard wagon's tailgate also fit into the same-width and -depth opening as the sedan's decklid. That's what, in fact, makes the body so tapered toward the rear. It's a characteristic that also leaves the Station Sedan's tailgate smaller than the 1973 Pinto wagon's.

The 1948-50 Pregnant Packard, whose pudgy lines seem to suit the wagon better than that era's sedans, has an unusual styling history. Edward Macauley, Packard's design vice president, was crazy about Sports cars. He admired Dutch Darrin's conversions of the early 1940s and was instrumental in giving factory support to the Packard-Darrin project. Ed Macauley had also built himself a series of Packard sportsters. One, called the Phantom, was begun in 1941, then modified in 1944 and again in 1947 to take on lines very similar to the Pregnant Packard. The Phantom became, in effect, a driveable test bed for Ed Macauley's ideas. Behind the scenes and very instrumental in both the 1941 Clipper and Phantom designs was Werner Gubitz, a man who apparently did much of Packard's real design work but, being shy and retiring, never got much credit.

Ed Macauley was no car designer but he had a good sense of proportion. John Reinhart, who was Packard's chief stylist from 1947 to 1951 (and who later did the Lincoln Continental Mark II under William Clay Ford), recalls the Pregnant Packard's design history this way:

"Ed Macauley was a good friend, a very fine man, and one of the last true gentlemen in the industry. What happened was this. The Clipper was taken over to Briggs Mfg. Co. around 1946. [Briggs stamped and built Packard bodies at that time.] There, Al Prance, Briggs's chief designer, filled in the areas between the front and rear fenders with clay. And that became the 1948 Packard. They didn't like the front end so they put a lower grille on it. The idea was to save money by reworking as few of the old Clipper's panels as possible, but before they got through with it, they'd redone almost everything, so they didn't save much after all. I think all they saved were the roof and decklid. Of course, some of the inner panels were held over—inner doors, cowl, floor, etc."

Ed Macauley then pushed for a station wagon for 1948 even though most other company executives weren't anxious to see one. Packard's most recent station wagon, the 1941 model, had sold only about 600 units, and that seemed par for an average year. Macauley, though, urged building the 1948 wagon with mostly sedan stampings, and despite lingering objections, he rammed it through. Result: a handsome wagon that suffered from cramped cargo space because of its sedan heritage.

Packard's 1948-50 Station Sedan turned out to be one of the two most expensive wagons of its day. It was even one of the more expensive Packards. Only the Custom 8s, Packard limousines, and 7-passenger sedans cost more. The Buick Roadmaster wagon was the Station Sedan's only price rival, and by 1950 even the Roadmaster cost $13 *less*.

Yet despite the Station Sedan's high price, it used Packard's smallest engine and spanned its shortest wheelbase. Also, during its entire 3-year production run, the car never changed. The 1949-50 Station Sedans are almost indistinguishable from 1948 models. The surest way to tell them apart is to look under the hood at their patent plates. The body number begins with 22 for 1948 models and has a 9 suffix for the early '49s. Late 1949s begin with 23, and the 1950 models have a 5 suffix.

Packard's Station Sedan *looks* like a woody, but it uses an all-steel body with bolted-on wooden ribs over simulated woodgrain panels. These painted-on panels were originally applied by rolling graining ink onto a colored enamel ground coat, then sealing the two with a clear, synthetic baked enamel. This wasn't the Di-Noc method, although the factory did suggest using Di-Noc decals if the sheetmetal had to be completely refinished (as in an accident). The factory also recommended restoring the wooden ribs every year or so by sanding them lightly, applying a toxic wood sealer (to kill fungus that might cause wood rot), then applying one of several recommended varnishes. The wooden cargo deck and inner tailgate needed similar periodic restoration. So despite being basically an all-steel wagon, the Station Sedan demanded as much upkeep as real woodies.

Many enthusiasts believe that Plymouth introduced the first all-metal production station wagon in 1949. *Its* first, yes, but *the* first, no. Packard beat Plymouth by some 18 months, but the 1946 Willys Jeep wagon beat Packard by two years. But then Chevrolet beat even Willys by 11 years. Chevy offered an all-steel wagon on a pickup chassis in 1935, and even that probably wasn't the first.

By today's standards, the Station Sedan's cargo area seems ludicrously tiny. With the second seat upright, the deck measures 42.75 inches long by 45.5 wide by 32.5 high. This comes out to 36.6 cubic feet or some 24 cubic

Except for roof and rear quarters, Packard's all-steel wagon uses sedan sheet metal, applied wooden ribs.

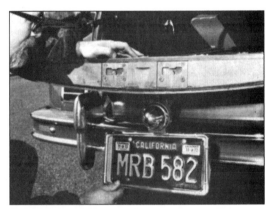

With tailgate open, license plate and light flip down. Open gate gives 25 inches of additional cargo floor.

DETROIT PUBLIC LIBRARY

Ed Macauley, Packard's styling director, built series of Phantom customs that became base for '48 design.

Since wagon's rear opening fits into sedan's former trunk, it's fairly tiny—smaller than Pinto wagon's.

Tapering rear section looks unusually sporting for so utilitarian a vehicle. Lack of drip rail over rear lift-gate causes leaks and rust.

All Station Sedans used Packard's new small 8. Bill Geyer's wagon has overdrive, which gives good flexibility, effortless highway cruising.

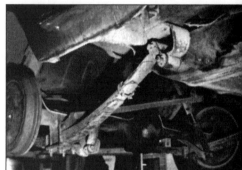

While 1949-50 Packards went to podded tail lamps, wagons stuck with 1948 lens all 3 years.

Pull-type handles make doors easy to open even if you have both arms full of grocery bundles.

Rear suspension uses anti-sway bar and inverted shackles. Wagon has more leaves than sedan.

Packard Station Sedan

feet less than inside the 1973 Pinto wagon with its second seat flat. In the Packard, you can leave the tailgate down for an added 25 inches of floor length. With the Station Sedan's second seat down, cargo volume rises to 63.0 cubic feet or about 2.5 more than in the Pinto wagon. Neither has provision for a third seat. The Station Sedan's spare tire rests underneath the stainless-steel-ribbed plywood cargo deck, and there's some extra hidden storage space beneath the second seat.

A major problem with the Station Sedan is that it leaks. All of them leak, and they leaked even when new. Since there's no rain gutter above the hinged rear window, water drips in when the lift-gate is raised. After the rubber weatherstripping dries out around the fifth door, dew and rain easily seep in and eventually rot the cargo deck floor, the sheet metal below the tailgate, and the bottom hinges. So it's rare today to find a Station Sedan without cancer of the rear floor area.

An early 1948 press release said that the Station Sedan's durable plastic-and-wood interior could be hosed out for quick cleaning. I can't imagine anyone actually doing that; I hope no one ever did. I found the wagon's upholstery sturdy looking and comfortable. All Station Sedans came with tan plastic/leatherette seats with woven plastic inserts. The rear-seat cushion flips up from the rear and rests on end against the back of the front seat. Then the rear-seat backrest unsnaps (a leather strap and eye buckle hold it) and lengthens the cargo deck.

Packard's engineering in almost every area was very straightforward, conventional, and rugged. The only far-out piece of engineering for the Pregnant series involved the Ultramatic. I place emphasis on rugged because Packard used one of the strongest X-member frames in the industry—an absolutely stable platform for an equally rigid body. Siderails were fully boxed behind and ahead of the big X, and the X itself was U-section with double gussets at each leg. Add to that five crossmembers plus a one-piece steel floor with pressed-in bracing and welded-on cowl and trunk, then braced and cross-braced sides, and you've got a monolithic structure. Packard bodies were thoroughly insulated with six different sorts of asphaltic compounds and padding—jute, celotex, fiberboard, asbestos, and

flocking plus combinations. The Station Sedan's 288-cid L-head engine became one of two re-engineered 8s for 1948 Packards, the other displacing 327 cid. Both were derived from the old 282, introduced in 1936. Chief research engineer Forest McFarland told *SIA* that Packard's decision to redesign the 282 into the new 288 and 327 came so the company could use common tooling and a minimum of different machining operations. The cylinder block was new but served both engines. All Packard engines now shared 3.5-inch pistons. Cylinder heads were common, although the 327 had greater clearance volume. Bore/stroke ratios became more nearly square. But the overriding consideration remained that Packard's smallest 8 (the 288) and its medium 8 (327) could be manufactured with common tools, from the same castings, and on the same production lines.

I should explain the various Packard series and designations at this point, because they've still got most people confused. First, please understand that Packard went along with conventional year-model dates (1948, 1949, etc.) only because everyone else did. But so far as the factory was concerned, year-model dates meant relatively little, and changes were heralded by series numbers. Packard's First Series began in 1923, and the Pregnant Packard, which bowed in Aug. 1947 as a 1948 model, kicked off the 22nd Series. The so-called 1949 Packard, introduced in Nov. 1948, simply continued the 22nd Series and looked almost the same. Except for a solid front bumper, there were no special changes at the beginning of the 1949 model year.

But in May 1949 came the celebration of Packard's 50th anniversary, so the company announced the 23rd Series that month. Styling changed very slightly (see chart), the Ultramatic transmission bowed, and a lot of fanfare and advertising attended Packard's Golden Jubilee. But when other automakers announced their 1950 models that October, Packard simply glided by with the 23rd Series, leaving it unchanged from mid-1949. After 1951, though, when the newly restyled bodies appeared to become the 24th Series, Packard's series changed year by year in step with other year models.

Within the 22nd and 23rd Series, Packard offered three distinct lines. Least expensive was the simple Packard 8 on a 120-inch wheelbase. This used the new 288-cid, 130-bhp engine. Above that came the Super 8 on the same wheelbase but with the 327, 145-bhp 8. Then at the top stood the Custom 8 on a 127-inch chassis, using a completely different,

Packard engineered a new 288-cid block for 1948 (shown), and it shared most components with also-new 327. Both derived from previous 282.

Packard's Electromatic clutch (arrow shows vacuum cylinder) rarely worked right. Most owners disconnected it. Ultramatic arrived in 1949.

Standard on Custom 8s, cormorant was available in lesser series, as were 3 other mascots.

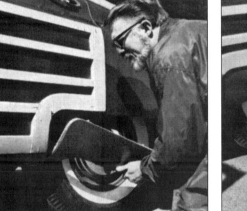

Rear tire changing isn't a sport for faint-hearted Packard owners. Bill Geyer demonstrates his technique by removing the two wingnuts that hold skirt on. To see them, Bill has to lie prone.

Spotter's Guide to Pregnant Packards

-1948: Introduced Aug. 1947 as Packard's 22nd Series. **Identity clues:** Bumper forms lower grille opening. Flush taillights with horizontal chrome dividers. Full-length chrome strips along rocker panels—one strip on Packard 8s and Super 8s, two strips on Custom 8s. Custom 8s also have eggcrate grilles front and rear.

-1949: Early 1949s were continuation of 22nd Series but had solid front bumpers. Body number 9 on patent plate. In May 1949, Packard's 23rd Series introduced (50th anniversary models). **Identity clues:** Solid front bumper. Horizontal trim spear runs full body length midway up doors. Chrome tail lamp pods. Custom 8s again have eggcrate grilles fore and aft, shared with new Super Deluxe. No suffix number on patent plate.

-1950: Continuation of 23rd Series. No visible differences from later 1949 models. Suffix number on patent plate became 5.

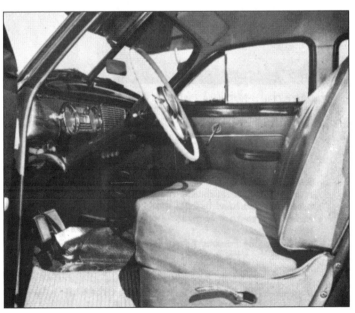

Uninspired gauge cluster makes all dials visible but seems out of keeping with tenor of that era's most expensive wagon. Upholstery is plastic.

53

Rear seat folds flat to nearly double deck space. Hasps lock seatback in place. Small valuables can be hidden in bins under bottom cushion.

Lovely wooden cargo deck uses stainless-steel ribs to protect finish. Factory said deck could be hosed out, but only a madman would do it.

Packard's smooth, soft ride means mushy suspension, which gives lots of lean in cornering. It's stable on the road, with plenty of brakes.

Spare rests under deck planking. This means you have to unload cargo for spare tire or tools.

Rear window locks with wingnuts. Fumes don't enter while driving with rear window open.

GM-like front suspension makes upper A-arms double as levers for indirect shock absorbers.

Packard Station Sedan

9-main, 356-cid 8 at 160 bhp, with hydraulic lifters and quite a few refinements in body, chassis, interiors, and trim. Yet even the Custom 8 used the same basic body as the lower lines, because the seven more inches of wheelbase came ahead of the cowl and showed up strictly in hood length.

Within the Packard 8 and Super 8 lines lay standard and deluxe trims. Body styles included a fastback 2-door club sedan, notchhack 4-door touring sedan, the Station Sedan in the smallest line only, then the two sedans plus a convertible in the Super and Custom 8s; and finally 7-passenger sedans and limousines in Super and Custom 8s on 141- and 148-inch wheelbases respectively.

Packard's board chairman during the 22nd Series' development was Alvan Macauley, Ed Macauley's father. Alvan was a strong, capable gentleman whose tenure (1916-48) paralleled the company's good years. He ruled benignly from a huge office in Packard's main building in Detroit that covered nearly a whole floor. Alvan Macauley always kept a roaring fire going, and he traditionally served coffee and doughnuts to visitors, be they employees or outsiders. His manner was friendly, worldly, and of the old school. He wouldn't be rushed, which perhaps helps explain the Series system—it was more important to get out a new car when it was ready than when the calendar dictated. Alvan Macauley's rather leisurely pace set the tone for the whole company, and former employees still remember the low pressure and Packard's freedom from tight deadlines.

Alvan Macauley retired in March 1948, and his place was temporarily taken by Max Gilman and then by George T. Christopher, a man quite unlike Macauley. Christopher had come up through Packard's manufacturing vice presidency and had fought the battles of postwar steel procurement. Those battles left him considerably less relaxed than Macauley had been. Colleagues describe Christopher as ambitious, pushy, hard-headed, not generally liked, but a man who did get things done. Under Christopher, Packard turned its first profits since WW-II. In 1949, his first year in office, Christopher saw the Ultramatic unveiled, the Golden Jubilee celebrated, and a record production of 116,995 cars.

SPECIFICATIONS
1948 Packard Station Sedan 4-door wagon

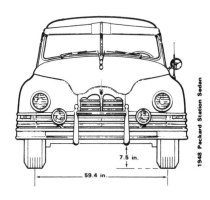

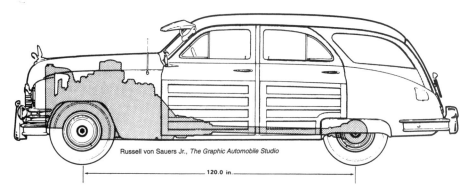

7.5 in.

59.4 in.

1948 Packard Station Sedan

Russell von Sauers Jr., *The Graphic Automobile Studio*

120.0 in.

Price when new	$3425 f.o.b. Detroit (1948).
Current valuation*	Xlnt. $3542, gd. $1550, fair $530.
Options	Radio, power antenna, heater, visor, Electromatic clutch, overdrive, fog lights, cormorant, whitewalls.

ENGINE

Type	L-head, in-line 8, water cooled, cast-iron block, 5 mains, full pressure lubrication.
Bore & stroke	3.5 x 3.75 in.
Displacement	288.64 cid.
Max. bhp @ rpm	130 @ 3600.
Max. torque @ rpm	226 @ 2000.
Compression ratio	7.0:1.
Induction system	Carter 2-bbl. downdraft carb.
Electrical system	6-volt battery/coil.
Exhaust system	Cast-iron manifold, single exhaust.

CLUTCH

Type	Single dry plate, woven asbestos lining.
Diameter	10.0 in.
Actuation	Mechanical foot pedal plus electro-vac assist.

TRANSMISSION

Type	3-speed manual with overdrive, all synchro, column shift.
Ratios: 1st	2.03:1.
2nd	1.28:1.
3rd	1.00:1.
Overdrive	0.61:1.
Reverse	2.65:1.

DIFFERENTIAL

Type	Hypoid, Hotchkiss drive.
Ratio	4.10:1.
Drive axles	Semi-floating.

STEERING

Type	Worm & 3-tooth roller.
Turns lock to lock	3.5.
Ratio	26.2:1.
Turn circle	44.0 ft.

BRAKES

Type	4-wheel hydraulic drums, internal expanding.
Drum diameter	12.0 in.
Total lining area	171.5 sq. in.

CHASSIS & BODY

Frame	Box & U-section steel siderails with central X-member, 5 crossmembers.
Body construction	All steel, wood overlays.
Body style	4-door, 6-pass. station wagon.

SUSPENSION

Front	Independent SLA, coil springs, hydraulic lever shocks, torsional stabilizer bar.
Rear	Solid axle, semi-elliptic leaf springs, tubular hydraulic shocks, anti-sway bar.
Tires	7.00 x 15 tube type, 4-ply whitewalls.
Wheels	Pressed steel discs, drop-center rims, lug-bolted to brake drums.

WEIGHTS & MEASURES

Wheelbase	120.0 in.
Overall length	204.6 in.
Overall height	64.1 in.
Overall width	77.5 in.
Front tread	59.4 in.
Rear tread	60.5 in.
Ground clearance	7.5 in.
Curb weight	4075 lb.

CAPACITIES

Crankcase	6 qt.
Cooling system	4.5 gal.
Fuel tank	17 gal.

FUEL CONSUMPTION

Best	16-18 mpg.
Average	12-14 mpg.

* Courtesy **Antique Automobile Appraisal,** Prof. Barry Hertz.

But all wasn't rosy under Christopher. According to FORTUNE Magazine, he under-produced the 1948 models and found his dealers screaming for more. Dealers had plenty of customers that year but no cars. On the other hand, they still had lots of leftover '47 Packards that they couldn't sell, and Christopher wasn't about to give any fancy allowances.

Then for 1949, Christopher told everyone he planned to produce 200,000 cars, and anxious dealers, believing him, began expensive expansion programs. They enlarged their showrooms, service areas, and so forth. But despite everyone's high hopes, Packard's 1949 registrations fell 19,000 cars short of production, and even at that, production was only half the 200.000 Christopher had talked about. So dealers were again stuck with leftovers.

Feeling unappreciated, Christopher resigned in Oct. 1949, which put Packard's reins in the hands of Hugh J. Ferry. Ferry had been the company's treasurer for the past 23 years. He served as a capable stopgap president, his most important moves being to commission the radical restyling of 1951 and to seek out a replacement for himself. This last turned out to be James J. Nance (see Postwar Packards, *SIA #4,* for a more detailed account of preceding and subsequent periods).

Bill Geyer met me in Elk Grove, California, in his 1948 Station Sedan. You'll recall that Bill kindly lent *SIA* his 1954 Dodge D-500 convertible for a similar driveReport in *SIA #8.* I'd seen his Packard wagon before, so when we decided to do our survey of woodies *(SIA #17),* I immediately thought of Bill's Station Sedan.

This car shows 70,855 original miles, and Bill, who's a legislative consultant in Sacramento, is its third owner. He bought the wagon from a hobbyist who outbid him at the auction of the original owner's estate. The Station Sedan's interior is especially well preserved, with no signs of water seepage into the cargo area. The exterior looks nearly new, too.

As in most Station Sedans, this one came with almost every option Packard offered in 1948. The cormorant was one of four hood ornaments listed. It was standard on Custom 8s and optional on lesser models. Also available were the "goddess of speed," irreverently known as the boy with the doughnut, the "Egyptian," which looked like a fancified 1949 Ford hood ornament; and the "Flying wing," a low streak of chrome on the Packard 8's nose.

Bill's wagon has overdrive and the Electromatic clutch. His over-

Packard Station Sedan

drive works fine and makes highway cruising a breeze, but the Electromatic has been disconnected, as in so many Packards. When working properly, it did away with the need for depressing the clutch when idling or shifting gears. But short circuits and vacuum leaks made most Electromatics unreliable.

If Ultramatic had been available in 1948, this wagon would surely have had it. Development of Packard's 1949 automatic began near the end of the

war under chief research engineer Forest McFarland. Herbert L. Misch, who's now a Ford engineering v.p., was just 3 years out of college at the beginning of the Ultramatic's development, yet Misch had the major responsibility of designing the torque converter, assisted by Warren Bopp. George Joly designed the gears.

Ultramatic became a particularly ambitious project for an independent automaker like Packard. They developed and built it without any outside help. Ford, in contrast, relied on Borg-Warner to develop Ford-O-Matic and Merc-O-Matic, and GM had Detroit Transmissions and later the Hydra-Matic Div.

Ultramatic used a torque converter similar in principle to Buick's Dynaflow but different in materials and construction. It had a direct-drive feature that engaged automatically above about 15 mph. the exact engagement speed being determined by load and pedal pressure. Once locked in direct drive, there was no more slippage, a fact that contributed to fairly good gas mileage. An accelerator kickdown kept Ultramatic from lugging and could be used for quick passing below 50 mph. In May 1951, CONSUMER RFPORTS rated Ultramatic the best of all torque converters available at the time. It added $225 to the price of a 1949 Custom or Super Packard.

Packard cloistered a very GM-like front suspension under its 22nd and 23rd Series—coils with SLA and integral lever shocks as the upper A-arms. The Station Sedan also used stabilizer bars front and rear. These might lessen lean on hard corners, but the wagon still leans pretty much, although it's not uncomfortable. All Packards of that era moved along with a very mushy, floating ride, and a lot of owners liked it that way.

Steering is extremely light and surprisingly responsive, with no tendency to wander on high-crown roads or in crosswinds. Bill Geyer's 2-ton wagon isn't a hot dog when it comes to acceleration, but I never had to push it either.

Starting comes by flipping the key and depressing the gas pedal, same as in Buicks of that day. The Packard's instrument cluster, while uninspired, makes all gauges legible, and all buttons are integrated into a protective horizontal trim rail near the bottom of the dash. The four big vent and heater controls stand beneath those, and whole the regular buttons look almost Nader-inspired, the four heater knobs look positively lethal.

Because of the Station Sedan's high price and modest carrying capacity, it never became anything like a best-seller. A total of 1,786 were produced in 1948, 1,100 in the 1949 23rd Series, and an unknown number for the 1949 22nd Series and in 1950. After that, Packard offered no wagons until 1957, with the Studebaker merger. Which means Packard never did build another wagon after 1950. 🙿

Our thanks to Bill Geyer, Sacramento, California; Burt Weaver and George L. Hamlin of Packard Automobile Classics, Box 2808, Oakland, CA 94618; John Reinhart and Herbert L. Misch, Ford Motor Co., Dearborn, Michigan; Forest McFarland, Flint, Michigan; William H. Graves, Ann Arbor, Michigan; and A. W. Prance, Bloomfield Hills, Michigan.

What a double–duty beauty!

THE stunning new Packard Station Sedan is truly an entirely *new kind* of car.

Here, for the first time, sedan luxury is combined with *the real carry-all utility of a station wagon.*

Previewers tried to place their orders for this car months before production began. Conservative, habitual buyers of black sedans saw it and exclaimed, "That's for me!"

You have to *see* this dazzling new motor car with your own eyes to know what all the excitement's about — because nothing else like it has ever rolled off *any* assembly line!

It's equally at home carrying six distinguished passengers to a summer theater opening, a formal country club dance, or skimming over a country highway loaded with farm produce or camping duffle.

You not only enjoy restful sedan comfort in the finest Packard tradition, but with a

twist of the wrist the rear seat folds forward, tail gate lowers, to form a cargo platform nearly eight feet long!

Roof, floor and structural side panels are of steel—strong, safe, rattle-free. The fine-grained wood panels are of selected northern birch.

Don't miss seeing this exciting new car —inside and out—at your Packard dealer's!

ASK THE MAN WHO OWNS ONE

THE NEW

PACKARD

STATION SEDAN

Out of this world . . . into your ♥ heart

Ad originally published in *Holiday* magazine, July 1948

by Robert Ackerson

1950 Packard DeLuxe Eight

ALL the mistakes, mishaps, and miscues of Packard's early post-war years seem to loom large in the Twenty-Second and Twenty-Third series of 1948-1950. Maligned for their appearance and their supposedly antiquated straight-eight engines, they are usually depicted as examples of the shortsighted marketing strategy that contributed to Packard's eventual demise.

What had happened? The prospects of peace in early 1945 and the consequent resumption of automobile production were as pleasant for Packard as for the entire industry.

As early as April of that year Packard stockholders were told that when production of both Rolls-Royce Merlin aviation engines and power plants for PT boats ended, their company expected "to double its prewar output of automobiles to 200,000 annually...." This unfulfilled promise dogged George Christopher (see sidebar, p. 64) for the rest of his years as Packard president. Yet, a review of the difficulties facing Packard in the late forties offers at least some grounds to suggest that no one could have done much more than

Christopher did to try and attain this 200,000 unit goal.

Before its first postwar models were shown in November 1945, Packard announced that without impairing its war effort, and with "the understanding cooperation of government agencies," it had made considerable progress toward returning to full peacetime automobile production. This somewhat ambiguous statement no doubt led some readers to conclude that a totally new Packard was on the way. If so, they were disappointed when they saw the 1946 edition. With the exception of a new center grille piece and license plate bracket, it was identical to the 1942 models. At a showing of the first postwar Packard in New York City's Astor Hotel, George Christopher said that Packard planned to manufacture 8,000 cars by January 1, 1946, and 100,000 by the first of August. Packard fell short on both marks, managing to turn out just 2,722 Clipper Eight four-door sedans in the last quarter of 1945 and 42,102 for all of 1946.

Regardless of the extremely limited availability of its cars, Packard, in 1945, was still a name that meant prestige, luxury and, to many, the best America

had to offer in the quality car field. The presentation of a DeLuxe Clipper by the US Conference of Mayors to retiring New York City mayor Fiorello La Guardia was indicative of Packard's continuing strong status. While having no bearing upon Packard history, La Guardia's response to his surprise gift displayed him at his verbal best. Remarking that he really did need a car, since his wife's Ford was getting shabby, he declined to pose behind the Packard's wheel, confessing, "I don't drive." He fended off photographer requests for him to lift the Packard's hood for photos, saying, "that would be looking a gift in the mouth." Even a man of La Guardia's position however, had to wait a bit for his new car to be delivered. On December 17, a Packard spokesman announced that the car "presented" to La Guardia the previous week had been a "display model" to show the mayor what he would be receiving. Packard promised La Guardia would be taking delivery of a "reasonable facsimile" by early spring.

In his annual report to Packard stockholders released in March 1946, Christopher spoke in candid tones concern-

The Last Of Packard's Postwar Pachyderms

photos by the author

Opposite page: Traditional Packard grille design was combined with horizontal bars on the '48-50 DeLuxe Eights, updating design of original '41 Clipper. **This page:** *Styling is nearly all curves and rounded surfaces, giving the car a somewhat bulbous appearance.*

ing Packard's present and future business prospects. While he was generally optimistic and saw Packard both as a producer of quality automobiles and a diversified company supplying marine and jet aviation engines, he also alluded to the future challenges Packard would be facing. "Although a seller's market currently exists," wrote Christopher, we recognize conditions will change in the relatively short time which it will take to permit capacity operations in the industry. We will then be faced with the necessity of meeting competition in a buyer's market."

But as 1946 unfolded, Packard found itself hamstrung by a seemingly endless number of production snags that prevented it from taking full advantage of the demand for automobiles. Early in the year some 7,500 members of its 8,500 man work force were idled for nearly two months because of a shortage of engine bearings caused by strikes at Packard's supplier. During this dismal first quarter Packard's final assembly line operated only nine days, turning out less than 1,500 Clippers. The economic consequences for Packard were severe.

In this quarter it lost $247,449, although before tax credits its actual loss was $3,469,449. Obviously exasperated at his inability to lead Packard to its production goal of 200,000 cars an-

nually, Christopher remarked, "we are equipped to handle the largest volume of business in Packard's 47 year history, but our volume necessarily depends upon uninterrupted flow of materials and parts from our suppliers." Packard's president also had harsh words for the Office of Price Administration's restrictions on new car prices, citing the unfairness of the government establishing price ceilings on cars but not on many parts furnished by suppliers outside the automobile industry. In his comments concerning labor conditions, Christopher was careful not to sound like a reactionary wishing to return to the prewar non-union era. "Nobody," he said, "ever would want to go back to those days." Yet the absenteeism rate during a 40-hour work week at Packard exceeded the rate of the war years, Christopher claimed, and he found this inexcusable.

Nevertheless, as he toured the United States, exploring markets and sources of supply, Christopher still held firm to his 200,000 car annual output goal. Packard, he promised, would reach this level once its $20 million expansion plan was completed. Describing it as half-finished, in November 1946 Christopher predicted that upon its completion Packard's payroll of 10,000 would double. Yet in the midst of this euphoric forecast Christopher found it necessary

to not only warn Packard dealers again that within a year the increased production of new automobiles would force them to become far more aggressive salesmen, but also to declare that Packard had no intention of leaving the luxury car field. It is significant that no Cadillac spokesman of this time felt it necessary to issue a similar statement concerning the future direction of that company.

At a November 15, 1946, Chicago news conference, Christopher announced that while Packard actually would lose $6 million on its 1946 manufacturing operations, it would show a profit because of tax carry-overs. Packard's gradually increasing production encouraged Christopher to comment, "We are quite happy at the showing we have made compared to what we thought we would show on V-J day."

Christopher confirmed at this time that Packard was planning a new model, but refused to give any details. A few days later in Dallas, Christopher was still not inclined to reveal what Packard had in mind, but he did tease his audience by telling them that the Packard, scheduled for introduction in March 1947, would be new "from the tires up."

Although Packard was far from reaching Christopher's highly publicized production objective, it had in 1946 outproduced Cadillac 42,102 to 28,144.

Traditional touches abounded in 1950 Packard. **Right:** Crosshatched pedal pads had been a Packard trademark for decades. Hood opens from either side à la Buick. **Below:** Packard's well-known pelican mascot points the way. '50 Packards were the last US car to use actual glass for taillight lenses.

1950 Packard

The following year the score shifted in Cadillac's favor, 59,436 to 55,477. These figures suggest that in the race for supremacy in the American luxury car field, Packard was still in the ring and on its feet. Both companies were proud to report that unfilled orders for their cars were in abundance. In 1946 Cadillac said it had on hand 96,000 orders for new models. At the annual stockholders' meeting in April 1948, George Christopher reported that Packard had a backlog of orders greater than could be filled in 1948, even If 30 percent were cancelled.

Obviously much rested on the reception the Twenty-Second series Packards would receive. For whatever it was worth, Packard got the jump on its rival by introducing its new Super-Eight convertible on March 29, 1947. The rest of the new series didn't bow until late September. Cadillac released its new models in February 1948.

In announcing the Super-Eight convertible Christopher again claimed, "Everything in the new vehicle is brand new, from the tires up." The subject of his comments was easily distinguished from the Twenty-First series Sedans that remained in production, but it was hardly all that new. It was readily identified as a Packard, a point that Packard used effectively in its famous "One Guess What Name It Bears" advertisement, and mechanically it was virtually a carbon copy of the Twenty-First series cars.

It has become almost mandatory to proclaim the Twenty-Second series Packard a styling blunder. Certainly the internal dissension their appearance fomented at Packard suggests this opinion is not inappropriate. Yet the unhappiness associated with the Twenty-Second series may not actually lie with their styling as such. For those critics of the "bathtub" Packards, perhaps a review of other contemporary d-signs is in order. It's hard to declare the first Kaisers or Frazers as more attractive, and the styling of the Chrysler Imperial

in its new 1949 skin was hardly a great achievement. Similarly. neither the contours of the 1949 Nash nor the form of the 1950 Studebaker's front end are remembered as paragons of timeless great design. Packard styling was restrained, and as Packard pointed out, "In this age of 'look-alikes' [its car] is still proudly *Packard* at a glance."

Cadillac was also well aware of the need and value of retaining marque identity in its new postwar car, and when the 1948 Cadillac (see *Special Interest Autos* #11) appeared it looked like a Cadillac, but it also represented a styling revolution. Packard styling offered nothing that could match the Cadillac's rear fins. Similarly Packard's relatively narrow, flat windshield was rendered instantly obsolete by the Cadillac's curved windshield.

Packard had been outflanked by its great rival, and in 1949 when Cadillac introduced its outstanding 331 cid overhead-valve V-8, Packard's disadvantage became even greater.

In essence, Cadillac had wrought a major marketing coup. In the public's mind, its products were intimately related to the glory of Cadillac's history. At the same time, it had established itself as both a styling and engineering leader, something the Twenty-Second series Packard was not.

Nonetheless Packard could and did benefit both from the still warm afterglow of an earlier age, and its totally deserved reputation for quality construction, ride, and interior appointments. In April 1947 Packard had produced its one millionth automobile, a Super-Eight convertible, and Christopher marked the moment by proudly proclaiming, "We expect to build as many cars in the next five years as we did in the past forty-eight." His promise of 200,000 cars a year output was getting somewhat hackneyed by this time, but that didn't deter Christopher from explaining, "Last year we expanded our facilities to build 200,000 cars a year.... However parts and material shortages, plus labor difficulties throughout the country, held Packard production in 1946 to considerably less than half the goal. It now appears we will not be able to build at the rate of 200,000 a year until the last quarter of 1947."

The first six months of 1947 were again unprofitable ones for Packard: its losses reached $1,872,634. But Packard seemed headed toward happier days: the new Super Eight, whose engine had been subjected to a run equal to what was described as a year's normal mileage at speeds between 75 and 80 mph before its tooling had been authorized, was joined by the rest of the Twenty-Second series in September. Available in 17 body styles in three series—Eight, Super-Eight and Custom-Eight—they were, said Christopher, "the final fruits of the $20 million program Packard started at the end of World War II."

In spite of labor problems at Bendix and Briggs and a wildcat strike in its own factory, Packard turned out 98,897 cars in 1948. Cadillac's output for the 1948 calendar year was 66,209. Packards still had a lot of sales appeal.

As Packard entered 1949 and the commemoration of its fiftieth anniversary, *The New York Times* commented, "Mr. Christopher has every right to feel encouraged about the outlook for his company." Having made over $15 million in 1948, Packard, in Christopher's view, could make 30 percent more cars in 1949. The actual 1949 output of 104,593 fell short of Christopher's prediction, but once again Packard had out-produced Cadillac, which reported a calendar year production of 81,545.

During the year Christopher was kept busy presiding over the celebration of Packard's Golden Anniversary and making public comments on a number of issues facing the industry. In response to the sales prospect of an American-built small car, Christopher

Packard's Super Eight

Rubbing elbows with the upper crust has always been one of the quicker ways up the social ladder, but it only takes a couple of missteps among your peer group, and watch out below! The hob-nobbing business seemed to pay off for Packard during the thirties, as sales of its Junior Series obviously kept the company solvent. But, even before Pearl Harbor, signs of stormy weather ahead for Packard were there for the looking.

Packard's basis for survival during the Depression was founded upon its One Twenty and Sixes. Its basis for prestige was rooted in the Senior cars whose public image was inevitably diluted by the success of the junior cars.

As well as any upper echelon Packard, the Super Eight not only reflected these dynamics of the marketplace, but also exhibited its own nasty little habit of nibbling away at the marque's core of public esteem.

After first use in 1933 as a new name for the former DeLuxe Eight, the Super Eight fell victim to a similar malady in 1938, disappearing in substance, but surviving as the "new name" for the Packard Eight. No doubt, more than a few Packard owners of yore were becoming just a little confused. But they hadn't seen anything yet. The next year the Super Eight began to cuddle up next to the Packard Twelve, with both series using virtually identical chassis. This was the type of familiarity that bred, if not contempt, then surely discontent among the Packard faithful who were also finding precious little in Packard's old-fashioned styling to get excited about.

The entire affair threatened to get totally out of hand when Packard began to encourage the purchase of a Super 8 (the change from Eight to "8" was made in 1939) on the basis of its $2,000 price tag.

When the 1940 models came on stream, the Senior cars were known as Super 8 One Sixtys and Custom Super 8 One Eightys. The old Twelve was gone, its place taken by the One Eighty. The difference between a One Sixty and a One Eighty? Not much, mainly relatively superficial trim and appointment features.

Yet, by calling both these lines Senior model Super 8s, Packard had shot itself in the foot. There were numerous intangibles inherent in the successful marketing of a luxury car, and excessive shifting of model designations wasn't one of them.

When the new "bathtub" Packard first appeared in mid-1947 as a convertible, it carried the Super Eight label. Packard was up to its old tricks once again. The first postwar Super Eights were close kin to the lower-priced Packards, and only the aficionado could readily distinguish the relatively subtle luxury differences between them at a glance.

In 1949 the Twenty-Third Series Super Eight shared both the sheet metal and wheelbase of the Custom model. By this time, perhaps it hardly mattered. For 1951 new names and numbers became the basis of class distinction at Packard. But Packard's tampering with the continuity of its labeling procedure confused the public, diluted its image and proved to be a habit not only apparently impossible to break, but also very costly.

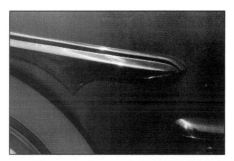

Left: *Sweepspear was a Packard design characteristic in use since the twenties.*
Below: *With 120-inch wheelbase, DeLuxe Eight was a medium-sized car for its time.*

illustrations by Russell von Sauers, The Graphic Automobile Studio

specifications

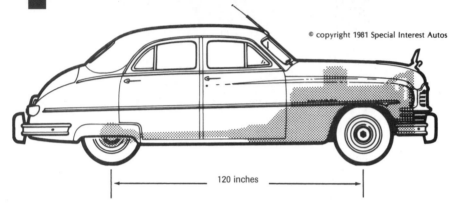
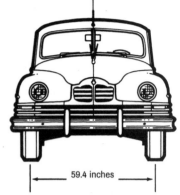

© copyright 1981 Special Interest Autos

120 inches

59.4 inches

1950 Packard Deluxe Eight

Price	$2,383 (base).
Standard equipment	Deluxe Eight interior and exterior appointments.
Optional equipment	Radio, heater, day/night mirror, maplight, engine compartment light, trunk light cormorant, Ultramatic, oil filter.

ENGINE
Type	L-head Straight Eight.
Bore & stroke	3½ inches x 3¾ inches.
Displacement	288 cid.
Max. bhp @ rpm	135 @ 3600 rpm.
Max. torque @ rpm	230 lbs./ft. @ 2000 rpm.
Compression ratio	7.0:1.
Induction system	1- 2-barrel Carter.
Exhaust system	Single.
Electrical system	6 volt.

CLUTCH
Type	Cork-faced.
Diameter	11 inches.
Actuation	Via vehicle speed and accelerator pressure.

TRANSMISSION
Type	Ultramatic 2-speed torque converter with direct drive lockup.

Ratios:	Low	4.37:1.
	High	2.4:1.
	Direct	1:1.

DIFFERENTIAL
Type	Hypoid.
Ratio	3.9:1.
Drive axles	Hotchkiss.

STEERING
Type	Worm, 3-tooth roller.
Turns lock-to-lock	35.
Ratio	26.2:1.
Turn circle	44 feet.

BRAKES
Type	Hydraulic, internal expanding, all 4 wheels.
Drum diameter	12 inches.
Total swept area	171.5 square inches.

CHASSIS AND BODY
Frame	Box and U-section steel side members, 5 crossmembers, X-member.
Body construction	Steel.
Body style	4-door sedan.

SUSPENSION
Front	Independent, coil springs, 4¼ inches inside diameter, tubular hydraulic shocks.
Rear	Leaf springs, 2 inches x 54⅜ inches, solid axle, sway bar, tubular hydraulic shocks.
Tires	7.60x5 inches tube-type.
Wheels	15 inches x 5 inches.

WEIGHTS AND MEASURES
Wheelbase	120 inches.
Overall length	204 11/16 inches.
Overall height	64.1 inches.
Overall width	77.5 inches.
Front tread	59.4 inches.
Rear tread	60.5 inches.
Ground clearance	7.5 inches.
Curb weight	4075 pounds.

CAPACITIES
Crankcase	7 quarts with filter.
Cooling system	16½ quarts.
Fuel tank	17 gallons.

FUEL CONSUMPTION
Av. city	12-14 mpg est.
Av. open road	20+ mpg.

MARQUE CLUB
Packard Club
Box 2808
Oakland, CA 94618

135-hp straight eight coupled to Ultramatic offers good but not startling performance.

1950 Packard

said, "The only successful small car would be one that has all the smoothness, comfort and performance of today's conventional vehicles. That kind of a small car cannot be built to sell at a price that would be materially below today's regulation size vehicles." Concerning Packard's future, Christopher was optimistic: "We foresee strong competition ahead," he said, "but we are confident our organization can meet it."

This opinion was not shared by the Packard Board of Directors or by many key Packard figures in styling. The newspapers for October 6, 1949, carried the result of the conflict between Christopher and his board: effective December 31, 1949, Christopher was retiring. "The announcement," said *The New York Times*, "coming in the midst of outstanding production and sales achievements by the company since the end of the war, caught the industry by surprise." The directors, *The Times* continued, had accepted Christopher's retirement "with regret." Fortune reported that Christopher's last retort to the board was: "Farming is a damned sight easier than the auto business—you don't have so many bosses on a farm."

As a result of this upheaval the Twenty-Third series Packards were both its Golden Anniversary models and the last product of the Christopher years. Just 42,640 of the 1950 version were produced, which hardly called for rejoicing at East Grand Boulevard. In the first six months of 1950, when the industry was enjoying its greatest boom in history, Packard lost over $700,000. Total American automotive output was up 30 percent, Packard's slumped by 20 percent and in sales it fell from thirteenth to fourteenth position, just ahead of De Soto and Kaiser.

Driving Impressions

In the face of this dismal showing, it's tempting to view the 1950 Packard as something of a has-been. The day we spent in, around, and driving Ron and Kathy Redden's DeLuxe Eight four-door sedan quickly dispelled this notion. Its overall quality of finish and detailing belied its position as a model structured in the lower strata of the Twenty-Third series lineup. Packard interiors were generally regarded as the best in the industry, and when you're seated in the rear, cuddled by a large retractable center arm rest or enjoying the view from behind the wheel of this Packard, the experience is a pleasant one. The wood-grained dash, large circular instruments, and array of chrome accessory buttons provides a decidedly dated but not unpleasant environment. The

*Above: It wouldn't be a Packard without the red hexagon in the hubcaps. Packard used the red hex since 1904. **Left:** Dashboard controls are true push-button in operation. **Below:** Dash has big, round speedo and clock, full gauge instrumentation.*

1950 Packard

gray lined upholstery, virtually unworn after 30 years of careful use, is similarly old fashioned but helps convey the Packard's overall character of quiet elegance.

The DeLuxe Eight was equipped with Packard's least powerful eight, of 288 cubic inches and 135 horsepower. With a 3-1/2-inch bore and 3-3/4-inch stroke and hydraulic valve lifters, its smooth, almost silent operation in combination with Packard's new for 1950 Ultramatic transmission provided us with an effortless tour in the foothills of the Catskill Mountains. Packard's automatic transmission combined a torque converter with a direct-drive clutch. There is a sensation of slushiness when the Packard has to make starts on fairly steep inclines, but the overall performance of the 30-year-old Ultramatic is excellent. The engagement of the direct-drive is noticeable only when the transmission is cold, and the ability of this 4,000-pound Packard with its supposedly antiquated engine to deliver 20 mpg at highway speeds speaks for itself.

When he introduced the 1948 Packards, Christopher had noted their new windshield wipers that, he said, eliminated the "swish and slap" of conven-

*Above: Even in their lower-priced lines, Packard interiors have always been superior in fit, finish and materials. **Right:** At the rear, more oblongs, ovals and rounded lines dominate the styling.*

George Christopher: Savior or Scapegoat?

"His passion for low-priced production has an echoing passion for low-priced cars, and in all ways open to him he exerts a strong downward pressure on pricing, so that he can make more cars, so that he can make each car cheaper, so that he can make more cars."

The man being thus depicted could be Henry Ford but it wasn't. The year was 1937 and *Fortune* was describing George Christopher. Three years earlier he had been hired by Packard for the express purpose of setting up its One Twenty Model production line. To hear some Packardites tell it, Christopher deserved the old tar and feather treatment both for his infamous "goddam senior stuff" statement and for his alleged "crimes" surrounding Packard's postwar experiences.

Coming from General Motors, Christopher wasn't steeped in reverence for Packard's past moments of glory. His job was to produce One Twentys efficiently, and he did his job extremely well. Then, when demand for the new junior Packards exceeded the supply, he saw to it that output was boosted by over 50 percent.

By 1942 he had succeeded Alvan Macauley as the undisputed boss at Packard. But his was the uneasy head that wore the crown. Some critics cite him for failing to restore Packard's eminence as a luxury car during the early postwar years.

Their argument seems persuasive. It was the type of seller's market any manufacturer dreams about, and obviously Packard could have sold as many top-line models as it was capable of producing. Instead, with his antipathy toward Packard's expensive offerings and propensity for mass-producing lower-priced models, Christopher followed the former path. Eventually forced to resign by what was in effect a palace revolt, he left Packard, if not in disgrace then certainly with a distinct lack of grace.

But to place blame on Christopher for Packard's assorted ills requires some clever sidestepping of the realities of the postwar automobile market. No matter what type of car Packard was producing at that time, severe labor and supply problems would have kept output below demand. To blame Christopher for failing to deliver on his promises is to both damn the man unfairly and to suggest he was capable of superhuman deeds.

Christopher's rehabilitation as a figure of automotive history requires one more look at the prospects for Packard's survival under any manager. Simply put, they weren't good. If the Senior Packards were to exist, then either a line of lower priced models or a sharply diversified company was necessary. Obviously Christopher, since he at least tolerated the Senior models, understood the former point very well. As to

broadening Packard's place in the industrial markets, he suggested at various times that such action was a possibility.

But to carry such a program forward required a high rate of investment, and it couldn't be assumed that Packard's stockholders would settle for smaller dividends for what then might have been viewed as a step in the wrong direction. The way out of the thicket then unseen but very real nevertheless, was merger. George Mason saw that, but for the most part his contemporaries at the other independents didn't. When James Nance finally got Studebaker and Packard together, the hour was very late. Even at that time Packard's economic health was still strong, certainly a legacy to be credited in large part to George Christopher.

Obviously, Christopher didn't always walk on water. His actions to bring all Packards, regardless of price, closer together in the public's view was a major marketing blunder, regardless of how much it contributed to cost effectiveness.

Yet, if Christopher wasn't part of the solution to Packard's ills, he also wasn't the only part of its problem. These went far beyond the scope of his control, and to suggest otherwise does a great disservice to a man whose talents at least ensured that after the war there still was a Packard Motor Car Company.

tional units. We hadn't expected to verify Christopher's claim, but, returning home after our photography session, a thunderstorm caught up with us. Sure enough, Christopher hadn't been fibbing. The pencil-thin wipers operated silently with nary a "swish or slap" to be heard.

From the driver's seat there's no mistaking the Packard for anything but an automobile of mid-twentieth century vintage. The view outward is restricted, and the thick corner posts seem excessively large. You can see the left front fender if you try hard, but most drivers of average height have to be satisfied with the sight of the Packard's slim hood and the famous Pelican that points the way in splendid fashion. At almost any speed the Packard's steering is surprisingly light and comfortable. The amount of pressure the brakes require seems at first rather high, but familiarity brings with it an easy acceptance.

The original owner of this Argentine Gray Metallic Packard was Clarence Frisbee, a descendant of one of the original settlers of Delaware County in New York State. Frisbee was 70 when he traded in a 1939 Packard One Twenty as partial payment for his new car. For the most part Frisbee used the DeLuxe

Eight Packard to visit his brother on Sundays. This journey Involved driving just eight miles (round trip!), and when Redden acquired the car from another collector in Binghamton, its total mileage was just 17,000.

The 1950 Packard DeLuxe Eight offers little evidence suggesting its maker was headed for trouble. Packard's early postwar cars were first-class products, but the temperament of Americans and the nature of the automobile industry were changing, and Packard didn't perceive those shifts until it was too late. What Packard was offering in 1950 was the product of an outdated philosophy. What was later labeled "pizazz" was alive and well in 1950, although no one had yet coined a term for it. Certainly the sound of a V-8 engine and the look of swoopy tail fins climaxing a rear fender line were two of its ingredients, and Packard had neither. It didn't matter just how quiet and smooth that straight eight was. In the eye of the public it belonged to yesterday.

Even Packard's way of doing business was passing by the boards, and that's one of the saddest parts of Packard's decline. There was no place for a company whose primary activity was the production of quality automobiles in an economy where capital investments

would soon be tallied in the billions and change for the sake of mere change would rule insanely, at least for a time. Packard, and all that it stood for and all that its leadership believed in, belonged to the past. For Packard there would, for a time, be a present, but there was no future. ☙

Acknowledgements and Bibliography
Business Week, *various issues, 1945-1948;* Current Biography, *November 1947;* Fortune, *various issues 1949-1950;* Newsweek, *various issues, 1949-1950;* The New York Times, *various issues, 1945-1950;* Time, *various issues, 1950;* Packard: A History Of The Motor Car And The Company, *edited by Beverly Rae Kimes.*
Our thanks to Richard Langworth, Contoocook, NH, and Margaret Butzu, National Automotive History Collection, Detroit Public Library, Detroit, Mich. Special thanks to Ron and Kathy Redden, Oneonta, NY

About the Author. Bob Ackerson lives in Schenevus, NY, with his wife, three daughters and three cats. His major interests besides collecting automotive literature and photographs are running (longest run thus far: 12.2 miles) and cutting wood (seven full cords last winter). Bob has also contributed to *Old Cars Weekly, Thoroughbred and Classic Cars, Cars & Parts* and *Automobile Quarterly.*

Above left: *The lap of luxury. Rear seat passengers enjoy a cushy center armrest, built-in armrests on each side of the seat, generous cushions.* **Above:** *Hood releases are on either side of car under the dash.* **Left:** *Steering wheel boss has beautifully crafted Packard coat of arms and modernized script.*

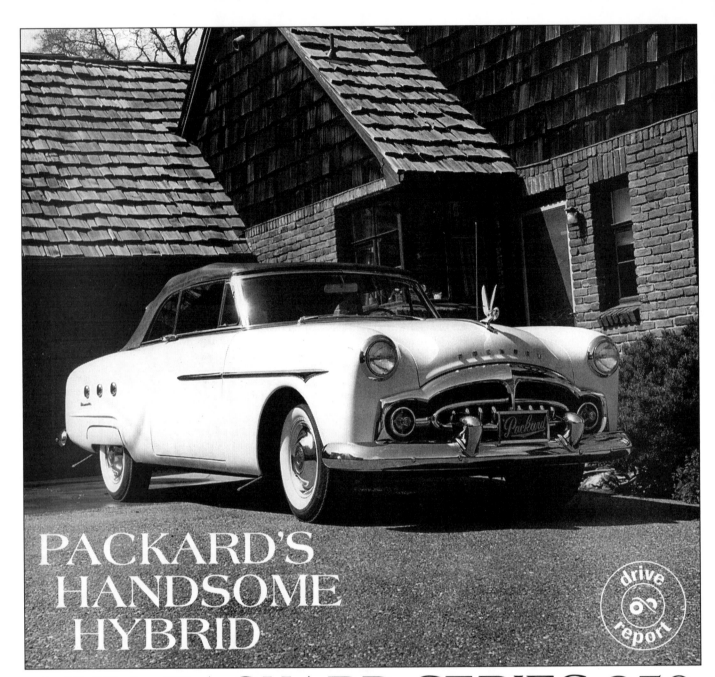

PACKARD'S HANDSOME HYBRID

1951 PACKARD SERIES 250

by Josiah Work
photos by Jim Tanji

FOLLOWING the surrender of Japan in August 1945, when — to paraphrase a poignant wartime song — "the lights came on again all over the world," the automobile industry found itself with a totally unprecedented backlog of orders. For four long years people had been wearing out their old cars, and there hadn't been any new ones coming off the assembly line to replace them. And for four long years paychecks had been fattened by the forced-draft wartime economy. Every automobile dealer in the country had a list of customers with cash in hand, each one anxiously awaiting the delivery of a new car.

Any new car! The manufacturers could sell anything and everything that they could manage to produce. The only

limitations had to do with labor problems and a severe shortage of certain critical materials — notably sheet steel. Strikes plagued some of the suppliers, as well as the automobile companies themselves. And, as Henry Ford II has observed, the productivity of labor was not nearly as great as it had been in prewar times.

So it took a while for the industry to regain its momentum, and meanwhile the customers waited. And waited!

It was a priceless opportunity for the independent companies, of course. During the thirties they had seen their share of an increasingly competitive market gradually diminishing, but the pent-up demand for cars raised their hopes, and their sights.

Studebaker elected to concentrate its efforts on re-tooling for a spectacularly restyled 1947 car, due for introduction in the spring of '46. They turned out only a comparative handful of 1946 models, all of the Champion series, while preparations were made for the big splash. The policy paid off; by 1948 they were selling more cars than ever before in the company's long history.

Hudson and Nash, on the other hand, lost no time in putting into full-bore production their warmed-over prewar designs. Nash became, in 1946, the only manufacturer to sell more cars than it had at anytime since 1929. And Hudson came within a whisker of its 1941 output.

But Packard stumbled. Production for 1946 amounted to only about a third of 1940's total, and 1947 wasn't much better. Not until 1948 would the company hit its stride again, and even then it was losing money.

Evidently there were a number of problems at Packard. For one, as Robert Turnquist has noted, "Three of Packard's prewar suppliers changed hands, forcing Packard to purchase odd lot steel at premium prices." (Meanwhile, of course, the price that Packard could charge for its cars was regulated by government fiat, under the Office of Price Administration.)

A second problem may have been, in the long run, even more critical. In 1944, while serving in the US Navy, it was this writer's good fortune to spend two months in a training program at the Packard factory in Detroit, where — among other war-related activities — the huge V-i 2 engines that powered the legendary PT boats were being manufactured. There, in a one-on-one conversation, a Packard engineer expressed concern for the company's future. He had no misgivings about the Packard automobile, he said, but the company's manufacturing procedures were — in his view, at least — grossly inefficient. He contrasted Packard's production methods with those of Nash, with which he had become familiar in 1940-41. There was no way, he declared, that Packard could be price-competitive and maintain a decent level of profit until the company adopted some of the efficient methods he had seen in Kenosha.

The man was prophetic. Packard lost money for three years in a row — 1946

through 1948 — while Nash, along with most of the rest of the industry, was posting substantial profits.

There have been other explanations of Packard's postwar malaise. The argument that the 1941 body dies should never have been sold to the Russians may have some merit, but the bald truth of the matter is that Packard's 1941-42 styling, apart from the Clipper (which of course was retained for the postwar market), was not that well received by the public. It may have been a new design, but (as noted in SIA #80) its styling theme was straight out of the mid-thirties. Alongside the fashionable fastbacks from General Motors, the Packard had looked old fashioned. Only the mid-season introduction of the sleek new Clipper (see SIA #59) had saved 1941 from being a complete sales disaster.

Packard entered the postwar market with a slightly revised version of the 1941-42 Clipper, built — as it had been before the war — in four series. Since nearly everyone else was following a similar course, and given the Clipper styling, which was among the freshest and most appealing of the prewar designs, Packard was really in a relatively favorable position. Whether the company exploited that advantage is another matter. Over half of Packard's 1946 production consisted of the moderately priced six-cylinder cars (including, to reinforce the public's perception of a down-market direction, taxicabs!), though they could easily have sold as many of the more expensive models as they chose to make.

Nor was Packard at pains to distinguish its senior cars from its medium-priced models, a grievous error in terms of maintaining its status as a luxury marque. For in 1946 a $3,047 Custom Super Eight could scarcely be told from a $1,730 Packard Six!

Mechanically, of course, there were

important distinctions between the senior and junior Packards. The former, both the Custom Super Eight and the Super Eight, were mounted on a wheelbase of 127 inches and powered by the silken, nine-main-bearing, 356-c.i.d. straight-eight that had first appeared in 1940. The Custom models were priced head-to-head with the Cadillac Fleetwood, while the Super Eight was pegged midway between the Cad 61 and 62 series. The Clipper Eight and Clipper Six, on the other hand, used a 120-inch chassis. The Eight, using the five-bearing, 282-c.i.d. engine of the prewar One-Twenty series, was positioned against the Buick Super, while the Six cost some $70 less.

But Packard had another design waiting in the wings. For 1948 the sides of the Clipper body were flared, and a short, stubby grille, while retaining the familiar Packard shape, lost the classic look of its tall, narrow predecessor. The new model won for Packard, among other awards, the Gold Medal of the New York Fashion Academy. But to many observers, including this one, it looked clumsy. The sleek appearance of the Clipper was gone, and before long the automotive press was referring to the new model as the "inverted bathtub" and the "pregnant elephant." No matter; it sold well!

There was some realignment of Packard's market in 1948. Except for taxicabs and export models, the company ceased production of six-cylinder cars. The public, as Chrysler and others were commencing to discover, was beginning to expect eight-cylinder power in its medium-priced cars.

And the Super Eight was downgraded a little that year, to a market position midway between the cheapest Cadillac and the Buick Roadmaster — evidently in an effort to provide Packard with a prestige automobile at a competitive

Comparison Table: 1951 Upper-Medium-Priced Convertibles

	Packard 250	Buick Roadmaster	Chrysler New Yorker	Hudson Hornet
Price[1]	$3,580	$3,283	3,941	$3,257
Engine, type	L-head straight 8	Ohv straight 8	Ohv V-8	L-head 6
Bore/stroke	3½ x 4¼	3.44 x 4.31	3.81 x 3⅝	3.81 x 4½
Displacement	327.0 cubic inches	320.2 cubic inches	331.1 cubic inches	308.0 cubic inches
Horsepower/rpm	155/3,600	152/3,600	180/4,000	145/3,800
Torque/rpm	270/2,000	280/2,000	312/2,000	257/1,800
Compression ratio	7.8:1	7.2:1	7.5:1	7.2:1
Automatic transmission	Ultramatic	Dynaflow	PrestoMatic[2]	HydraMatic
Axle ratio	3.9:1	3.9:1	3.73:1	4.1:1
Steering	Worm/roller	Worm/nut	Worm/roller	Worm/roller
Steering ratio	22.3:1	23.6:1	20.4:1	20.4:1
Braking area	208.2 square inches	207.5 inches	201.1 square inches	158.7 square inches
Drum diameter	12 inches	12 inches	12 inches	11 inches
Tire size	8.00/15	8.00/15	8.20/15	7.10/15
Wheelbase	122 inches	126.2 inches	131½ inches	123⅞ inches
Overall length	209⅜ inches	211 inches	213¼ inches	208.14 inches
Shipping weight	4,040 pounds	4,355 pounds	4,460 pounds	3,780 pounds
Horsepower/c.i.d.	.474	.475	.544	.471
Pounds/Horsepower	26.1	28.7	24.8	26.1
Pounds/c.i.d.	12.4	13.6	13.5	12.3

[1]Including automatic transmission, an extra-cost option on Packard and Hudson
[2]Semi-automatic

Below: Packard's handsome pelican mascot was standard feature of the 250.
Right: John Reinhart's adroit styling of the 1951 cars resulted in Packard's first truly horizontal grille design and a much more square contemporary shape compared to earlier postwar Packard bodies. Below right: Traditional red hexagonal design was retained for wheel covers.

1951 PACKARD

price. Two cost-cutting measures made the change possible: The shorter, 120-inch-wheelbase chassis was used, and power came from a new, five-bearing, 327-c.i.d. straight-eight. Much cheaper to manufacture than the nine-bearing powerplant (which was retained for the Custom Super Eight), it utilized the same bore and stroke as the old Packard Six.

Evidently the ploy worked. Something did, at any rate. for Packard sold more cars in 1948 than at any time since 1937. And in 1949, Packard's Golden Anniversary year, they did even better, racking up what proved to be the company's all-time sales record. The cars were virtually unchanged that year, except that on May 1, 1949, Packard made available its Ultramatic transmission (see sidebar, page 71). The only automatic to be developed by an independent automobile manufacturer, it was standard equipment on the Custom Super Eight, optional at extra cost on all other models.

Packard's first full restyling in a decade came with the 1941 models. Designed by John Reinhart, these cars have been variously described as "bulbous" (by Robert Turnquist) and "praiseworthy" (by Richard Langworth). *Motor Trend* spoke of the design as "one of the

best of the current offerings," and in general the contemporary automotive press agreed.

Again there were three series, though their names were changed. The 200 series, priced against the Buick Super, was powered — as its counterpart had been since 1948 — by a 288.6-c.i.d., five-bearing straight-eight. The 300, competitive with the cheapest Cadillac, used the 327-cubic-inch mill. And the 400, some $300 cheaper than the Custom Super Eight of the previous year, was priced just above the Cadillac 62. The big, silky-smooth, expensive-to-build 356-c.i.d. engine was gone. Powering the 400, instead, was a nine-bearing version of the 327. Power was down just a little — 155 horsepower instead of the previous 160 — but the weight was correspondingly reduced, so there was no great penalty in performance.

Packard's emphasis, by this time, was clearly on its smaller cars. The 300 and 400, both utilizing the 127-inch chassis, were offered only as four-door sedans, and the stretched-wheelbase models of prior years were dropped. The 200 series, on the other hand, came as both two- and four-door sedans in either standard or deluxe trim, and even a business coupe was available. Packard's first 1951 catalog showed a 200 series convertible, but evidently that model was never built.

Some six months into the 1951 season the 250 series was added to the line. Comprising Packard's only convertible that year and its first hardtop coupe, the 250 mated the shorter (122-inch) wheelbase of the 200 series to the 327-c.i.d. engine of the 300. Distinguished by the toothy grille of the senior cars, as well as the shell-like rear fender ornaments and the gorgeous pelican radiator mascot of the 400 series, the 250 series cars were sumptuously trimmed. Lovely automobiles they were, and powerful. But far from cheap!

Packard continued into 1952 with its cars substantially unaltered. But in May of that year came a fateful change in the company's management: James J. Nance, recently of Hotpoint, took the helm as Packard's president. Nance brought with him a number of ideas with respect to Packard's future, some of them good and some disastrous.

For one thing, Packard's management team was getting on in years, and evidently little had been done to develop new, younger leadership from within the ranks. Nance set about to encourage a number of retirements, recruiting new talent — much of it from Hotpoint — as replacements.

Perhaps the best of Nance's plans was to return Packard to the prestige market, in part by sharpening the distinction between the senior and junior cars. The top-of-the-line car was re-named the Patrician, and its engine was stroked to 358.8 cubic inches for 1953, while a spectacularly beautiful, limited production convertible — the Caribbean (see *SIA* #4) — was introduced. By 1954 the smaller cars were known simply as Clippers, the Packard name being reserved for the senior models.

A broad-scale expansion program was another part of Nance's game plan. Packard sales were faltering when he took over as president, but the company's financial condition was sound. There was cash available to underwrite his aspirations. He built a multi-million-dollar engine plant for the manufacture of the new V-8 that was then under development, agreeing to supply engines to the newly formed American Motors Corporation and in return to patronize AMC's new stamping plant.

But then, almost immediately, Nance bought a stamping plant of his own, abrogating the reciprocal agreement with American Motors. Packard's newly acquired facility turned out to be cramped and inadequate, leading to some quality control problems. And as Nance should have foreseen, AMC quickly commenced production of its own V-8 engine, cancelling what had become a one-sided contract with Packard. With its output severely limited, Packard's new engine plant ran deeply in the red, and what Nance had intended as a prime asset to the company became a serious liability. The new V-8 engine first appeared in Packard's 1955 models, along with a revised Ultramatic transmission and a highly sophisticated (not to say incredibly complex) self-leveling torsion bar suspension system. The entire package came to market before the glitches had been worked out, unfortunately, and irreparable damage was done to Packard's reputation for quality.

Meanwhile, James Nance had gone shopping again. People speak of the Studebaker-Packard "merger," but it would be closer to the truth to say that Packard *bought* Studebaker. And in so doing they bought trouble.

On the face of it, the plan looked like a good one, for it gave the combined organization full-market coverage, from the low-priced field to the luxury market. And Studebaker probably had the strongest dealer body among the independent manufacturers at that time. Nance foresaw strengthening that group by transforming it into a series of dual Studebaker-Packard dealerships. But Studebaker, riddled with both financial problems and production hangups, became virtually a bottom-

1951 Packard Prices and Weights

200 Series	Price	Shipping Weight
Business coupe	$2,302	3,550 pounds
Club sedan, 2-door	$2,416	3,600 pounds
Sedan, 4-door	$2,469	3,665 pounds
Club sedan, deluxe	$2,563	3,605 pounds
Sedan, deluxe	$2,616	3,660 pounds
250 Series		
Mayfair hardtop coupe	$3,234	3,820
Convertible	$3,391	4,040 pounds
300 Series		
Sedan, 4-door	$3,034	3,930 pounds
400 Series		
Sedan, 4-door	$3,662	4,115 pounds
(Prices are with standard equipment, and include federal excise tax)		

Right: Fender skirts were standard equipment on 250 series cars. **Below:** *Sweepspear motif had appeared on Packard hoods and fenders since their Classic era.* **Bottom:** *Massive bumper and guards, big vertical taillamps dominate rear-end styling.*

Production Figures

Model year, all Packard series/body styles....	100,132
Model year, this series/body style only	2,572
Calendar year, all series/body styles	76,075

1951 PACKARD

less pit into which Packard was forced to pour much too much money.

We'll draw the curtain of mercy over the story of Packard's final agonies and its ignominious end. Suffice it to say that with prudent and farsighted management — both by James Nance and his predecessors — it could have been avoided. Had the right merger been undertaken at the right time, and had some other foolish mistakes been avoided, Packard might well be with us yet.

Driving Impressions

Our driveReport Packard was originally purchased from a Red Bluff, California, dealer by an elderly gentleman who must still have possessed something of a sporting spirit. He had driven Packards for many years; this one would serve him for the rest of his life. And following his death it was taken over by his daughter.

Evidently neither father nor daughter put a lot of miles on the Packard. The odometer was broken at 38,000 miles when the car came into the possession of a body shop owner named Gary Murray, and there are indications that the total mileage may not have been much more than that.

Murray undertook a complete cosmetic restoration, including paint, plating,

carpeting, upholstery, and top. And so, by the time Haskell Young bought the car in early 1983 its appearance was like new. Haskell then set about to bring its mechanical condition up to the same standard as its cosmetics. The engine, radiator, transmission, front end, and brakes were all completely refurbished. Taper in the cylinder walls came to less than .005″, so reboring wasn't necessary, but new pistons, rings, and pins were installed. The crankshaft was ground and new bear-

ings were fitted — both rods and mains. And of course the valves were refaced.

Today the engine runs like a brand new one. Perhaps it lacks just a little of the smoothness of the nine-bearing Packard straight-eights, but the margin of difference seems to be a narrow one.

Young has made two minor mechanical modifications to this car, both calculated to enhance its usefulness as a "driver": The electrics have been converted to a 12-volt system, and a solenoid under the dash has replaced the original starter control, which was coincidental with the accelerator. Haskell and his wife Pat intend the Packard to be used and enjoyed; it's not primarily a "show" car, though it has taken first-in-class honors at a couple of local concours.

The driver is comfortably seated in a fairly erect position. Front leg room is adequate, though from a tall person's perspective we wouldn't call it generous. Back seat passengers, in addition to enjoying unusually easy access through

Left: Despite plush riding qualities, 250 can dig in and hold a line through a corner with a minimum of fuss. Below left: Rear fender "jetports" were unique to the 250 cars. Below: By contrast to the taillamps, back-up lamps are tiny.

the very wide doors, find plenty of leg and knee room. Their seating position is very low, however, and the cushion is too soft for adequate support.

A conventional dash layout faces the driver. Lights are used for battery and oil pressure warning signals, while gauges indicate the fuel level and engine temperature. A clock balances the speedometer dial, giving a symmetrical effect to the panel.

Like the early automatics from General Motors, the Ultramatic places reverse at the bottom of the quadrant. A "Park" position is provided in order to lock the transmission, and "H" (for "High") is

Slushbox with a Difference: The Ultramatic Transmission

It takes time, talent and lots of money to develop an automatic transmission. And so when "shiftless" driving became popular in the years following World War II, most of the independent automobile companies turned to outside suppliers for their gearboxes. Hudson, Kaiser-Frazer and Nash all bought HydraMatic units from General Motors, while Studebaker used a Borg-Warner-based automatic.

There was one exception. Given its reputation for engineering excellence, it comes as no surprise that alone among the smaller firms, Packard developed its own automatic transmission. Nor is it remarkable to find that it was significantly different from anything then on the market.

They called it the Ultramatic, and it was introduced on May 1, 1949, just in time to take part in Packard's Fiftieth Anniversary celebration. Like Buick's Dynaflow and Chevrolet's soon-to-be-announced Powerglide, it was of the torque-converter variety, but with a difference. The torque multiplication was a little greater: 2.40:1 compared to 2.25:1 in the Dynaflow, 2.20:1 for the Powerglide. But the big difference lay in the Ultramatic's "lock-up" feature.

For unlike the Dynaflow, the Ultramatic's torque converter is used only for acceleration; it is cut out automatically by means of a direct-drive clutch when the car is at speed. Thus, under most driving conditions there is a direct mechanical coupling between the engine and the driving wheels.

The direct clutch is applied hydraulically through the action of a centrifugal governor. Since the mechanism responds to a combination of governor and throttle pressure control, the driver can overrule the governor at will, under most driving conditions. With maximum throttle, then, the torque converter remains in operation until a speed of about 50 miles an hour is reached. And on the other hand, if the driver "feather-foots" the throttle, the direct clutch will engage at around 15 miles an hour, eliminating any slippage caused by the torque converter — and no doubt contributing significantly to fuel economy.

When faster acceleration is desired, at any speed short of 50 miles an hour the driver may overrule the governor — i.e., the lockup — by simply kicking the gas pedal past full-throttle position, thus returning the transmission to converter drive. In order to safeguard the mechanism, however, governor action is such that at 50 miles an hour sufficient pressure will be developed to overrule the pedal pressure and force the transmission to engage direct drive.

One of the unique characteristics of the Ultramatic is the fact that the lock-up feature permits push-starting the car in the event of a dead battery. To accomplish this the selector lever is placed in neutral position, remaining there until car speed reaches approximately 20 miles an hour. The lever is then moved to

H — corresponding to D on most automatic transmission quadrants — whereupon the mechanical clutch will engage and the engine will turn over.

And unlike most of the early automatic transmissions, the Ultramatic provides a Park position — enabling the driver to hold the car on a hill, for instance, by means of a complete mechanical lock-up with the rear wheels.

A planetary gearset, encompassing both reverse and "emergency" low, is also employed, the former having a ratio of 1.64:1. Packard intended the emergency low gear to be exactly what the name implies: a device for emergency use only. In practice, however, drivers often hand-shifted the car into low range — just as users of the early Dynaflow and Powerglide transmissions did — in order to provide an additional measure of "punch." One test driver complained that, "while the unit gives smooth and effortless operation, acceleration in driving range is sluggish with the torque converter apparently churning wildly yet going no place." The lower range, with its 1.82:1 ratio, changed the picture considerably, cutting more than three seconds off the Packard's 0-60 time.

Later Ultramatics, like their counterparts from General Motors, were rigged to start from rest in low range, then shift automatically to high — an important improvement. But even in its original form the Ultramatic was a sophisticated transmission, very advanced for its day and a credit to its designers.

specifications

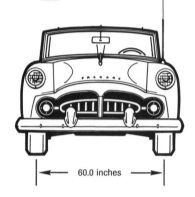

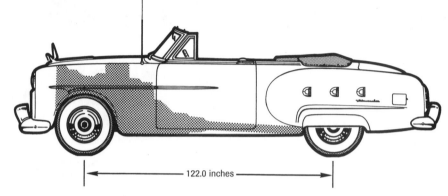

60.0 inches

122.0 inches

1951 Packard 250

Price	$3,391 f.o.b. factory, with standard equipment
Options on dR car	Ultramatic transmission, radio, heater

ENGINE
Type	L-head straight-eight
Bore and stroke	3½ inches x 4¼ inches
Displacement	327 cubic inches
Max bhp @ rpm	155 @ 3,600 (150 with std trans)
Max torque @ rpm	270 @ 2,000
Compression ratio	7.8:1 (7.0:1 with std trans)
Main bearings	5
Valve lifters	Hydraulic
Induction system	Carter WGD, Model 767S dual downdraft carburetor
Exhaust system	Single
Electrical system	6-volt originally, converted to 12-volt on driveReport car

TRANSMISSION
Type	Ultramatic, torque converter with planetary gears
Ratios: 1st:	1.82:1
2nd	1.00:1
Reverse	1.64:1
Max ratio at stall	2.4 @ 1,500

DIFFERENTIAL
Type	Hypoid
Ratio	3.54:1
Drive axles	Semi-floating

STEERING
Type	Worm and roller
Wheel diameter	18½ inches
Turns lock to lock	4½
Ratio	22.3:1
Turn circle	43 feet

BRAKES
Type	Hydraulic, drum type
Drum diameter	12 inches
Total swept area	208¼ square inches

CHASSIS AND BODY
Frame	Box section with X-member
Body construction	All steele
Body style	Convertible coupe

SUSPENSION
Front	Coil springs and wishbones
Rear	Semi-elliptic longitudinal leaf springs, solid axle
Tires	8.00 x 15
Wheels	Steel disc

WEIGHTS AND MEASURES
Wheelbase	122 inches
Overall length	209⅜ inches
Overall height	62.69 inches
Overall width	77⅝ inches
Front tread	60 inches
Rear tread	61.22 inches
Ground clearance	8.66 inches
Shipping weight	4,040 pounds

CAPACITIES
Crankcase	7 quarts
Cooling system	20 quarts
Fuel tank	20 gallons
Transmission	12 quarts

PERFORMANCE
Top speed (av)	98.5 mph
Acceleration: 0-30	4.35 seconds
0-60	13.82 seconds

(Starting in Low, manually upshifting to H)

Braking	21 feet from 30 mph
Braking	104 feet from 60 mph

*Based on a *Speed Age* road test of a 1952 Packard Cavalier sedan, having the same drivetrain and approximately the same weight as the driveReport car.

Right: *Safety mavens would approve Packard's padded sun visors.* **Below:** *Rear ashtrays are neatly hidden in top well. Below right: '51 Packards have easy-reading instrument cluster.*

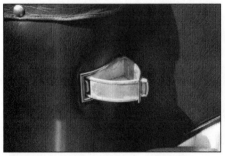

1951 PACKARD

used in place of the customary "D" for what is usually thought of as "Drive" position.

In H position the Ultramatic relies entirely on the torque converter to boost the car's acceleration when starting from rest. It is as smooth as cream, but the pace is so leisurely that almost instinctively the driver pulls the lever down one notch In order to engage the planetary "emerge low" gear. This results in substantially better acceleration, but the driver who makes it a regular practice may find that his car is a candidate for premature transmission repairs. The lower gear, with its 1.82:1 ratio, provides excellent engine braking when descending steep grades, but a

*Left: Robust flathead straight eight was thoroughly understressed at less than half a horsepower per cubic inch. **Below:** Packard's very sensible answer to the glove compartment: a big, sliding bin. **Bottom:** 250 convert boasts easy access to rear seat.*

distinct jerk is felt when the lever is moved back to H position.

Once having got under way, the Packard quickly gathers its forces and commences to stretch its long legs. The engine, with its 4-1/4-inch stroke and its great, 103-1/2-pound crankshaft, is a veritable powerhouse! The car will cruise indefinitely at speeds that would leave most modern cars far behind, and there is ample torque for climbing hills. There would be even more, but for the fact that the Ultramatic on this particular car is adjusted to lock into direct drive much sooner than it is supposed to.

Engine noise is minimal, thanks to the Packard's hydraulic tappets, and the ride is limousine-smooth. So softly sprung is this big car that we were pleasantly surprised to find that it takes the corners without leaning very much, and handles such irregularities as dips and railroad tracks with commendable aplomb.

Packard had not yet adopted power steering in 1951, and the driver is aware of the car's considerable weight when it is being parked. But under way the huge (18-1/2-inch) steering wheel responds to a light touch. The necessary trade-off to this is that it takes 4-1/2 turns of that big wheel to wind it lock-to-lock. So a right-angle turn takes a lot more wheel-winding than most of us are accustomed to

From the Pinnacle to the Pits

Both the best and worst cars I've ever experienced have been fifties' Packards. A 1951 200 sedan with stick/overdrive was left in my care by a friend when his family moved to California. I was in high school at the time, and having a Packard to park in the student lot among all the Chevy and Ford V-8s was akin to bringing a two-headed mongrel to the local dog show — you were certain not to see another one there.

That 200 sedan was fast. Or at least it seemed fast in those days. Second gear would wind to forever, and it acquitted itself very well in impromptu combat with Mercs, Fords and such, sometimes beating some of them quite badly. The trick was to get the big Packard in second and just leave it there with your foot mashed on the accelerator. Not exactly formula-one racing technique, but bloody effective under the circumstances.

The 200 was also reliable as an anvil and nearly as strong. The interior was vast and comfortable; it didn't do badly on gas if driven at all prudently; it handled exceptionally well for a big car; it was nicely put together; and I was very sad to have to relinquish it to a Ford dealer's lot where my friend eventually sent it on consignment.

Remembering my happy experiences with the '51 Packard, I bought a used '55 Clipper Constellation hardtop a few years later. Gad, what a *mistake!* It must have been a car like this which prompted Stephen King to write *Christine.*

I owned that worthless bit of rubbish for all of three days. In that modest time span the following occurred:

1) The fuses for the rear torsion bars failed. Result: instant lowrider.

2) Its hydraulic valve lifters suddenly began playing the 1812 Overture.

3) After curing these problems, at least temporarily, the third day of ownership brought the *piece de resistance* in Packard peculiarities. When I stopped for gas on a winter's evening, the bright lights of the station began to reveal a weird oozing from under the car, as though it was parked over the La Brea Tar Pits. The Clipper was started and moved, and there on the ground for all to see and admire was a nearly precise out-line of the car's chassis in automatic transmission fluid.

I'm told the '56 Packards came to market with all these problems cured. Maybe so. I've never cared to find out.

DWB

*Below: Square shape of car virtually guarantees scads of trunk space, and the Packard 250 doesn't disappoint. **Right:** 250 is one convertible which really does have room for five adults to ride in comfort.*

1951 PACKARD

these days! On the other hand, the wheel is nicely positioned for the driver's comfort.

The brakes are very effective, but they take a fair amount of leg muscle to bring the car to a halt. For a car of this heft a power booster would be helpful. But *Speed Age* noted in their road test of a Packard 300 that the brakes withstood 25 panic stops from 40 miles an hour without fading. And *Motorsport* described the Packard's brakes as "considerably above average." We have to agree. They have a lot of weight to handle, and they do their job well.

Touches of luxury abound: four ashtrays, for instance, two in front, two to the rear. The dash compartment is a lockable drawer that slides out for access, so even when it's overloaded it

won't dump its cargo on the floor. A slim bar across the top of the radio dial changes stations at a touch of the finger. And chrome-plated window sills complement the high-quality interior.

The trunk is cavernous! All the more reason for the Youngs to look upon the Packard as a superb tour car.

We've never really been partial to big, heavy cars like the Packard 250. Yet we like this one. Its smart styling, coupled with its comfortable ride and quiet operation, makes it an appealing automobile, especially for long-distance travel. We would much prefer the available stick-and-overdrive combination to the rather sluggish Ultramatic, however, in the interest of better economy as well as livelier performance.

But that's being picky, and personal. The Packard 250 was an excellent product, a marvelous "road locomotive," and a solid value in a luxury convertible. ᛞ

Acknowledgements and Bibliography
Automotive Industries, *May 1, 1949: September 1, 1950: September 15, 1950: March 15, 1951:* Bill Callahan, "Packard Packs Pep," Motorsport, *January 1951:* John Gunnell (ed.), Standard Catalog of American Cars, 1946-1975; *Jerry Heasley,* The Production Figure Book for US Cars; *Ted Koopman, "Packard for 1952."* Speed Age, *July 1952;* Richard M. Langworth, Encyclopedia of American Cars, 1940-1970; G. Marshall Naul, The Specification Book for US Cars, 1930-1969; Speed Age, *May 1952 (table);* Ralph Stein, The American Automobile; Robert E. Turnquist, The Packard Story; Walt Woron, "Packard 200 Is the One to Beat," Motor Trend, *February 1951:* Packard factory literature.

Our thanks to Ralph Dunwoodie, Sun valley, Nevada; Chuck Holmes, Stockton, California; Special thanks to Haskell and Pat Young, Sutter Creek, California.

Never a car like Packard!

...and never a Packard like this!

Above: Packard Patrician '400'— the most advanced, most exciting motor car in the world.
One of nine daring new models for '51.

The way people are crowding into our showrooms to see the new 1951 Packard, you'd think they had never *seen* a new car before! And they *haven't!* *Never* a car like this daring new Packard!

Your first glance tells you why Hollywood's famed Society of Motion Picture Art Directors selected the 1951 Packard as *the most beautiful car of the year.* And so *practical,* too —from the new low-level bonnet and Guide-line fenders (for safer parking and passing) to the mammoth new luggage compartment!

You'll get another lasting thrill from the stunning new Fashion Forum interior. So amazingly *roomy,* so luxuriously appointed. Plus—new visibility that brightens your entire outlook!

And what a joy it is to *handle!* Effortless steering — and effortless performance! New Packard Thunderbolt engines—teamed with Packard's exclusive Ultramatic Drive (now even finer for '51)—give you America's most advanced automatic motoring!

By all means—come *drive* this wonderful car!

It's more than a car ·· it's a PACKARD *-the* <u>one</u> *for '51!*

ASK THE MAN WHO OWNS ONE

Ad originally published in *The Saturday Evening Post,* December 9, 1950

1951 PACKARD

drive on report

JOHN REINHART'S MASTER STROKE

PACKARD emerged from World War II financially strong and still the perceived leader in the luxury car field, even though the lesser Packards comprised the lion's share of production from 1946 through '48. Packard's president, George Christopher, was convinced he could sell 200,000 cars a year. He might well have sold half that many were it not for materials shortages and labor problems. As it was, Packard produced 30,793 cars for the 1946 model year and 81,879 for 1947. Production rose to 146,441 for 1948, down to 116,248 for 1949.

Cadillac was closing in fast with its new ohv V-8 engine. For 1950, Packard production dropped down to 42,627 against 103,857 Cadillacs, and Packard slumped from fourteenth to sixteenth place in the industry. This was the first time Cadillac had ever outsold Packard by such a margin.

While hardly anticipating such a sales dropoff for 1950, Christopher did have the foresight to hire the brilliant young stylist, John Reinhart, before retiring in late 1949. Reinhart was one of those great natural artists of the industry's golden years. He came from the GM design school. then worked under Gor-

**by Tim Howley
photos by the author**

don Buehrig and later Raymond Loewy. From there he moved to Packard to design the 24th Series for 1951. Reinhart, who died suddenly in February 1986, is best remembered for the Continental Mark II. His 1951 Packard may have been an even greater achievement. It might easily be argued that this was the most advanced looking car of the year and the number one reason why the floundering Packard firm survived as long as it did. It is to Reinhart's credit that Packard was still using the 1951 body (although much reworked) through 1956.

Reinhart's 24th Series Packard was introduced August 24, 1950. making it one of the earliest 1951 models unveiled to the public. On October 12, 1950, it was named "the most beautiful car of the year" by the Society of Motion Picture Art Directors. Showroom reception to the 1951 Packard was exceeded only by the 1949 Ford.

In spite of the car's contemporary

styling, the classic Packard look was retained, mainly through restrained use of trim and a new horizontal grille that gracefully updated the earlier vertical design and distinctive Packard bonnet. The hood was lowered a full 4-1/2 inches and was now level with the fenders. For the first time in Packard history the hood opened from the front rather than from either side. The styling, combined with greatly increased visibility, allowed the driver to see all four fenders. The new Packards averaged two inches lower with no sacrifice in head room or ground clearance; were two inches wider and five inches longer, on the average, than the 23rd Series. Increases in interior dimensions were even greater, almost to the point of excess.

The entire frame and body, including the side rails, roof rails and pillars, were built of box-section steel for greater rigidity, greater safety, and a savings in weight of about 200 pounds. The box-section X member frame was suspended in front with coil springs and wishbones and in the rear with 54-3/8-inch-long, 2-1/2-inch-wide longitudinal leaf springs. An anti-sway bar was employed in front and tubular shocks were used all around. These were not revolu-

Driving Impressions

Our driveReport car is a 1951 Packard 300 touring sedan with Ultramatic. It has slightly less than 70,000 original miles and is mostly original other than paint and chrome. This car is a Bill Lauer restoration and should be familiar to most Packard enthusiasts in Southern California. The owner is Joe Whitaker, a man of many old car interests. He owns three other Packards including a 1940 Packard 120 touring sedan and a 1949 Custom Eight touring sedan, plus a 1969 Continental Mark III and a 1958 Chrysler Imperial. Joe works for the San Diego Water District at the Otay Lakes Reservoir where the road test was conducted and many of the photos were taken.

While the car lives up quite well to Packard's tradition of living room comfort, the front seat might not be as comfortable on long trips as one would like it to be. Possibly slightly greater height at the front edge might have been the solution. Both front and rear seats are extremely roomy, with more than ample leg, hip and shoulder room for six adults. If it was interior space you were after in '51, Packard offered it by the yard. But the narrow drop armrest in the rear is uncomfortable for the person sitting in the middle. Other than these minor points, the body is exceptionally well dimensioned — no doubt the John Reinhart touch. Door openings are large and head room permits a person to wear a hat, even in the back seat. Shades of Chrysler's KT. Keller.

Vision is excellent all around (about 30 percent better than 1950), and instruments are carefully positioned so that there is no night reflection in the windshield. Controlling the map lights with a single headlamp switch and controlling the windshield wipers with a knob on the steering column are real conveniences. The glovebox is quite a novelty. Instead of the door opening forward to dump the compartment's contents in your lap, the glovebox pulls out like a drawer. Neat!

I had never driven an Ultramatic before. While it is smooth and effortless, acceleration at low speed in driving range is pathetically sluggish, especially on the steep San Diego hills we encountered. Starting in the low range offers a much more positive approach, especially for zero to 30 mph performance. There's also a kick-down gear so you don't have the effective drive of third speed as in the standard transmission. I would take the standard transmission with overdrive any day, but Joe points out these are not easy to find. To really appreciate this car with Ultramatic you have to get out on the interstate. Joe says this car comes into its own at about 70 mph and performs beautifully all the way up to 100 mph. His comments are confirmed by 1951 road tests.

Regardless of the roughness and twisting of the back roads down near the Mexican border, this big Packard loved the punishment. The faster you drive the better it handles, and the suspension is tops for its time. Steering through the tightest turns is effortless, and the body remains near level at all times. You really only need power steering for very slow speeds and parking. Power brakes, which reduce pedal pressure by 60 percent, would have been a big help for a little guy like me. But actually bringing this brute to a halt is no problem, and brake fade is nil after many panic stops. However, I definitely agree with Wilbur Shaw that the steering ratio should have been quicker.

Throughout the hill country, speeds were maintained regardless of grades; the Ultramatic shifted so effortlessly you hardly noticed it. And the car is so silent, virtually no engine noise or wind noise, no thumps and bumps coming through to the passenger compartment. You really have to wonder if there have been any real ride improvements since 1951. This Packard is every bit as well behaved as a Cadillac or Chrysler of the same year and is a much better handling car than the 1951 Lincoln Cosmopolitan. Many readers know that I am a diehard Lincoln nut, but this Packard was making a convert out of me by the day's end.

By fifties standards this was one of the safest cars on the road: a minimum of sharp projections from the steering column, knobs and door handles; really very little inside the car to harm you. Accidents in these Packards have proven their body and frame rigidity time and time again. There are a few people walking around today because the big accident in their youth was in a Packard.

If you want to see how indestructible these cars are, get a video cassette of the 1952 movie *Sudden Fear*, with Joan Crawford stalked by Jack Palance in a series of 1952 Packard Mayfairs. He slams into walls, goes off cliffs, plows into cars, chasing her up and down the hilly streets of San Francisco, *Bullitt* style. It's a little hard to watch these beautiful cars in a Hollywood destruction derby. But they come through remarkably intact despite all the terror crashes.

Above left: Balanced good looks, restrained use of trim, modern interpretation of traditional Packard styling touches characterize the all-new 1951 design. *Above right:* Packard radiator "shoulders" have evolved into this curvaceous bit of trim. *Right:* Generous use of glass for light, airy greenhouse is a total departure from the turtletop look of previous postwar Packards.

1951 PACKARD

tionary changes over 1950. They were more like refinements.

Packard, the first automobile company to place a straight eight in mass production in 1923, introduced the highest compression engine in the industry, 7.8:1 and still a straight eight. With a new type of automatic spark control and a leaner mixture, Packard boasted three more miles from a gallon of gas in the 20-45 mph range. Above that, the increase was negligible probably because the car was hardly good aerodynamic design.

The venerable 356 engine was discontinued in favor of the 327, introduced in 1948. This was now Packard's largest engine. The 288, also introduced in 1948, was continued as the small power offering. The bore of both these engines was the same at 3.50 inches. The difference in displacement came from the stroke, 3.75 inches for the 288 and 4.25 inches for the 327. Four ranges of horsepower — 135, 138, 150 and 155 — were obtained by matching these engines with varying compression ratios.

The 288 was the standard engine offered in the 200 Series. With a conventional transmission, the compression ratio was 7:1 and the horsepower was

135. With Ultramatic, the compression ratio was up to 7.5:1 and the horsepower was 138. The 250, 300, and 400 all used the 327 engine, but in the 400, the engine had nine main bearings instead of five. In the 250 and 300 manual the compression ratio was 7:1 and horsepower was 150. In the Ultramatic versions, it was 7.5:1 and the horsepower was 155. (This engine was optional in the 200 but was seldom asked for.) With high performance heads, the compression ratio of the 327 was given a boost to 7.8:1. The Patrician 400 327 engine was also rated at 155 horsepower with a 7.8:1 compression ratio. This engine was optional in the 300 Series only, as with its nine main bearing crankshaft it could not fit into the smaller chassis. The 250, 300, and 400 engines all used hydraulic lifters. The 200 engine had mechanical lifters, with hydraulic lifters optional.

Even though Cadillac, Oldsmobile and Chrysler all had overhead-valve V-8 engines in 1951, Packard with its 7.8:1 compression ratio L-head straight eight was an engine to be reckoned with. The three ohv V-8s only had 7.5:1 compression ratios. But Packard was not to retain its performance edge for long.

Packard's Ultramatic transmission, introduced in 1949, had undergone many refinements. Its oil cooler was re-

moved from the engine radiator and mounted below the water pump. This improved accessibility and helped prevent oil leakage. The governor in the control system had new gearings and the bearings were steel backed to increase life. Pistons in the control system were bigger. Only the Patrician 400 came with Ultramatic as standard equipment. All other models had a three-speed manual transmission with the option of overdrive for an additional $102 or Ultramatic for an additional $189. Standard transmission Packards of this era with overdrive are much sought after by collectors today, but very few seem to be around. Much-needed power brakes came in 1952 and power steering in 1953.

Gone in 1951 was the Eight, Deluxe Eight, Super Eight, and Custom Eight nomenclature. There were now the 200 and 250 on 122-inch wheelbases, and the 300 and 400 on 127-inch wheelbases. The 200 Series included a business coupe with no back seat. It had 31-1/4 cubic feet of storage in the rear seat area plus a cavernous 30-cubic-feet of trunk space, same as all other 200 and 250 models. The 300 and Patrician 400 trunks were slightly larger. At $2,302 this was the lowest priced Packard. It may have been a practical replacement for the station wagon which was discontinued that year. The coupe, which

was no different from the club sedan body, was discontinued in 1952. There was also a four-door sedan in the 200 Series plus a 200 Deluxe four-door sedan and club sedan. Beginning in 1953, all of the 200 Series models would be designated as Clippers.

The 250 Series, on the same 122-inch wheelbase, was a mid-year introduction. This series consisted of the Mayfair hardtop coupe and the convertible coupe. The 250s retained the vertical taillights and side trim of the smaller series.

From the front, the 250, 300, and 400 can be distinguished by the cormorant hood ornament and vertical grille bars. The 300 shares the 400's twin horizontal taillamps. The Patrician 400 is distinguished by three jet louvers over a low strip of stainless on the rear quarter panel plus a stainless mud guard. The 300 and 400 were offered in four-door touring sedans only.

The 400 interior is as posh as in any previous Packard Custom Eight. But all the Packard interiors were quite handsome with excellent fit and detail even in the 200 Series.

Normally, a first year body might be expected to have a lot of minor flaws. Not so with the 24th Series Packards. Body fit, trim fit, paint, and detail were all up to previous Packard standards. What was so amazing was that you could buy all this Packard quality in the 200 Series for about the price of a Buick Super or for $400 to $500 less than the lowest priced Cadillacs.

In the summer of 1950, ex-race-driver, Indianapolis Motor Speedway president and *Popular Science* test driver Wilbur Shaw tested a Packard 200 and 300 on Packard's famous proving grounds track. He was assisted by *Popular Science* photographer Bill Morris and associate editor Devon Francis. On hand to greet the *Popular Science* crew and answer questions were Ed Macauley, chief engineer of Packard styling, J.R. Ferguson, Packard's chief automotive engineer, and Bill Graves, vice pres-

Packard's Ultramatic

In 1949 Packard became the only independent to offer an automatic transmission of its own. This was Ultramatic, which had been in the works since the thirties. It was a pretty reliable unit from the outset and a fairly simple setup. It was a torque converter with a direct drive clutch, which would engage at around 15 mph, eliminating a lot of the slippage and gas waste found in other automatics such as Buick's Dynaflow. It was designed in such a way that the driver had a lot of control to keep the torque converter in operation up to about 50 mph if he so desired. A positive neutral position prevented creep while the car was idling. In addition there was a push-start feature. In the event of a dead battery, a Packard with Ultramatic could be pushed up to about 25 mph, at which speed the engine would turn over.

Column quadrants were Park (rare in those days), Neutral, High, Low, and Reverse. In addition to Ultramatic there was the very popular overdrive feature which was greatly improved in 1949. In 1951 overdrive was available on all models except the 400. With overdrive the owner could expect about three mpg better gas mileage than with a conventional transmission and, theoretically, longer engine life.

In its 1951 motor trials, *Motor Trend* described Ultramatic In this manner: "The Ultramatic, which we were giving a test as much as the car itself, is a combination of a hydraulic torque converter, planetary gearshift, and friction clutch. For all normal driving, the gearshift con-trol is set in H (high) and left there. The transmission is operating in torque converter up to 15-17 mph (for normal acceleration, higher speeds for faster acceleration), at which speed the clutch automatically engages, causing the crankshaft to link up directly to the driveshaft. Any downshift that becomes necessary can be made by additional throttle pressure, provided you're below 50-55 mph. (Above these speeds, you're always indirect drive.) L (low) is used for extremely hard pulls, added acceleration or braking. At any speed below 50-55 mph you can move the gearshift selector from H to L for immediate braking. This is decidedly advantageous down a steep incline, for in L the transmission won't shift to a higher range until you make a selector change."

illustrations by Russell von Sauers, The Graphic Automobile Studio

© copyright 1987, Special Interest Autos

specifications

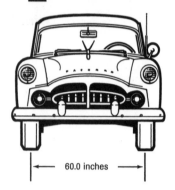

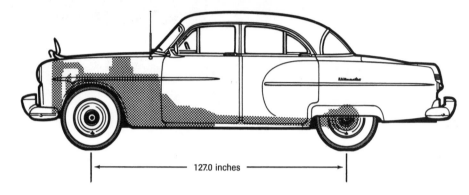

60.0 inches

127.0 inches

1951 Packard 300 four-door touring sedan

Price when new	$3,034
Options	Ultramatic, heater/defroster, rear fender skirts, radio

ENGINE	
Type	L-head eight
Bore & stroke	3½" x 4¼"
Displacement	327 cubic inches
Max bhp @ rpm	155 @ 3,600
Max torque @ rpm	270 lbs. ft. @ 2,000
Compression ratio	7.5:1
Induction system	Carter dual downdraft carb.
Exhaust system	Cast iron manifolds, single exhaust
Electrical system	6-volt coil

TRANSMISSION	
Type	Ultramatic Drive, 3-speed with direct drive lockup

DIFFERENTIAL	
Type	Hypoid
Ratio	3.54:1
Drive axles	Semi-floating

STEERING	
Type	Worm and three-tooth roller
Turns lock to lock	4¾
Ratio	22.3:1
Turn circle	43 feet

BRAKES	
Type	Hydraulic, cast iron drums
Drum diameter	12 inches
Total swept area	208¼ square inches

CHASSIS & BODY	
Frame	Pressed steel, I-beam, box section X-type
Body construction	All-steel
Body style	Four door, six passenger sedan

SUSPENSION	
Front	Coil springs and wishbone independent parallelogram
Rear	Semi-elliptic longitudinal leaf springs, solid axle

Shock absorbers	Delco direct acting
Tires	8.00 x 15
Wheels	5-lug pressed steel disc

WEIGHTS AND MEASURES	
Wheelbase	127 inches
Overall length	217¾ inches
Overall width	77 11/16 inches
Overall height	62 29/32 inches
Ground clearance	8 21/32 inches at rear axle
Front track	60 inches
Rear track	61 7/32 inches
Shipping weight	3,875 pounds
Curb weight	4,025 pounds

CAPACITIES	
Crankcase	7 quarts
Cooling system	20.5 quarts with heater
Fuel tank	20 gallons
Transmission	12 quarts

PERFORMANCE	
Top speed (av.)	98.5 mph
Acceleration: 0-30	4.35 seconds
0-60	13.82 seconds

Below: Sweepspear motif goes back to Classic-era Packards. *Right:* Hex design on wheel covers goes back even further, all the way to 1904!

1951 PACKARD

ident of Packard engineering.

Packard's test track was the fastest of its kind in the world. Two-and-a-half miles around, the parabolic curves enabled you to turn the track at up to 110 mph with absolutely no side thrust to the car. If you were brave enough you could actually take your hands off the wheel and let the car find its proper height in the turn. But the track was no good for racing as there was only one high speed groove.

The first car Shaw tested was a 200 with standard transmission. He went up to 90 mph on the track without even trying. He was impressed with the car's solid feeling and directional stability but complained about the slow turning ratio.

He then put the 300 with Ultramatic through the paces, commenting that "she took those switchback turns like a well mannered boat in rough water.... This car has a good solid feel, that's for sure. Then he took the 300 all the way up to 100 mph on the high-speed track with Morris and Francis hanging on in the back seat. After several times around, he noted that the heat indicator wasn't sweating at all. He commented that while it wasn't the fastest ride he'd ever taken it was one of the most pleasant. He closed his report by stating, "I'd finally driven that magnificent Packard track, and in a fine automobile."

He tried out the Ultramatic on Packard's killer-hill, a 35 degree grade. With three people in the car, they sailed over the top at 15 mph. Then Shaw backed down with the lever in Drive position using the forward driving power as braking power. He said the Ultramatic performed "fantastically."

Tom McCahill tested two Packards on the same proving grounds for *Mechanix Illustrated*. The cars were a 200 club coupe and a 400 sedan, both with Ultramatic. Commenting on the 200's performance, he wrote, "I have never driven an American car at actual speeds above 95 mph that handled better and showed less high-speed stress. I was doing an actual speed of 96 and 97, which is all this car has. The steering was firm and the car was as confident as Charles Boyer.... This car is big, comfortable, fast and luxurious, and my personal favorite of the line."

He drove the 400 around the high-speed rim until the speedometer stopped showing any rise at 105 and 106 mph. The actual speed he calculated was slightly in excess of 100, about the same as Shaw's speed.

Virtually every motoring magazine tested the 1951 Packard, and all were enthusiastic about its performance, ride, handling characteristics and im-

Above: L-head straight eight is understressed with just 155 horses coming from 327 cubic inches. **Left:** Flush mounted door handles in beltline are elegant solution to a usually awkward detail on any car. **Below left:** Vacuum wipers operate from knob on steering column. **Below:** Unique and sensible bin-style glove compartment.

The Frenchman's Packards in Mexico

The Frenchman Jean Trevoux finished sixth in the first (1950) Mexican Road Race in a 1950 Delahaye. After that he turned to Packards and Packard specials which he campaigned throughout the series. In the 1951 free-for-all in which the Italians, Taruffi and Ascari, finished first and second in Ferraris, Trevoux came in fifth in a 1951 Packard. Troy Ruttman, who finished fourth in a hopped-up 1948 Mercury, wrote in *Motor Trend*, "Trevoux actually looked better to me than any of the Italians, since the car he was driving required a greater degree of skill to stay in competition. The way he led that Packard through the turns was masterful; he's an extremely smart driver. The best Mexican driver was also behind the wheel of a Packard: Douglas Ehlinger of Puebla. His Judgment was far superior to that of any of his countrymen. Ehlinger finished in fourteenth place; with a speedier machine he would have done better."

In 1952, driving a 1952 Packard, Trevoux finished ninth in stocks and fifteenth overall. Two other Packards finished thirteenth and fifteenth in stocks. Don and Betty Pope made the following note in *Motor Trend* of Trevoux's ill-fated 1953 attempt: "Jean Trevoux's special Packard, with body by Moto of Italy, was much admired. Kept the Packard lines, in miniature. Trevoux was plagued with broken valves, which he attributed to the wrong fuel mixture, and he had to drop out at Durango." In the final race of 1954, Trevoux finished thirteenth overall in a Packard special and Ehlinger finished twenty-first overall in a stock Packard. None of these Packards were factory backed like the Lincolns. They were all Mexican entries, including Trevoux, no doubt with a Mexico city Packard dealer support.

courtesy Gerald Farber

Above: *Styling clay shows '51 in nearly final form. Trim looks like it belongs on '53 Pontiac.* **Right:** *entry and leg room are spacious up front.* **Below:** *Lovely upholstery, robe rail, ashtray, and lighter are standard.*

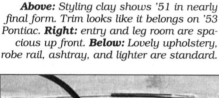

proved Ultramatic. In the 1951 Mobilgas Economy Run, a 1951 Packard 200 four-door sedan averaged 22.093 mpg, better than 12 other entries in the same class.

1951 was Packard's last great year: a brand new model, 100,132 units produced, and a comfortable six-percent profit. Packard remained in sixteenth place. The 25th Series Packards for 1952 were introduced with great fanfare on the Red Skelton Show, November 14, 1951. Unfortunately, neither Red's wisecracks nor the spectacular Pan American show car were enough to keep Packard humming on all eight. The Korean War materials shortages and government controls, plus increasing competition from the new pack of ohv V-8s saw Packard production tumble down to 62,921. It had nothing to do with the car itself, which had only minor trim changes from 1951. It was factors from without plus the moribund state of Packard management.

John Reinhart left Packard in 1951 to head up styling for Ford's top secret new Special Projects Division. This was soon renamed the Continental Division, which produced the Continental Mark II. Throughout 1950 and 1951 Packard's interim president. Hugh Ferry,

John Reinhart: 1916-1986

Three years ago, in writing a history of the Continental Mark II for another publication, I had the pleasure of interviewing John Reinhart by telephone. I was not then aware of the key role he played in designing the 1951 Packard. By the time *SIA* assigned this project to me, John had passed away. It's a shame that he never put his career in automobile design on paper and that he was seldom interviewed by auto historians. John Reinhart was one of the finest who practiced the art. He is best remembered for the Continental Mark II. His brilliant career went way beyond that contemporary classic.

John Reinhart was born in 1916 in Cincinnati, Ohio, where his father was fire chief. His lifelong fascination with cars started with pedal cars, fire trucks, and his father's fire chief roadster. By the time he was 12 or 13 years old, he was making drawings of exotic European styled classics of his own design. He studied auto design at the Central Academy of Commercial Arts in Cincinnati and then the GM design school. He worked on the instrument panel of the Cadillac 60 Special (see *SIA* #62) and also worked for Gordon Buehrig in Auburn, Indiana (see *SIA* #65). This was at the end of the Auburn-Cord-Duesenberg era, so Buehrig had set up his own design firm. Reinhart then went

photo by Gerald Farber

to Packard, where he worked under Werner Gubitz as a junior designer on the first Packard Clipper (see *SIA* #59). It is not clear whether he ever worked directly at Studebaker. He did work for Raymond Loewy doing design work on the 1947 Studebaker.

At the end of World War II he went with Loewy to England to restyle the whole Rootes line, which included the Hillman, Humber, and Sunbeam Talbot. Reinhart

returned to Packard in 1949 to become the chief stylist for the 1951 model. While at Packard he worked with Charlie Phaneuf, who would follow him to Ford to assist in styling the Continental Mark II. Interestingly enough, Gordon Buehrig worked under Reinhart at Ford.

I regret that I never discussed the 1951 Packard with John. We talked at great length about the Continental Mark II and his frustrations with Ford's top management (specifically Henry Ford II, Ben Mills, and the executive board of directors). He contended that they killed the Mark II without really giving it a fair chance.

John wrote to me in 1985, "Bill Ford (in disgust) bought the Detroit Lions, and I went to U.S. Steel as director of automotive design and marketing, railroad and agriculture, with steel shows at Cobb Hall. I had the greatest design staff (hand picked) I ever had in my life, and we couldn't sell those great cars [The Mark IIs]. What a severe frustration. I had ulcers a mile wide."

Reinhart rejoined Ford in the mid-seventies. He was assigned to the interior design studio, working on special-project cars. He retired in 1980 at age 64 and died quite suddenly in early February 1986. The legends he styled live on.

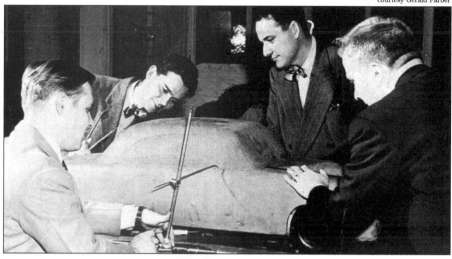

searched for his own replacement. He thought he found his man when James J. Nance, the Hotpoint hotshot, took Packard's helm in 1952. What followed was expansion, the separate Clipper Series for 1953, Studebaker-Packard, an ohv V-8 finally in 1955, and the slow, agonizing decline and fall of one of Detroit's mightiest giants. This in no way diminishes Reinhart's 1951 design, which, with modifications, was good enough to compete through 1956. With an ohv V-8 in '53 or '54, Packard might have had a fighting chance. As it turned out, the 1951 Packard marked not so much a new beginning but the beginning of the end. ∂?

Acknowledgments and Bibliography

Mechanix Illustrated *Tests the '51 Packard, November 1950;* "Take a Ride in the '51 Packard, with Wilbur Shaw," Popular Science, *September 1950;* "The Packard 300 is the One to Beat," Motor Trend, *February 1951;* "Testing the Packard for 1952," Speed Age, *July 1952:* The Packard: 1942-1962, *by Nathaniel T. Dawes.*

Special thanks to Lloyd King and Joe Whitaker of the San Diego Region of Packards International Motor Car Club.

Above: *Reinhart's crew works on preliminary clay of '51 design. John is third from left.* **Left:** *Packard passes the Tom McCahill trunk capacity test with ease!* **Below left:** *Back seat area is huge and cushy.* **Below:** *Vital instruments are grouped directly in front of driver.* **Bottom:** *Reinhart's father's fire department Buick may have provided the inspiration to send John into an automotive styling career. He's behind the wheel in this early photo.*

SHOULD YOUR NEXT CAR BE
The 1953 Caribbean?

by Michael Lamm, *Editor*

Originally published in Special Interest Autos #4, Mar.-Apr. 1971

First-year Caribbean is more sought-after than later models because of clean styling. It's a driveable collector's car with family room.

Bill Lauer's convertible served as Rose Parade grand marshall's car. Hydraulic top fits snugly when up, can be lowered in 30 seconds flat.

PHOTOS: ROSS MAC LEAN

Left-hand key starting, slide-out bin glovebox, rather plain, round gauges mark dashboard. This car boasts power windows and 4-way seat.

Enormous trunk gets that way with continental spare. Tire tips rearward, still causes awkward reach. Gas filler is on the left rear fender.

THIS RECENT SWING to small economy cars—the Pinto, Vega, Datsun, Gremlin, Toyota, etc.—by people who want *economy*, well it's a false hope. Because if you're really after economy, you don t buy a car that depreciates $1,000 its first two years on the road. You buy one that *appreciates*. And right now you're looking at one.

The 1953 Caribbean isn't the only such car, of course. But it's an example—an automobile you can drive as everyday transportation as long as you like, then turn around and sell it for at least as much as you paid. Probably more.

This drivability is one of the great advantages special-interest cars enjoy over antiques and classics. Most antiques can't keep up with traffic, and even if they could, who'd be silly enough to leave one parked unattended on a city street? Same goes for most classics—they can keep up with the traffic but they're just too tempting for the lollipop-and-fingerprint crowd. But the Caribbean and hundreds of other S-I cars like it are: 1) completely modern to drive, 2) individual enough to satisfy the collector, 3) not yet fantastically conspicuous or overpriced. This last, though, might change in the near future, and we realize that by merely publishing this article, we could be contributing to the spiral. That's not our purpose, though.

But to us, the Caribbean, among postwar Packards, does seem more desirable than most. It's pretty, there weren't many made, most were sold with the options we've since come to consider standard equipment (power steering, power brakes, automatic trans), they're convenient and fun to drive, roomy enough for the entire family, and relatively easy to work on.

The basic idea for the Caribbean came from Russell Feldmann, who headed the Henney Body Co. of Freeport, Illinois, in the early 1950s. Henney built ambulances and hearses on Packard chassis back in that day. Feldmann, knowing that Cadillac and Buick were about to start offering fancy new convertibles (and that Chrysler was toying with the K-310 coupe), suggested to Packard president Hugh Ferry that Henney build a showcar in the luxury-convertible vein. This was in late 1951. Ferry agreed,

and Feldmann had Henney designer Richard Arbib draw up sketches for a jazzy Packard ragtop showcar.

Ferry approved the design and this car became the 1952 Packard Pan American. Eventually, four or six were built (records are unclear), and the Pan American made its debut at the New York International Motor Sports Show in April 1952. The Pan American's purposes were to give Packard a more youthful image, to promote Packard generally, and to test public reaction to a fancy convertible like the 1953 Eldorado and Skylark. Ferry figured that if the Pan American stirred enough serious interest, Packard would go into limited production.

Reaction turned out to be very favorable, so Packard did indeed produce *not* the Pan American but a more "family" version called the Caribbean. The Caribbean was designed by Dick Teague, now AMC's vice president of automotive design. He'd come to Packard in August 1951, and this was his first major assignment there.

The Pan American had been a 3-passenger convertible, with a metal cover to hide the top when it was down. The Caribbean became a full 6-passenger convertible, its styling much nearer the regular 1953 Packard line. What set it apart, though, were the bold full wheel cutouts, heavy bright wheel lip moldings, chromed wire wheels, airscoop on the hood, completely uncluttered expanses of sheet metal, and the continental kit. This trunk-mounted spare was supplied by the Hudelson-Whitebone Co., which made tack-on continental kits for most other U.S. cars of that era.

The Caribbean also got a distinctive interior treatment—very bold and bright for the day—but except for those blandishments, all mechanical and engineering aspects remained stock Packard. Packard merely shipped 122-inch-wheelbase convertibles over to Mitchell-Bentley in Ionia, Michigan, and had the cars finished there. The first Caribbean was announced in January 1953, but delivery didn't begin until March.

In its first year, the Caribbean used the 180-bhp 327 Straight 8 with the big 4-barrel carb. Unlike the 1953 Eldorado and Skylark, all Carib-

Henney-built 1952 Pan American showcar led to production Caribbean. This 3-passenger convertible was styled by Richard Arbib of Henney.

Experimental 1954 Packard Panther-Daytona carried fiberglass body and 275-bhp engine, bowed at that year's Daytona 500, clocked 131 mph.

Another experimental, this Balboa hardtop used fiberglass roof with reverse slope. Except for the roof, it was a standard 1953 Caribbean.

Soft springs give easy ride, some lean. Packard introduced torsion suspension in 1955. This car uses coils and leaves.

Big 327-cid Straight 8 delivers 180 bhp. Although air cleaner hides it, the engine is very easy to service. For 1954, this 8 put out 212 horses.

Heavy wheel-lip moldings accentuate chrome wires. The Caribbean was Packard's answer to Buick Skylark, Cadillac Eldorado convertibles.

1953 Caribbean

bean power accessories were optional, even Ultramatic. Of course, the Eldorado sold for $9,000 and the Skylark for $5,600, whereas the Caribbean's base price was projected at $5,200 (by 1954 it rose to $5,600). For 1954, Packard upped the big 8 to 359 cid, raising compression to 8.7:1 (aluminum head) and drawing a whopping 212 bhp from it. Then in 1955, Packard went to its completely new body/chassis, and the Caribbean got the 275-bhp V-8. And for 1956, available in both convertible and hardtop form, the Caribbean packed 310 bhp under its hood.

We borrowed Bill Lauer's 1953 Caribbean to get an idea of how suitable this car really is as everyday transportation.

Bill lives in Santa Ana, California, runs a restoration shop there, owns 12 Packards, and is a director of Packards International.

With Ultramatic and power everything (brakes, steering, windows, seats), his Caribbean feels and handles just like a brand-new car. It's a delight in town, and it's just as great out on the road. You couldn't ask for more room for the family and, with the top down, you just can't get the kids to leave. The trunk is huge, thanks to the exterior spare.

Plenty of acceleration, good brakes (if a bit touchy with Easamatic, but you get used to it), nice steering (but slow to return to center), quiet,

SPECIFICATIONS
1953 Packard Caribbean convertible

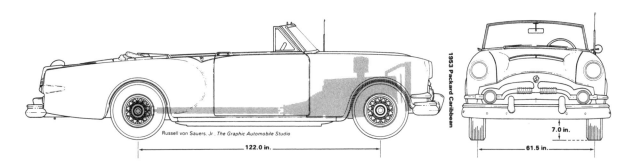

Russell von Sauers, Jr. The Graphic Automobile Studio

122.0 in.

1953 Packard Caribbean

7.0 in.

61.5 in.

Price when new . . . . $5209 f.o.b. Detroit (1953).

Current valuation . . . . Xlnt. $3100; gd. $2300. *

Options . . . . Ultramatic, power steering, power brakes, power windows, radio, heater.

ENGINE
Type . . . . L-head, in-line 8, cast enbloc, water-cooled, 5 mains, full pressure lubrication, hydraulic valve lifters.
Bore & stroke . . . . 3.50 x 4.25 in.
Displacement . . . . 327.0 cu. in.
Max. bhp @ rpm . . . . . . 180 @ 4000.
Max. torque @ rpm . . . . 300 @ 2000.
Compression ratio . . . . . 8.0:1.
Induction system . . . . . . 4-barrel downdraft carb (Carter), cast-iron manifold, single exhaust & muffler.
Electrical system . . . . . . 6-volt battery/coil (Delco).

CLUTCH
Type . . . . None.

TRANSMISSION
Type . . . . Ultramatic 2-speed automatic with torque converter, planetary gearsets, column-mounted selector.
Ratios: Low . . . . 1.82 x converter ratio.
Drive . . . . Direct.
Reverse . . . . 1.64 x converter ratio.
Converter . . . . . . 2.55 at stall.

DIFFERENTIAL
Type . . . . Hypoid, spiral bevel gears.
Ratio . . . . 3.54:1.
Drive axles . . . . Semi-floating.

STEERING
Type . . . . Linkage-type power steering (Bendix).
Ratio . . . . 18.6:1.
Turns lock to lock 4.4
Turn circle . . . . 41.0 ft.

BRAKES
Type . . . . Hydraulic, vacuum assisted, 4-wheel drums, internal expanding.

Drum diameter . . . . 12 0 in.
Total swept area . . . . . . 208.3 sq. in.

CHASSIS & BODY
Frame . . . . Channel-section steel, double-dropped, central X-member, reinforced.
Body . . . . Steel.
Body style . . . . 6-passenger, 2-door conv. cpe., hydraulic top.

SUSPENSION
Front . . . . Independent A-arms, coil springs, tubular double-acting hydraulic shock absorbers.
Rear . . . . Semi-elliptic leaf springs, tubular double-acting hydraulic shock absorbers, anti-sway stabilizer bar.
Tires . . . . 8.00-8.20 x 15 whitewalls, tube type.
Wheels . . . . Nipple-spoke wire wheels, drop-center rims, chromed, bolt-ons.

WEIGHTS & MEASURES
Wheelbase . . . . 122.000 in.
Overall length . . . . 220.281 in.
Overall height . . . . 64.000 in.
Overall width . . . . 77.875 in.
Front tread . . . . 61.500 in.
Rear tread . . . . 60.500 in.
Ground clearance . . . . . . 7.000 in.
Curb weight . . . . 4960 lb.

CAPACITIES
Crankcase . . . . 7 qt.
Cooling system . . . . 20 qt.
Gas tank . . . . 20 gal.

PERFORMANCE (from **Motor Trend,** Aug. 1953 test of Cavalier 4-dr. sed. with 180-bhp 8 & Ultramatic):
0-30 mph . . . . 5.0 sec.
0-60 mph . . . . 16.7 sec.
Standing ¼ mile . . . . . . 67.0 mph & 20.0 sec.
Top speed . . . . 100.93 mph.

FUEL CONSUMPTION
Average . . . . 11-15 mpg.

* Courtesy **Antique Automobile Appraisal.**

comfortable, superbly crafted; the dash is simple and doesn't reflect in the windshield; no rattles, handsome interior detailing, and we got a number of admiring and inquisitive glances from passersby, especially when we passed them. Altogether, there's no reason to buy a newer car and plenty of reasons not to.

It's true—you get no warranty, and there's not a dealer in the world who'll welcome you with open arms. But the old L-head 8 gives you plenty of elbow room under the hood even with all that power stuff (except for getting at the generator, which they've hidden under the battery and oil filter). So if you've got the time, might as well spend it doing the maintenance

yourself—better than pacing some dealer's TV room.

It's also true that the Caribbean doesn't get tremendously good gas mileage. But if you sit down and figure cost per mile on this car, taking into account the $150 a year or so that it's appreciating, the answer becomes perfectly clear. If you want an economy car, this looks like the way to go. ∾

Our thanks to Bill Lauer, Santa Ana, Calif; Packards International, Box 1347, Costa Mesa, CA 92626; Burt Weaver and George Hamlin of Packard Automobile Classics, Inc.. Box 2808, Oakland, CA 94618; and Dick Teague, vice president of automotive design, American Motors Corp., Detroit.

Was Packard's last true luxury sedan worthy of its name and responsibility?

drive report

1956 Packard Patrician

by Michael Lamm, *Editor*

Originally published in Special Interest Autos #36, Sept.-Oct. 1976

Packard originally dominated the luxury car market by a careful blend of engineering, sumptuous styling, extraordinary dependability, and sheer snob appeal. But by the end of WW-II, Packard had definitely lost its magic formula, and what sales success Packard did enjoy in the postwar years happened mainly by virtue of the now-legendary "sellers' market."

Packard president George Christopher had, during this postwar period, a fine chance to recapture the snob appeal by producing luxury cars only. He purposely shunned that opportunity in his pursuit of turning Packard into a mass producer of medium- and high-priced cars. Unfortunately Packard couldn't get all the postwar steel and raw materials it needed to realize that dream.

When Christopher left the company in October 1949, Packard drifted aimlessly for over two years while the interim man, Hugh Ferry, cast about for another president. Ferry saw himself as unfit for the job, and history has proved his judgment sound. When he found his man—James J. Nance of Hotpoint—Packard was already programmed to fail, although few recognized it at the time.

Nance, seeing a chance to put the four largest U.S. independent automakers into a combine bigger than Chrysler Corp., and encouraged in his thinking by Nash's George Mason, took the job anyway. The V-8 Packards of 1955-56 began life when Nance moved into his new offices in May 1952.

This driveReport's purpose is to examine the strong and weak points of the last *True Packards* and to analyze—so far as they can be analyzed—the reasons why Packard ultimately failed.

Many notable automobiles have rightly been called the product of a single person. The 1955-56 Packard wasn't one of them. Although Nance gave Packard the long-overdue push to produce the V-8, the car's many new ideas came together from a variety of sources.

The credits read like an automotive playbill: styling by Richard Teague; suspensions by William D. Allison; engines under William H. Graves, with the V-8's actual design by W.E. Schwieder, who shares credit with J.R. Ferguson and E.A. Weiss; transmissions under Forest McFarland, assisted by Herbert L. Misch and Warren Bopp. Gadgets came under the direction of Jim Nance himself.

Gadget No. 1 of the 1955-56 Packards was—and is and ever will be, of course—the Torsion Level suspension. It took the lion's share of press coverage, generated the most conquest sales, and wore out most of the showroom carpets. The ride it gave was unprecedented, and its automatic leveler tickled the fancy of many an automotive writer.

Although torsion bars weren't new in 1955, they'd never been installed in such a way that the front and rear wheels were interconnected. The result of this idea—front and rear forces trying to twist a free bar in different directions—was to load down the rear wheels whenever the front wheels hit a bump, transmitting the force upward into the frame at the front and rear equally. The car tended to rise evenly, and only half as much.

The only drawback to the system was that, unanchored as it was, the car came to rest wherever its weight distribution balanced the bars' preload. To counter this it was necessary to add a leveler, an electric screwjack, which wound up the main bars at the rear to bring the car back to a level position. Such a device, far from being a sales drawback, was by its ingenuity and uniqueness, an overnight hit, providing miles of press copy and hours of entertainment for the neighborhood kids.

"*The* car for '55," said *Auto Age*. "Most comfortable ride I've ever had," said Floyd Clymer in *Popular Mechanics*. "The car of the year in its class," exuded *Car Life*. "What a fantastic ride!" added *Motor Trend*.

It had long been in the works, and this suspension proved the merit of listening to an idea from the outside. Outside was one Bill Allison, a young engineer employed at the time by Hudson, who knocked on doors all over the auto industry in 1946-1951 trying to interest someone in his crazy torsion-bar system. Nobody saw any need of it, though, particularly at companies whose sales were adequate.

Packard's McFarland finally showed interest and fostered an agreement in December 1951 for the construction of some prototype models. When Nance came aboard the next year, he saw the idea as a perfect attention-getter. Although offered with a certain hesitancy (Packards only, then optional on the top Clippers, then optional on other Clippers, then optional on everything, finally standard equipment), the suspension did everything Nance wanted for it. It sold well and has proved durable in use.

The new 1955-56 styling was attention-getting, too. It derived basically from the 1951 job by John Reinhart and represented pulling maximum mileage out of an old body shell. In one swoop, Packard had come up with wraparound windshields, Fifties Moderne ornamentation, really tastefully done items like the taillights, and a few touches your neighbor didn't have, like sidemarker lights. On the Caribbean convertibles there were 3-tone paint jobs. Interiors were upgraded dramatically, and Dick Teague found a way to modernize Packard's traditional grille design.

With a package like this, Packard lacked only performance. Although the company traditionally had offered a great deal of horsepower (175 in the V-12, for example, and 165 in the 1940-47 Super 8), the rules of the game changed when the horsepower race of the 1950s began. Packard found itself caught up in the race with a Straight 8, flathead, 327-cid block dating from 1940.

"Give us V-8s!" said the American public. By 1954, the aging Packard 327, stroked to 4-1/2 inches and bored to 3-9/16, was producing 212 bhp with its new displacement: 359 cubic inches. (Why 212? To beat the 1953 Cadillac output of 210. Too late; Cadillac offered 230 bhp for 1954.) Packard had thrown everything at that engine: aluminum head, 8.7:1 compression, and hot cam. It was the ultimate Straight 8, But it wasn't enough to interest buyers. "There's no news in a V-8," growled Nance, but that was what everyone wanted and those were the people Packard was trying to sell to. So Packard built a V-S for the first time.

Everything on the '56 Packard is bold and massive—the final evolution of a basic body begun in 1951. Both Clipper and Packard lines featured hooded headlights, a Dick Teague touch that was a carryover from 1955.

1956 Packard

The company had tinkered much earlier with the idea of using V-8s in the One-Twenty, but they wouldn't fit. The new engines, begun in 1946 but deriving not at all from those early ones were, in a word, *big*. A V-8 Packard block was a beefy thing set beside its competition. Packard's V-8 engineers Schwieder, Ferguson, and Weiss had determined that this block was going to last out the horsepower race, and they saw at least 440 cid in it without resorting to cylinder siamesing or other drastic measures.

It was an open secret that Packard was going to *build* a V-8. Buick, after all, had given up in 1953 and Pontiac in 1954 on their Straight 8s. The only mystery now was, How radical is it?

Industry pundits occupied their time speculating on all the far-out features this engine would have. When it turned out not to have any, they were disappointed in print. Well, there was a radical new intake manifold which resulted in unprecedented free breathing, but who gets excited about things like that?

Nevertheless, for all their lack of radical design features, Packard V-8s did perform well. They led the production-car field, both in Packard's class and in Clipper's, for the two years they were built. They turned in solid records in such diverse fields as drag racing and marine applications. They've seen millions of miles of street use with no major shortcomings. In one pre-production stint, a prototype Patrician was run 25,000 miles (a distance chosen for its relation to the circumference of the earth) around the Packard proving ground track at an average speed of 104.737 mph.

Completely new engines have a history of teething problems. Yet Packard's new engine needed no redesign once it was on the road. Sustained, very high speeds finally showed the need for better oil pumps and better valve-spring retainers, which were incorporated, but many original engines are still running happily today, unmodified.

Performance, of course, requires more than a big engine. It also takes an efficient transmission. Packard had begun work in that direction in mid-1954, when it modified the Ultramatic so it did what the street racers were doing anyway: start in low and shift to high. This design, the basic elements of which were carried into 1955 and bolted behind the new engine, gave Packard a most unusual transmission arrangement: low-gear start, shift to high (1:1) by means of a timed release of low band plus engagement of high-range clutch pack, and finally torque-converter lockout by means of a direct clutch. It was patchwork, making the original 1949 Ultramatic into a sort-of 3-speed thing for competitive purposes. And it worked. But it didn't work well enough.

When locked into direct drive, the so-named Twin Ultramatic did not offer a quick kickdown under moderate throttle. The car frequently ended up lugging at comparatively low rpm as a result. Worse, the careful linkage setup required for the precise timing of the 1-2 shift was often ignored in the field. The result too often was flare between shifts, followed by premature burning of the high-range clutches. Says ex-chief engineer McFarland: "The 9-inch direct clutch should probably have gone up to 10.0 or 10.5 or used a more durable material, as it is the only thing that lacked capacity which didn't show up in proving-ground testing."

The Twin Ultramatic has taken a beating on the rumor mill for many years, and there's no doubt that it was Packard's weakest link. Properly set up and maintained, these units have served well, many with over 100,000 miles. But several unfortunate happenings hit the Ultramatic all at once.

First and most important was the demise of the dealer force upon the decline and fall of the Detroit-built Packard. With no friendly local expert to care for their cars, owners fell prey to backyard mechanics, gas-station operators. dealers in other makes, independent transmission shops, and ordinarily competent mechanics with no experience in Ultramatics or even a manual to go by. The all-important linkage adjustment was forgotten, shlock parts were used, factory-recommended torque specifications for things like aluminum valve bodies were ignored. Such mechanics usually failed to replace the bushings so critical to the maintenance of proper operating pressures in this transmission, either because they never heard of such things or because it cost too much. Thus the Twin Ultramatic's greatest shortcoming proved too frequently to be: once taken to the shop for major or minor fixing by the average mechanic, the thing didn't *stay* fixed. It would go down again and again, with the owner eventually giving up and telling his neighbor, "Can't fix 'em!"

Second, the horsepower race. The old canard about Twin Ultramatic is that the engine was too powerful for it. This it an over-simplification, but as over-simplifications go, it's fairly close. More to the point, the torque characteristics of the V-8 differed from those of the Straight 8 for which the transmission was originally designed. In addition, the mid-1950s saw more emphasis on performance. Repeated full-throttle starts, sometimes coupled with manual low/high shifts which frustrated the governor and promoted slippage, were common.

All things added up, the Twin Ultramatic should not be termed a hopeless or even a bad transmission. Properly set up, properly driven,

Packard's Fuel-Injection Experiments

It's been a well kept secret that Packard was working on a fuel-injection system for the 1956 model. Experiments began in early 1954 under Henry E.J. Pringham at the direction of chief engineer Forest R. McFarland. If all had gone to plan, f.i. would have become standard equipment on the 1956 Packard Caribbean and studebaker Golden Hawk and optional on other S-P cars.

ROSCOE C. STELFORD, JR.

Early experiments involved Lucas and American Bosch. Later Packard developed its own f.i. system, and at some time during the program Simmonds Aerocessories, Carter, Bendix, and Marvel-Schebler also demonstrated their f.i. systems to Studebaker-Packard.

Tests showed only slight acceleration increases in a Packard-injector-equipped Clipper (shown). Fuel economy increased, however, an average of 9%, with a whopping 14% gain at 60 mph. Top speed also went up—from 103 mph in a carbureted car to 116 with f.i.

After 1956, S-P continued activity on f.i., but the program shrank in priority. Bendix at one point quoted Studebaker a price of $50 per unit on its Electrojector system for 1957, but test failures forced Bendix to retract its estimate. Other units fell into the $250-$350 price range, which topped S-P's target by a multiple of five. Eventually f.i. dropped from S-P's plans altogether. At least one prototype unit still exists in the hands of a Packard collector.

Above: Stephen Melges's 1956 Patrician stays firmly planted through fast corners. Below: For '56 decklid was squared off and decoration refined. Taillamps and parking lights are visible from sides. The V symbolizes V-8.

Left: Rear seat has lots of leg room. Armrest and hassock add to feeling of luxury. Melges's car has silver-threaded black upholstery. Right: Asymmetrical dash looks like a juke box, but layout is well-planned, and gauges are easy to read. Monstrous steering wheel seems ill-suited to power steering.

and properly maintained, it was among the best available. But it was unforgiving of a lapse in any one of these requirements: as such, it was a failure. Packard might better have saved itself the R&D costs on this unit; it was no small feat for a company of this size to manufacture its own automatic, a fact matched by only three other companies at the time (GM, Chrysler, and Borg-Warner, all larger than Packard). Yet the use of Borg-Warner and GM transmissions lost Ford no customers.

Packard did, however, hate to send work out, at least under Nance. Nance made every effort to produce as much of the car as he could, and he did succeed in getting Packard back into the body business, even though the circumstances were less than happy. When the Briggs Mfg. Co. went on the block in 1953 (*SIA #19*), Chrysler became its new owner and principal customer. Chrysler informed Nance that it wouldn't supply Packard with bodies but did agree, in a burst of generosity, to do so through the 1954 model year. This situation put Packard in a box at a bad time, forcing it to lease a former Briggs plant from Chrysler. But not just to make bodies—that would have been too easy. Instead, Nance decided to move the whole assembly line over to Conner Ave., escaping from the 6-story layout on East Grand Blvd., which had been in place for nearly 50 years.

The resulting assembly line was one of the most modern in the business, and Nance did make his start-up deadline, to the amazement of the industry. But the plant was small. So small, in fact, that Nance's lieutenants had to quell several rebellions among middle management when the move was decided on. One of the dissidents even forecast that it was impossible to build cars in that plant. He was wrong, but the obstacles proved monumental. The line had to be detoured around fixed objects, there wasn't enough loading/unloading space, there were too many hand operations getting the chassis started. At times quality-control problems had the dealer force in near revolt.

Nance eventually came to the conclusion that he couldn't build Packards and Clippers on the same line. Either Packard quality suffered, or the Clippers took a cost penalty. A cost penalty was the last thing the company needed at that point. So, for that matter, were quality-control problems. As a matter of fact, the whole cost/quality headache was something Nance didn't need. Because, with the startup of 1955 production, he suddenly had to worry about another whole automobile company: Studebaker.

Above: Packard's beefy V-8 has proven itself over the years. Below: Unique suspension was designed by Bill Allison. It used long, interconnected torsion bars plus an electric screw leveling device. Torsion Level, with its unprecedented ride, pulled many customers into Packard showrooms.

IMAGE INTERNATIONAL

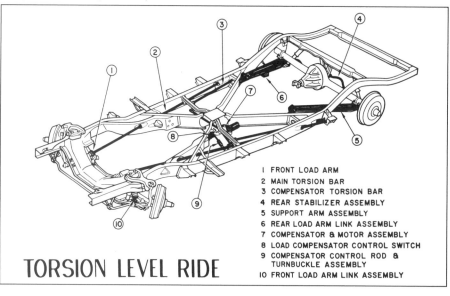

TORSION LEVEL RIDE

1 FRONT LOAD ARM
2 MAIN TORSION BAR
3 COMPENSATOR TORSION BAR
4 REAR STABILIZER ASSEMBLY
5 SUPPORT ARM ASSEMBLY
6 REAR LOAD ARM LINK ASSEMBLY
7 COMPENSATOR & MOTOR ASSEMBLY
8 LOAD COMPENSATOR CONTROL SWITCH
9 COMPENSATOR CONTROL ROD & TURNBUCKLE ASSEMBLY
10 FRONT LOAD ARM LINK ASSEMBLY

Above: Small lamp graces rear door. Packard collectors call bright strip "Reynolds Wrap." Below: Decklid ornament is also trunk release.

Above: Electric windows and door locks came together. Gear selector locks at 5 mph. Below: Glovebox has pouch for maps and cigarettes.

1956 Packard

The new Studebaker-Packard Corp. was the first step in a grand plan to combine Studebaker, Packard, Nash, and Hudson into one full-line company. It was also the last step, both because George Mason died and because Packard had bought, without adequate investigation, a company in debt up to its smokestacks. A full discussion of the financial problems of Studebaker is out of scope here, but we can note that Packard, crackerbox plant or not, expensive pre-delivery fixups notwithstanding, made money for 1955. Studebaker's losses, meanwhile, wiped that out to the tune of a net minus nearly $30 million.

Things were going to be better for 1956. Or else. Again ignoring Studebaker, because there was no integration to speak of, a new program, with a shared shell, was planned for 1957.

Meanwhile, the 1956 Packard line was fully refined, and many models are now sought out by collectors on several points, not the least of which, of course, is the fact that they represent the last luxury Packards. However, the many little details on these cars intrigue collectors, too. For one thing, Packards and Clippers were finally separated completely, reversing the original mistake of 1935 and its reaffirmation in 1946. Nance made internal changes to that effect: the name of the Packard Div. was changed to Packard-Clipper, in imitation of Lincoln-Mercury down the street. The Packard name was removed from the Clipper decklid (late in the year it went back on); the franchises were physically split, although there was no effort to franchise separate Clipper dealers; and the 48 states were notified that Clippers should be separately registered and titled.

Sales, responding to the refinements and some added gadgetry, were satisfactory until Packard hit still one more quality-control snag, namely defective rear axles. The 1956 Packards and Clippers had the company's first flanged rear axles, and they were supplied by Dana. They began failing proving-ground tests just before introduction, and Packard was forced into a costly and embarrassing recall campaign at precisely the wrong moment. Although Dana agreed to a cash settlement, the lost confidence was never regained. And by this time, with every division of Studebaker-Packard operating at a loss, it was obvious that the company would have to be either liquidated, sold, merged, or subsidized.

The government, which had been quick to pull the defense contracts S-P needed so badly, hesitated to offer any aid. Every firm contacted declined purchase or merger. The only halfway attractive offer came from Curtiss-Wright, the airplane manufacturer, which rescued the company's stockholders at the price of the Packard car, all the remaining defense business, and the corporation's best plants in Utica, Michigan, and South Bend, Indiana.

While all this was going on, what kind of car was the 1956 Packard? Powered by an even bigger version of the 1955 engine (now 374 cid), the *Greatest Packard of Them All* offered also a pushbutton transmission. The new idea in shifting was what *Popular Science* referred to as "the piano," mounted on a pod to the right of the wheel. Packard rejected the Chrysler system, also offered in 1956, of making the driver shift left-handed. Packard's system was electric, like the Edsel's and Rolls-Royce's that followed. The elec-

tric shifter, a bolt-on modification to a standard Twin Ultramatic, worked as well as can be expected for a mass-produced device of critical tolerances and precision adjustments. There were failures, partly due to moisture getting into the motors, and again there were some botched jobs by mechanics unfamiliar with the things. Anyway, Packard's reputation for reliability took another punch on the nose.

Styling changes consisted of little things in 1956. The decklid was squared off, decoration refined, the backlight modified to minimize the appearance of what was, after all, a 1951 shell. The stainless-steel bright strip, known to Packard collectors as "Reynolds Wrap," no longer ended at the running light as in 1955 but now continued to the tail. The Caribbeans had reversible upholstery (leather on one side, cloth reverse). The headlight peaks were extended as far forward as practical.

Underneath, the Torsion Level suspension was refined to minimize electrical troubles. Mechanical aspects were unchanged. The industry's first limited-slip differential, Twin Traction, became available. The electrical system was changed from positive to negative ground, Packard being one of the last holdouts.

Accessories abounded. Four-door cars could be equipped with another industry first, electric door locks controlled by the driver. There were rear-window defoggers, underseat heaters, and power absolutely everything. Patrician sedans continued to be equipped with a genuine relic of the past: carpeted hassocks.

Packards for 1956 came in four varieties: a sedan, the Patrician; a 2-door hardtop, the Four Hundred; and a pair of luxurious, all-out 2-door Caribbean models—hardtop and convertible. Late in the year, in an effort to bring in one last buck, Packard stopped producing medium-priced Clipper Customs and put Packard fronts on them, calling them Packard Executives. But the Executive wasn't in the original program.

Never mind Lincoln, never mind Chrysler's Imperial—although it's always nice to outsell *somebody*—Cadillac was the target; had been since the battle between Packard and Cadillac got under way in the 1930s. It wasn't exactly an even match—Packard's four models to Cadillac's 10. Against the Patrician was Cadillac's 62 sedan on a 2-inch-longer wheelbase; against the Four Hundred, a pair of series 62 hardtops (standard and Coupe deVille); against the Caribbeans, the Eldorados (Seville hardtop, Biarritz convertible). Packard had no competition for the 62 convertible, the 62 4-door hardtop (Sedan deVille), or anything on a longer wheelbase. The demise of the Henney Motor Co. had deprived Packard of all its long-wheelbase cars, and even though they didn't sell in great numbers, just having them in the catalog was good for prestige. Where the models were comparable, however, Packard had a good score.

Packard didn't offer the Autronic Eye but lost no other points in the gadget race; Cadillac couldn't counter the electric door locks, pushbutton transmission, Twin Traction differential, Torsion Level suspension, automatic leveler, or the Caribbean's reversible upholstery. Packard had the advantage, albeit slight, in horsepower (310 to 305 in the limited-production jobs, 290 to 285 in the main line); displacement (374 vs 365); torque (405 vs 400); and compression ratio (10.0 vs 9.75). Interior and exterior dimensions were within aces of each other, the two greatest differences being in the Cadillac 62's 2-inch-greater wheelbase and Packard's 4-inch-greater overall length.

In short, the 1956 Packard had everything except sales, and the question remains, Why did it lack those? We'll get to the answer in a mo-

specifications

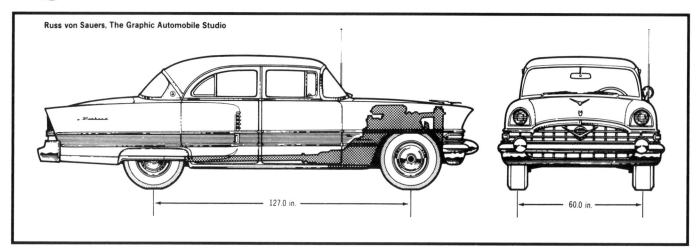

Russ von Sauers, The Graphic Automobile Studio

127.0 in.   60.0 in.

1956 Packard Model 5682 Patrician 4-door sedan

Price when new ....$4160 f.o.b. Detroit (1956)
Standard equipment ....Ultramatic transmission, power brakes, Torsion-level suspension.

ENGINE
Type ....Ohv V-8, water cooled, cast iron block, 5 mains, full pressure lubrication.
Bore & stroke ....4.125 x 3.500 in.
Displacement ....374 cid.
Max. bhp @ rpm ......290 @ 4600.
Max. torque @ rpm ....405 @ 2800.
Compression ratio ......10.0:1.
Induction system ......4-bbl. downdraft carburetor, mechanical fuel pump.
Exhaust system ....Cast-iron manifolds, twin mufflers & resonators.
Electrical system ......12-volt battery/coil.

CLUTCH
Type ....None.

TRANSMISSION
Type ....Pushbutton Twin Ultramatic 2-speed planetary automatic with torque converter and direct-drive lockup.
Ratios: 1st ....1.82:2.
        2nd ....1.00:1.
        Reverse ....1.63.1.

DIFFERENTIAL
Type ....Hypoid gears.
Ratio ....3.54:1.
Drive axles ....Semi-floating.

STEERING
Type ....Worm & roller, Bendix power assist.
Turns lock to lock ......3.875.
Ratio ....19.9:1.
Turn circle ....43.0 ft.

BRAKES
Type ....4-wheel hydraulic drums, internal expanding shoes.
Drum diameter ....12.0 in.
Total swept area ....208.25 sq. in.

CHASSIS & BODY
Frame ....Channel-section steel, central X-member.
Body construction ......All steel.
Body style ....4-door, 6-passenger sedan.

SUSPENSION
Front ....Unequal A-arms, anti-roll bar, full-length torsion bars with automatic load level, tubular shocks.
Rear ....Solid axle, full-length torsion bars with automatic load level, tubular hydraulic shock absorbers.
Tires ....8.00 x 15 4-ply tubeless.
Wheels ....Pressed steel discs, drop-center rims, lug-bolted to brake drums.

WEIGHTS & MEASURES
Wheelbase ....127.0 in.
Overall length ....218.54 in.
Overall height ....62.3 in.
Overall width ....78.0 in.
Front tread ....60.0 in.
Rear tread ....60.9 in.
Ground clearance ......8.0 in.
Curb weight ....4660 lb.

CAPACITIES
Crankcase ....5 qt.
Cooling system ....28 qt. (with 2 heaters).
Fuel tank ....20 gal.

FUEL CONSUMPTION
Best ....15-17 mpg.
Average ....610-12 mpg.

PERFORMANCE (from **Auto Age**, May 1956):
0-30 mph ....4.1 sec.
0-40 mph ....6.0 sec.
0-50 mph ....9.0 sec.
0-60 mph ....11.9 sec.
Standing ¼ mile .....17.7 sec. & 78.0 mph.
Top speed (av.) ......111.0 mph.

ment, but for now, the fact remains that when the end did come in June 1956, it came with a whimper: 28,835 cars sold, only 18,482 of them Packards. This was against a break-even of 60,000 and against Cadillac's formidable 154,000 sales that year.

AS a representative of Packard's last glory year, our driveReport Patrician, owned by Stephen Melges, seems amply qualified. It's got every accessory under the sun except air conditioning. Interior appointments make it the sort of car that could get away with a $4,310 price tag 20 years ago. (The published base on the 1956 Patrician was actually $4,190, but Torsion Level was listed as a mandatory option at $150 extra. Other prices: push-button shift $52, dual heaters and defroster $131, 3-way-tuning radio with electric antenna and rear speaker $135, power brakes $40, power steering $115, electric windows $108, electric door locks mandatory with power windows $30, whitewalls $39, tinted glass

$45, and Twin Traction axle $44.)

The car starts and idles quietly, and the engine is so well muffled that if you listen hard you can hear the transmission and generator whirring. Touch one of the piano buttons—H for smoothness or D for gear assisted pavement rippling—and away you float.

It is a floating ride, the sort that you expect to wallow a lot through hard turns. No such thing. The car stays horizontal and firmly planted through fast corners. It's an amazing feeling and totally unexpected. Stiffer shocks aren't needed, and Packard owners who've tried them say they only make the ride jiggly without improving cornering. We didn't drive this car hard enough to check tire adhesion, but with that heavy V-8 up front, there's bound to be plenty of understeer.

One anachronism is the huge steering wheel, which seems out of place with the sensitive power steering. You do have some road feel, though, and it's a fine system. It's just that the monstrous wheel isn't necessary.

Another thing that's monstrous is interior spa-

ciousness in this Patrician. Rear leg room rivals any limousine, and the instrument panel stands far forward to heighten the illusion of space (it's no illusion). This dash, by the way, has a slightly unnerving asymmetry, plus a busyness and a perforated, damascened silveriness that's more than a little jukeboxy. All gauges, however, are easy to read, and it's a well planned layout—central glovebox and twin ashtrays at each end of the panel.

Seats are extremely comfortable, the first postwar Packards ever to have overstuffed cushions—a direct response to the competition, whose seat material had not been drawn down so tightly as Packard's. Controls are easy to use, and Packard had an oversized power brake pedal for 1956 to make that operation even easier.

Particularly handy is the pushbutton control, although it does take some getting used to. There's an answer for those who feel that putting this control at the right might tempt young passengers into trying it. Yet at above five mph, the P, N, and R buttons don't do anything if

1956 Packard

pushed. An additional safety feature, not necessarily loved nor retained by today's 1956 Packard owners, is an automatic relay which puts the transmission into park whenever the ignition is shut off.

Packard did have a fairly serious safety program going in 1956, as this car demonstrates. Besides the limited-slip differential, the easy-tracking suspension and pushbutton transmission, there's a dished steering wheel, but with a center medallion that looks as if it could do a job on your sternum if given half a chance. There's also a padded dash top.

The wraparound windshield shows minimal distortion, and the taillamps and parking lights are visible from the sides (as are body side-markers). And all S-P (Studebaker-Packard) cars came with seatbelts that year, although our driveReport car had them removed.

The 1955-56 S-P seatbelt system was indeed interesting. The central anchor point was a steel cable loop bolted to the floor, while the outside anchor points stood on the lower trailing edges of the front doors. This system, claimed S-P, kept the doors shut in a crash. Well, probably so, if your internal anatomy could stand the resulting squeeze. Anyway, when not in use, the door-mounted halves of the belts clipped into place toward the fronts of the doors.

To sum up our impressions, the Patrician excels in every detail that counts in a luxury car: silence, smoothness, performance, ease of control and handling, roominess, attention to detail, sumptuousness of decor, and totality of power assists. It's also, in our opinion, a fine looking car inside and out.

So the question remains, Why did Packard fail? Why were sales so low? Was this car worthy of its name and price?

The life of a car is every bit as complicated as the life of a breathing organism, so it's impossible to list everything that contributed to Packard's demise. But foremost among the reasons was a lack of public confidence in a company that for so many years *seemed* to be sinking (seeming makes it so); also the founded and unfounded rumors of mechanical difficulties surrounding the Twin Ultramatic, the axle-breakage problem, and an assumed delicacy of a suspension system that mysteriously whirs up and down at curbside for no apparent reason. Packard's dealer network was weak, its advertising budget slim when compared to the Big 3, and its cash situation severely pinched by the coming aboard of Studebaker.

The company foundered and sank, but cars like this 1956 Patrician will probably sail along smoothly for as long as Packard collectors are willing to devote a reasonable amount of attention to them. They're not temperamental cars by any means—quite the opposite. They're very hardy and amply qualified to wear the red Packard hex. ☙

Our thanks to Dick Teague, John Reinhart, and William D. Allison, Detroit; Forest McFarland, Flint, Michigan; William L. Graves, Ann Arbor, Michigan; John R. Bond, Escondido. California; Burt Weaver and Steve Cram, San Francisco; and Packard Automobile Classics, Box 2808, Oakland, California 94618.

Quite a contrast to our driveReport Patrician, these two Packards—the Request and the Predictor—were built at the same time.

Loyal Packard owners begged the firm to bring back the classic vertical grille. Dick Teague (l.) and Bill Braves discuss the very appropriately named Packard Request of 1955. Designed by Teague for the Chicago Automobile Show, the Request was built on a Packard 400 chassis—color was opalescent pearl with a copper-toned top and side accent molding. The car, a one-off by Creative Industries, disappeared after the Chicago show. Favorable show response to the Request led Packard to consider a V-12 revival, but the ideal stalled for a lack of development financing.

William M. Schmidt and Dick Teague conceived the Packard Predictor. The Ghia execution was completed in just 90 days; Creative Industries rushed the electrical work, finishing just in time for the 1956 Chicago Automobile Show. Packard president Jim Nance used the Predictor to forecast planned engineering innovations. Car featured retractable roof panels and had energy-absorbing vertical grille; all instruments were overhead or in console between seats. The hood extended through the windshield to form the dash. Car used independent rear suspension with a Twin Ultramatic transaxle. the Predictor survives today in the Studebaker Historical Collection, South Bend.

Portrait of Craftsmanship in Action

The all new *Packard Hawk*

THE MOST ORIGINAL CAR ON THE AMERICAN ROAD

You will find no other car like the Packard Hawk. It is the most original and distinctive automobile crafted in America, styled to match the tempo of our times. Its unique flowing lines are aerodynamic. Its fins: functional. It is designed with that imaginative flair you only expect to find in Europe's most fashionable automobiles. Faithful to its thoroughbred breeding, the Packard Hawk is a *luxury* automobile with smooth, soft leather seats and elegant, tasteful interior appointments.

Extra Power from Built-in Supercharger

Its appearance is complemented by power from a highly efficient V-8 engine with a built-in supercharger, capable of instantaneous acceleration, or smooth performance under the most trying conditions of stop-and-go traffic. The supercharger with variable speed drive cuts in automatically as needed, for acceleration or extra power for passing or hill climbing, but when not in use, costs nothing extra in gasoline. It is a design for power, with economy.

The Packard Hawk is *the* new car with a regal air that immediately distinguishes its owner as a man of position. Put yourself in that position . . . behind the wheel of a Packard Hawk, soon.

Studebaker-Packard offers the most varied line of cars in America. See them all . . . economy cars . . . sports cars . . . station wagons . . . luxury sedans and hardtops.

Visit your Studebaker-Packard dealer today!

Studebaker-Packard
CORPORATION
Where pride of Workmanship comes first!

Ad originally published in *Chicago Sunday Tribune*, December 8, 1957

1958 PACKARD

FIN-ALE FOR A PROUD NAME

by Tim Howley
photos by the author

ON July 13, 1958, the last car to bear the prestigious Packard nameplate rolled off the line. Many bemoan the final fate of Packard dressed in Studebaker armor. Few know that Packard might have survived as a reborn 1956 or 1957 Lincoln. This is the story of those last fated days and the turmoil that led to the not so grand finale.

In 1944 Packard was in a better financial position than almost any other manufacturer to meet the postwar demand for luxury cars. In 1954, when Packard merged with Studebaker, Packard was still solvent. This was not the case with Studebaker. It was the car of the proletariat that dragged down His Lordship, and not the other way around. But there were also many other circumstances growing out of the time and Packard's precarious position in the fickle marketplace.

The underlying causes of Packard's demise in the late fifties is well chronicled in the 1956 Packard Patrician driveReport by George Hamlin (see *SIA*

#36); so we will only highlight that account here. Hamlin begins his report by stating, "Packard president George Christopher had, during this [early] postwar period, a fine chance to recapture the snob appeal by producing luxury cars only. He purposely shunned that opportunity in his pursuit of turning Packard into a mass producer of medium- and high-priced cars. Unfortunately Packard couldn't get all the postwar steel and raw materials it needed to realize that dream.

"When Christopher left the company in October 1949, Packard drifted aimlessly for over two years while the interim man, Hugh Ferry, cast about for another president. Ferry saw himself as unfit for the job, and history has proved

his judgment sound. When he found his man [in early 1952] — James J. Nance of GE Hotpoint — Packard was already programmed to fail, although few recognized it at the time.

"Nance, seeing a chance to put the four largest US independent automakers into a combine bigger than Chrysler Corp., and encouraged in his thinking by Nash's George Mason, took the job anyway. The V-8 Packards of 1955-56 began life when Nance moved into his new offices in May 1952."

SIA #4, March-April 1971, further chronicles the decline and fall of Packard. Dick Teague, who headed Packard styling in the fifties, said, "Nance knew when he came that he was going to be in for some tough sledding. And I think he felt he had to gamble. He was going to play either black or red. He played red and it wound up red — real red. He did everything he could to make it work, but he just extended the corporate finances so far that...."

While it is difficult to recognize them as such, the 1955-56 Packards are mas-

Driving Impressions

For 1958 Packard built just 1,200 sedans. Given the average survival rate of one percent for any make, that would mean that only 12 still exist Even that could be a high figure, since this was not the sort of car anyone would be motivated to save. We considered ourselves very fortunate to find an all original 1958 Packard sedan in Oceanside, California. The 109,000 miles on the odometer is very likely to be original. We don't know who owned this car originally or why it was so well preserved for so many years, but we are fairly certain that it is a California car that somebody put away for years. At some point it was purchased by actress Elizabeth Montgomery and her husband Robert Foxworth, who donated it to an Old Globe Theater, San Diego Auction in 1987. The buyer later resold it to Gerry Capp, collector of fifties cars in Oceanside. What you see in the photos is a '58 Packard pretty much as they looked in 1958, and what we experienced were the driving and riding qualities of a '58 Packard when they were new. The owner notes that the car is extremely tight and rattle free, which was unusual for a Studebaker of this vintage. He further points out that the silver Mylar side trim was originally gold, but has faded over the years. The steering and front end had the firm kind of feel of a low mileage car. We noticed no blowby, sluggishness, transmission slippage or valve noise which is so typical of cars of this era. We also noted no oil spots in the places where we parked it for photos. Wind noise at higher speeds was extremely low. So this car was either very well maintained or was professionally rebuilt mechanically.

Slipping behind the driver's seat, we were rather disappointed at the upholstery, trim and detail for a car bearing the name of Packard. It struck us as more of a super Studebaker President. The instruments were rather plain for a luxury car of this period, but totally convenient and easily readable. The aluminum facing on the dashboard looked kind of cheap. About the only reminder of Packard luxury of bygone days was the lap robe cord on the back of the very well cushioned front seat.

For 1958 both Studebaker and Packard were lowered two inches and underwent considerable suspension changes. There was a front anti-sway bar fitted between the lower control arms for more stable cornering and to control nose dive in fast stops. The variable rate front coil springs were re-engineered for a softer and more stable ride. Rear springs were somewhat unorthodox at the time. They were offset with respect to the mounting of the rear axle — the rear axle being mounted forward of the leaf spring centers rather than on dead center as in most other cars. The result was greater rear-end stability, less tendency to sway or break away under extreme handling conditions, decreased tail end dipping on acceleration or rising on hard braking.

All of these improvements showed up when we were putting our car through the paces 36 years after it left the factory. While you could hardly call it a great handling or riding car today, it is an excellent family car to drive by late fifties standards. One would think the Packard would have had a somewhat more sophisticated suspension system than Studebaker, particularly after Packard offered Torsion-Level suspension in 1955-56, but it was pure Studebaker. Coupled with the 289-c.i.d. V-8 and Flight-O-Matic transmission, this meant we were testing a '58 Studebaker President with a Packard badge. The finned brake drums were another feature shared with the Studebaker President and Hawk. Little wonder that the 1958 motoring press didn't bother testing it. This was a darn nice car by any '58 measure, but a far cry from a Packard in every department but grillework. In 1958 the base price of the Studebaker President four-door sedan was $2,639, which meant the Packard name cost an extra $573. The only justification for this sharp price differential we can come up with is the distinction of driving the last year Packard, which in 1958 carried about as much weight as a speech by Herbert Hoover!

Still we liked the car overall for these reasons: 1) Simplicity of engineering, ease of getting at everything mechanical and no pushbutton automatic transmission to worry about. 2) Styling that has stood the test of time remarkably well compared to the likes of many other '58 chrome monsters. 3) Truly distinctive road recognition; when was the last time you saw a snout like this coming down the street, and wearing a Packard name to boot?

1958 PACKARD

terful facelifts of John Reinhart's 1951 design. The front and rear clips were entirely new, the windshield wrapped around, the instrument panel was new, but the chassis and inner body structure were all a car that had been around for four model years. The Clipper on the same chassis incorporated the same basic body changes as the senior Packard. It remained a Packard subseries in 1955 and became a separate make in 1956, something which should have happened in 1951.

The number one attraction of the 1955-56 Packard was Torsion-Level Ride, highly touted by the press and quite reliable in service. Torsion-Level was a self-equalizing, self-leveling suspension system with long torsion bars

running nearly the length of the car. It was discontinued after 1956.

In 1955, better late than never, Packard debuted its long awaited ohv V-8. Introduced in a 320-c.i.d. version for the Clipper and 352-c.i.d. version for the Clipper Custom and senior Packards, then bored out to 374-c.i.d. for the 1956 Patrician, 400 and Caribbean, this powerplant was as reliable as any in the industry. It was the product of engineering research and development dating back to 1946. Packard V-8 engineers Schwieder, Ferguson and Weiss had determined that the block was good for at least 440 cubic inches. This engine would have been more than adequate for any Packard built in the 1957-58 era. Unfortunately, Studebaker management chose to drop it after 1956, turning the plant's facilities over to defense production.

If the engine had a drawback, it was

1955 Twin-Ultramatic. There was nothing wrong with this unit when properly maintained. But with the weakening of Packard's dealer organization in the mid-fifties, service fell prey to non-factory trained hands. Unlike HydraMatic, or even Lincoln's Turboglide, this transmission was unforgiving when serviced by the ignoramus. To further complicate matters, it had electric pushbutton controls for 1956. Packard might have been better off buying its transmissions from Borg-Warner or GM. Lincoln used HydraMatics from 1949 through 1954 and never lost a buyer because of it.

Then, for whatever his reasons, Nance decided to move the entire body assembly line from the East Grand Boulevard location where it had been for 50 years over to much smaller quarters on Conner Avenue. While the new plant was modern, it was small, and, due to

its layout, made the production of automobiles in even Packard's kind of quantity difficult at best. Eventually Nance concluded that he couldn't build both Packards and Clippers on the same line. Either Packard quality suffered or the Clippers took a cost penalty. His ultimate decision was to throw the whole problem in South Bend's lap, which eventually resulted in a Packard turned into a Studebaker.

As for the Studebaker-Packard merger in 1954, again quoting our 1976 *SIA* article, "The new Studebaker-Packard Corp. was the first step in a grand plan to combine Studebaker, Packard, Nash and Hudson into one full-line company. It was also the last step, both because George Mason died and because Packard had bought, without adequate investigation, a company in debt up to its smokestacks. ...We can note that Packard, crackerbox plant or not, expensive pre-delivery fixups notwithstanding, made money in 1955. Studebaker's losses, meanwhile, wiped that out to the tune of a net minus of nearly $30 million."

The 1956 Packards were much improved over 1955 except for serious rear axle problems and pushbutton Ultramatic. By this time Packard was getting a reputation for having considerably less than traditional Packard reliability (see sidebar, page 104). For these and a lot of other reasons Packard sales slumped monumentally during 1955 and 1956, two fantastic years for the industry at large. On June 25, 1956, the last *real* Packard was assembled in Detroit. Our 1976 article concluded: "With every division of Studebaker-Packard operating at a loss, it was obvious that the company would have to be either liquidated, sold, merged or subsidized."

Backtracking a bit, in 1955 William F. "Bill" Schmidt resigned from his long-standing position as head of Lincoln-Mercury styling to become vice president of Studebaker-Packard design. Dick Teague now headed Packard styling under Schmidt; Duncan McRae

1958 Packard Hawk

The most amazing of all the Hawks of that period was the 1958 Packard Hawk, with only 588 built. It carried a Studebaker Hawk body with the fiberglass Packard nose bolted on. To further differentiate it from the Studebaker Hawk it carried arm rests on the outside of the doors, Mylar fins, a continental kit impression on the deck lid, functional airscoop in the hood, a full leather interior, and most important of all a McCullough supercharger that boosted horsepower from 225 to 275. The decklid was actually a return to that of the 1953 Studebaker Starliner with a continental kit impression. The car was done by Studebaker stylist Duncan McRae who was also responsible for the 1958 Packardbaker sedan, wagon and hardtop. Shared with the Studebaker Hawk were unusually large brakes with finned drums.

The Packard Hawk was never originally intended to be a production car. At first just one was built for Roy Hurley, the Curtiss-Wright president who made the last-ditch effort to save the venerable Packard name, but not the car, as mentioned earlier. The Packard Hawk was then reluctantly put into production; a bit surprising considering the pathetic state of Studebaker/Packard finances at the time and Hurley's mixed feelings about continuing the Packard.

One of the most impressive features of the Packard Hawk is the tooled instrument panel with full instrumentation including tachometer and manifold pressure gauge. A more simplified version of this instrument panel would have gone far to set the other 1958 Packards apart from their Studebaker brothers, but it just wasn't in the cards.

Portrait of Craftsmanship in Action

The all new Packard Hawk

illustrations by Russell von Sauers, The Graphic Automobile Studio

specifications

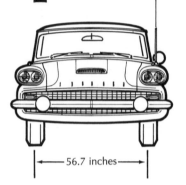

← 56.7 inches →

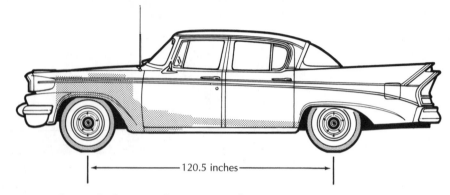

← 120.5 inches →

1958 Packard four-door sedan

Body number	58L-7818
Base price	$3,212
Options on dR car	Flight-O-Matic, power steering, power brakes, pushbutton radio, heater, oil filter, dual exhausts, white sidewall tires, two-tone paint. Price as equipped, $3,773

ENGINE

Type	90-degree ohv V-8
Bore x stroke	3.56 inches x 3.63 inches
Displacement	289 cubic inches
Compression ratio	8.3:1
Horsepower @ rpm	225 @ 4,500
Torque @ rpm	305 ft./lb. @ 3,000
Main bearings	5
Induction system	Carter model 2575S four-barrel
Fuel	Camshaft driven vacuum pump
Exhaust system	Cast-iron manifolds, dual exhausts
Ignition system	12-volt

TRANSMISSION

Type	Borg-Warner three-speed automatic, column shift,. Maximum torque converter ratio: 2.15
Ratios: 1st	2.40:1
2nd	1.47:1
3rd	1.00:1
Reverse	2.00:1

DIFFERENTIAL

Type	Hypoid final drive, Spicer-Thorton limited slip
Ratio	3.31:1
Drive axles	Semi-floating

STEERING

Type	Saginaw integral recirculating ball, power assist
Turns lock-to-lock	4.5
Ratio	18.2:1
Turning circle	41 feet

BRAKES

Type	Hydraulic drum type
Drum diameter	12 inches
Effective area	172.8 square inches

CHASSIS & BODY

Construction	Box section steel, double-drop side rails
Body construction	All steel, welded
Body style	4-door sedan

SUSPENSION

Front	Independent, unequal-length upper and lower control arms, coil springs, tubular hydraulic shock absorbers
Rear	Rigid axle, semi-elliptic leaf springs, tubular hydraulic shock absorbers
Tires	8.00 x 14
Wheels	Stamped steel, five bolt

WEIGHTS AND MEASURES

Wheelbase	120.5 inches
Overall length	213.2 inches
Overall width	77 inches
Overall height	57.5 inches
Front track	56.7 inches
Rear track	55.7 inches
Weight	3,505 pounds

CAPACITIES

Engine oil	5 quarts
Cooling system	18.5 quarts
Fuel tank	18 gallons

PERFORMANCE*

Acceleration: 0-30 mph	3.9 seconds
0-45 mph	7.2 seconds
0-60 mph	11.2 seconds
50-70 mph	9.6 seconds
Top speed	100 mph plus
Fuel mileage	18 mpg best; 14 mpg average

* *Dell's 1958 Car Buyer's Guide*

This page: Packard's venerable red hexagon design is retained in wheel covers. *Facing page, top:* Surely the most bizarre tailfin design from an era when nothing succeeded like excess. *Below:* The front end is certainly memorable, too.

1958 PACKARD

headed Studebaker styling. Schmidt and Dick Teague did the Packard Predictor (see sidebar, page 102) plus a handsome line of 1957 Packards and Clippers in full-size clay model form. They actually got as far as die models, but dies were not started due to lack of finances. These models borrowed from both the Predictor and the 1956 Lincoln. You must remember that before leaving Ford, Schmidt had done the 1956 Lincoln, the 1955 Lincoln Futura show car and quite a bit of facelifting for the 1957 Lincoln which in one form or another would have carried Futura style fins. Schmidt got into an argument with Lincoln-Mercury management over the 1957 Lincoln styling and decided to resign and go over to Studebaker-Packard. For the rest of his life he totally disowned the 1957 Lincoln, although his drawings suggest that he had a lot more to do with the final product than he ever admitted. Clearly, he still had 1956 and 1957 Lincolns foremost in mind when he joined Studebaker-Packard.

In a last ditch effort to provide a new Packard for 1957, Nance approached Ford on the possibility of using 1956 Lincoln dies. According to Schmidt, Ford would have sold them because the 1958 Lincoln was unitized construction and a completely different car from the 1956 and 1957. Not long before his death in 1990, Schmidt told this author that the project never got any further than some renderings by him and a few meetings between Nance and Ford management. Dick Teague has also claimed doing the Lincoln/Packard renderings.

We do have some idea of what a 1958-59-60 Packard with a Lincoln body would have looked like. It would have had a Packard chassis with Torsion-Level suspension. It would have continued using the Packard 374 engine and Twin-Ultramatic transmission. The grille probably would have continued the 1955-56 Packard theme and the taillamp treatment would have been 1955-56 Packard. The unique 1956 Lincoln instrument panel might have been retained, but more likely it would have been changed to a Packard-style instrument panel. The interiors would have been completely redesigned. The car would have carried the 1956 Lincoln body, not the 1957 Lincoln body. Packard would have defied the industry trend to fins and thus would have provided luxury car buyers with a unique, conservative alternative to Detroit's gaudiest creations in history.

At about the same time as Nance promoted the idea of a Lincolnesque Packard, in early 1956, he approached New York bankers and investors hoping

The Last Time I Saw a 1958 Packard

1958 is a year that somehow still sticks to the roof of my mind like peanut butter. It was the year I graduated from the University of Minnesota and took my first job as a radio announcer with station KSUM in Fairmont, Minnesota. I felt I deserved a new car that year but barely had enough change in my pockets to keep gas and girls in my '55 Chevy. Still I visited all the showrooms, studied all the cars, collected all the brochures, and still have a couple left — brochures, not girls or cars.

Anyway, one of the sales ladies at the station did, indeed, have a brand new Packard sedan, black, with the same silver interior as our driveReport car. We all thought it was strange looking, and even used to joke about in on the radio. I can't remember her name but do know why she bought the car. After Packard production stopped on July 13, the dealer couldn't give it away. She said she got it for no more than the price of a Studebaker. Well, that's what she said. Nobody ever thought of it as rare or worth saving, just strange looking, like something you wouldn't want to run into on a dark road late at night. About the time I left Fairmont she left her husband and headed north for Alaska in that car. Thinking I was somehow in on her plot, he followed me with a shotgun as far as Mankato, and that's the last time I ever saw him, her, KSUM or a '58 Packard!

Above: Textured fabric is reminiscent of early Kaiser-Frazer interior efforts. Below: 289 Stude V-8 gave Packard respectable scat. Facing page: Anti-sway bar and innovative rear spring/axle location help Packard handle quite well.

The Packard Predictor
Was this where Packard was going?

SIA #47, October 1978, carries the story, "Predictor, Packard's Last Dream Car," by Gerald Perschbacher. For those with further interest in what Packard might have been, it's worth rereading. The Predictor idea originally came from Bill Schmidt, with Dick Teague and Dick McAdam doing the actual design work. This was a fully operational, full-sized car built on a Packard Clipper chassis and utilizing 1956 Packard running gear. The Predictor was a two-door coupe with a classic Packard grille, T type top, reverse angle backlight and swivel front bucket seats. The car was completed in steel by Ghia in Turin, Italy, and rushed back to the United States in time for the January 1956 Chicago Auto Show. A careful study of this car will reveal more than a few similarities with Schmidt's Lincoln Futura which made its debut a year earlier.

The car was promoted to dealers and the public as something that was soon to come out in production. But it was full of electronic bugs, especially the sections over the doors that retracted into the roof, and at the time Packard didn't have the money to pay the $70,000 cost of this creation, let alone ready it for production.

After touring the 1956 show circuit, the Predictor went into the Packard collection which included the 1955 Request (a standard 1955 Packard with a classic-era grille), and two early model Packards.

Despite the turmoil at Packard during its last days as an entity, the Packard Predictor survived. Sometime in 1956 it went to South Bend to be added to the Studebaker car display, and we understand it survives in the Studebaker Museum in South Bend to this day.

1958 PACKARD

to raise raise $50 million. He was turned down cold. He then tried for $35 million and was turned down again. At this point Nance left Studebaker-Packard. He later went to Ford as head of the Lincoln-Mercury Division, a position which he held very briefly. To the helm as Studebaker/Packard president went Harold Churchill, formerly Studebaker chief engineer who, with Mike DeBlumenthal, was responsible for such achievements as free-wheeling, overdrive and hill-holder.

Finally, Roy Hurley, president of Curtiss-Wright, agreed to consider Studebaker-Packard as a complex $70 million tax loss. He hoped to keep Studebaker at a roughly break-even point for two years, write off its losses as a bad Curtiss-Wright investment and then collect roughly $40 million (the difference between what he'd agreed to pay and the real selling price) on what would be 45 percent of Studebaker-Packard stock by the time he exercised his option. All of this maneuvering precluded continuing plans for a separate Packard in 1957-58 but did not preclude continuing the Packard name in the hopes of pushing Studebaker production up to and beyond the break-even point. This, in essence, is how the Packard became a Studebaker.

The separate Packard engine was out as being too costly. The Lincoln/Packard plan was totally out of the question. What came down the line for 1957 was the "Packardbaker," styled by Duncan McRae who basically grafted the styling cues from the Clipper mockup onto the Studebaker body. The instrument panel was a 1957 version of the 1955-56 Packard panel. It was not a bad looking creation, but it was no Packard.

After a sneak preview at the New York auto show in December, the 1957 Packard made a late January appearance in dealer showrooms carrying a 289-c.i.d. Studebaker President/Hawk V-8 engine, with a distinctly Packard grille and taillamps and unmistakably Studebaker body. The front bumper was actually a reworked 1956 Packard bumper. So were the taillamps and hood ornament. It was called the Packard Clipper, the separate Clipper line being dropped, and it came in only two body styles, a four-door Town Sedan on the 120.5-inch wheelbase Studebaker Hawk chassis and a four-door Country Sedan station wagon on the standard 116.5-inch-wheelbase Studebaker chassis. This was the first Packard wagon since 1950. Production was a mere 3,940 sedans and 869 wagons. The engine achieved its 275-horsepower rating via McCulloch supercharging, same as the Stude-

options were standard on the Packard. These included blower, Studebaker automatic transmission, Studebaker variable rate front coil springs and dual exhausts. But power steering, power brakes, power windows and power seats that you would expect to be standard on a car bearing the Packard nameplate were optional.

Motor Life noted in a brief report in their February 1957 issue, "The principal differences [between Packard and Studebaker] are the plushier appointments and the use of distinctive Packard-type details in trim, taillights, dash and so forth. In fact, the Packardizing of the cars ran as some kind of a minor miracle in view of the relatively short period of time allowed for the redesign and preparation for production.

"Although there has been no official S-P announcement to this effect, it is quite evident that the cars merely are a temporary measure. Something completely new, and very possibly based upon the Predictor experimental Packard, no doubt is in the works."

All that was in the works was a second year facelift on the Studebaker body which was again introduced late, in January. Now two more body styles were added — a hardtop and a Packard Hawk (see *SIA#25*), the latter utilizing the Studebaker Hawk body. The Clipper name was dropped. The McCulloch supercharger boosting horsepower to 275 was now standard only on the Hawk. All other Packard engines developed 225 horsepower, same as the Studebaker President. Unfortunately all of these cars moved further away from looking like Packards. The hood, aprons below the dual headlamps and cowl section in front of the radiator were fiberglass. On the Hawk the entire nose was fiberglass. Hoods carried an air scoop, functional only on the Hawk. Dual

1958 Studebakers

photo by Fred K. Fox

For 1958 Studebaker continued its Scotsman, Champion, Commander and President lines as well as the Silver and Golden Hawks, but the model line was pared down to eliminate the short-wheelbase President sedan and club sedan. There were two wheelbases, 116.5 inches for the Scotsman, Champion, and Commander, 120.5 inches for the President and Hawk. The new President Starlight hardtop was put on the shorter, 116.5-inch wheelbase chassis. Like the Packard, all Studebakers were lower due primarily to new roofs and floor pans and 14-inch wheels on the Commander and President. The Scotsman and Champion still rode on 15-inch wheels as standard equipment. You could order 14-inch wheels on the Champion but not the Scotsman.

Dual headlamps and tailfins, the latter being inspired no doubt by the Hawk, were now featured on all models and body styles except the Scotsman. A step up from the Scotsman was the Champion with dual-headlamp option. An L-head six was the only engine available on both the Champion and Scotsman. Studebaker-Packard was now betting heavily on economy cars which management sincerely believed

would bring them out of a four-year slump.

Outer body shells of all models were greatly reworked by Vince Gardner, and not necessarily for the better. Their pedestrian looks covered a multitude of suspension improvements that finally made Studebaker a respectably good handling car. All of these improvements, no more or less, were shared with Packard. Optional even on the Studebakers this year was Twin Traction limited-slip differential, a Packard innovation introduced in 1955. Engines remained virtually unchanged from 1957.

Inside, the cyclops-eye speedometer remained on an instrument panel that was even busier than that of 1957. Toggle switches continued to be used for auxiliary controls; windshield wipers and heater/air vents were operated by levers. Upholstery colors and patterns were much changed from 1957.

This was not a good year for Studebaker. With a mere 44,759 units produced for the US market, this was Studebaker's poorest year of the postwar era. Losses were a hefty $13 million. A few better years with the Lark were ahead.

Above: Seats use unusual door-to-door pleating. Right: There's plenty of luggage room. Facing page, top: Oil filter was an optional extra! Center left: Dash carries big, round gauges. Center right and bottom: There's no mistaking a '58 Packard for any other car.

headlamps were on all body styles except the Hawk. Tail fins were grafted on the rear. It was a strange rear treatment with fins on top of fins. The side trim was Mylar.

In an effort to make all 1958 Studebaker and Packard sedans look lower, there were new roofs and floor plans. This necessitated a change to a two-piece propeller shaft with three universal joints. Lower transmission tunnels were the result. Wheel size was reduced from 15 inches to 14 inches except on the Studebaker Scotsman (see *SIA* #81). Prices were $3,212 for the sedan, $3,262 for the hardtop and $3,384 for the wagon. All convenience items considered to be standard on luxury cars were optional, and now even the Studebaker Flite-O-Matic was a $189 extra, although it is doubtful that any Packard left the factory without it. Little wonder that production was down to 1,220 sedans, 675 hardtops, 159 wagons and 588 Hawks. All Packard production ended July 13. But as late as February 1958, Churchill had a 1959 program for Packard which again would have been a facelifted Studebaker. What killed the plan was Studebaker's shift in 1959 to the compact Lark which totally precluded a luxury line. Even the Studebaker Commander and President got the axe for 1959, as all Studebakers (except the

Clipped by a Clipper
by Dave Brownell

All through my high school years I'd owned or driven some kind of Packard, starting with a 1936 One-Twenty convertible sedan with Dietrich body plates, through a '36 Standard Eight sedan and a '51 Clipper 200 sedan with stick and overdrive which could give Chevy V-8s a very hard time through unofficial and slightly illegal quarter-mile sprints.

By the time 1959 had rolled around Packard was out of the car business. I was starting college and casting around for a V-8 Packard. And then I saw it on the Lincoln-Mercury dealer's lot: a yellow and black '55 Clipper Panama hardtop with all the baubles and bangles. It had been a locally owned car since new and I had admired it when the original owner — who ran the big franchise shoe store — went gliding by. Parts and service shouldn't be a problem since the local Packard dealer was still around, albeit selling Edsels. That should have told me something about him, but it didn't!

After the requisite test drives and hard bargaining, the Packard had a new home. It was a difficult relationship from the start. The first morning it developed an awful engine clatter from dry hydraulic lifters. Then after a short ride something let go in the torsion bar electrics and it settled down like the world's original lowrider. A trip to the ex-Packard dealer got these problems sorted out while causing grave damage to my checkbook.

A few nights later I was headed to a party near Boston. A glance in the mirror revealed that the Clipper was laying down a smokescreen like James Bond's trick Aston Martin. Oil pressure looked o.k., though, and the engine sounded well, the torsion suspension was on an even keel; maybe, I thought, it's just a temporary condition that will cure itself. Some moments later that turned out to be an exercise in self-delusion as the car began surging, slipping and struggling to maintain speed on the four-lane.

I left at the next exit, pulled into a nearby service station, shut off the Packard, which was now almost fully enveloped in smoke, and stepped back,

waiting for the explosion. None came, but after the smoke had drifted off there was the most precise outline of the Clipper's chassis on the ground that you could imagine — all done in transmission fluid. The highly-touted Twin Ultramatic had decisively puked itself!

In less than a week this rolling calamity of a Clipper had managed to develop major problems in all the areas that were new for Packard in 1955: V-8 engine, torsion suspension and "improved" automatic tranny. Contrast this sorry performance with the totally reliable service which the '51 Clipper gave this heavy-footed high school loony and you begin to understand why Packard lost not only its traditional long-time, loyal customers but those who bought new Packards in 1955-'56 thinking that they were stepping up to a half-century tradition of superb quality and impeccable engineering.

I never owned another Packard. And I never bought another pair of shoes from the former owner's store again,

Hawk) became either Deluxe or Regal models. However, the Corporation continued to call itself Studebaker-Packard until 1962.

Could Packard have survived? Not very likely given all the circumstances. But it could have been continued for a few more years had the Lincoln body plan materialized. A 1956 Lincoln/Packard might have sold in numbers of possibly up to 20,000 a year through 1960 because Lincoln buyers shied away from the 1958-60 models. There was a market out there for the '56 Lincoln, and it might have had even more appeal with a Packard name. That market was never tested beyond 1957. However, the question is, could Packard have built enough of these cars to break even? We'll never know. ❏

Acknowledgements and Bibliography
"Postwar Packards," SIA #4, March-April 1971; 1958 Packard Hawks," and "How Studebaker Came Not to Be," SIA #25, November-December 1974; 1956 Packard Patrician driveReport, by George Hamlin, SIA #36, September-October 1976; "Predictor, Packard's Last Dream Car," by Gerald Perschbacher, SIA #47, October 1978; "1958 Studebaker and Packard," Dell's 1958 Cars; "Packard in Decline," and "The Turbulent Life and Times of the Packard Hawk," by G.H. Zimmerman, Packards International Magazine, Fall 1985; "The 1957 Packard," Motor Life, February 1957; "1958 Studebaker and Packard," Motor Trend, November 1957; Standard Catalog of American Cars, 1946-1975, by the Editors of Old Cars Publications. Special thanks to Gerry Capp, Oceanside, California, for furnishing our 1958 Packard driveReport car.

PACKARD BY VIGNALE

Italian Elegance/American Engineering

by John F. Katz
photos by Roy Query

WHAT'S this? A ravishing, *rosso chiaro* chariot sporting Italian lines and American proportions? The round-shouldered grille says "Packard," but the fender badges bear the dome, spire, and initial "V" of Carrozzeria Vignale. A Vignale-bodied *Packard?* There *has* to be a great story behind this car!

Undoubtedly there is, but we weren't able to find it. Incredibly, this unique and remarkable automobile drew virtually no notice at all from the English-language media. A single photo of it appeared in the March 1951 *Road & Track*, as part of a scantily captioned feature called "Salon of Italian Coachwork." Then this magnificent custom Packard dropped out of sight, to reappear on a Los Angeles used-car lot in 1953 or '54. So its origin remains a mystery — although current owner Mark Smith has developed a very plausible theory.

Mark has repeatedly contacted the Vignale family about his treasure, but for reasons of their own they have chosen not to respond. In fact, the history of the entire Vignale operation, like that of our driveReport car, is somewhat obscure. Published sources are thin and contradict each other, making it difficult for us to be certain of our story.

Still, it appears that Alfredo Vignale was born in Turin on June 15, 1913, the fourth of seven children. Even then, his father worked as a car painter, and two of Alfredo's older brothers also found employment in the embryonic Italian auto industry. At 11, Alfredo himself traded his desk in the classroom for an apprenticeship in a sheet-metal shop, and by 17 he was beating fenders for master coach-builder Alessio Farina.

Alfredo learned what he could from Farina, then left in 1939 to set up his own carrozzeria in partnership with his brothers. The war ended that venture almost before it began, but Alfredo started over again in 1946, fabricating bicycle and motorcycle parts in one dingy room while he waited for automotive orders to trickle in.

Early on, an odd bit of luck helped to promote his name. The British journal *The Autocar* mistakenly attributed one of Vignale's first efforts, an aluminum-bodied Fiat 500, to another coachbuilder, but Vignale's fame blossomed when the magazine printed an apology and word got around that the stunning little car was really his. Then, in 1948, a Vignale spider body for the Fiat 1500 chassis won the coachbuilding *Grand Prix d'Europe* at Juan les Pins, firmly fixing Alfredo's reputation.

By then, Alfredo had persuaded his brothers Giuseppe and Giovanni, a partner named Angelo Balma (or Balma Angelo, depending on the source), and a number of ex-Farina craftsmen to join him in larger quarters on Turin's via Cigliano. For their emblem, they chose the outline of the *Mole Antonelliana*, the great tower that dominates downtown Turin.

At that time, Vignale favored the designs of a young freelancer named Giovanni Michelotti. To save money and materials, Vignale craftsmen generally eyeballed Michelotti's full-sized drawings into three-dimensional sheet metal without full-sized models or body bucks. As a result, Vignale bodies tend toward asymmetry, but Alfredo himself once defended the practice by pointing out that no one can look at both sides of a car at once.

Soon, Vignale received orders for coachwork on more expensive and exotic chassis. He built 100 Ferraris in 1950-53, three of which won various Mille Miglias, while two more scored a one-two victory in the second-ever Carrera Panamericana in 1951. (A number of sources credit Michelotti with the oval-shaped, egg-crate-textured grille that remains a Maranello hallmark today.) He bodied Briggs Cunningham's road cars, built one-offs on Aston Martin and even Rolls-Royce chassis, and produced short runs — 50 cars or less — of special bodies for Fiat and Lancia.

We found but a single photo of Alfredo Vignale during this period. It reveals a wiry Latin with thinning hair swept back from his face, and a bristly mustache protecting soft lips. His dark, deep-set eyes look not at the photographer but off into the distance. His coverall hangs open from the collar almost to his waist, and a cigarette casually dangles from his left hand. It is the pose of an eccentric artist — except that his entire body crouches slightly, as if ready to pounce, catlike,

PACKARD

Above: *Vignale retained side-opening hood feature as used on stock Packards of the time.* **Below:** *Vignale badges and "Eight Special" nameplates are mounted on lower front fenders.* **Bottom:** *With top up, car has a formal yet sporty profile.*

upon whatever has caught the attention of those far-away eyes.

If we accept its 1948 registration as accurate, then our driveReport Packard would represent one of Vignale's earlier efforts. The chassis came from a prewar One-Twenty, serial number 309582, which marks it as a 1939 model. The mechanical pieces are absolutely stock save for some slight modification to the heater. Noting the unusually glossy finish on the frame and running gear, Smith postulates that 309582 was a display chassis that somehow survived the war to come into Vignale's possession.

We found one cryptic reference to an unspecified prewar chassis bodied by Vignale for the *Concorso di Eleganza di Torino* in 1947. Vignale may have created our featured Packard for that affair, or for a particular, anonymous customer. Or, as Mark believes, he may have built it as a demonstrator, hoping to sell a limited production run of similar bodies, perhaps through Packard's own dealer network. Certainly Southern California, where the car ultimately turned up, would have been a prime market for such a project. It's an elegant theory, one that fits all the known facts. But it's *only* a theory. The truth is, we just don't know.

Vignale's relationship with Ferrari ended in 1953, as Maranello turned increasingly to Pinin Farina for body design and construction. Vignale still thrived for a while on limited runs of bodies for Fiat, Abarth, and Maserati,

among others, and by designing mass-production cars for Standard-Triumph. He moved again in 1961, to a 127,000-square-foot factory adjacent to the Fiat Mirafiore plant in Grugliasco. But fortune turned against Vignale in 1966, when he won, then quickly lost, the contract to build the Chrysler-powered, Touring-designed Interceptor for Jensen. Then he blundered into a relationship with Greek-Cypriot gambling magnate Frixos Demetriou, who agreed to import Vignale-bodied Fiats into England. The trouble was, while Vignale seriously planned to sell cars, Demetriou only needed a business front in Great Britain to facilitate the renewal of his gaming license — and he backed out of the import deal once that renewal was secure. In November 1969, short on cash and orders, Alfredo Vignale reluctantly sold his factory to Alejandro de Tomaso. Vignale died three days later, in a suspicious single-car accident.

With financial backing from Ford, de Tomaso built Pantera bodies, and later complete Panteras, at the Grugliasco factory. Ford acquired the Vignale name along with de Tomaso's Ghia operations in 1973, and still affixes it to the odd show car or special edition.

Driving Impressions

William F. Montigel, the gentleman who rescued our driveReport car from a used-car lot in Los Angeles, brought it home to Riverside and cared for it for nearly four decades. Current owner Mark Smith bought it from him in early 1990, in partnership with Norman Wolgin. They found the Packard in very

Above left: Spare chews up most of the available trunk space. *Right:* Taillamps are Fiat units. *Below:* Hand-formed bumpers and guards are graceful but substantial. *Bottom:* Top goes up and down with minimum of fuss.

specifications

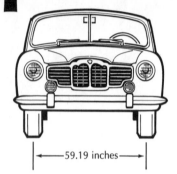

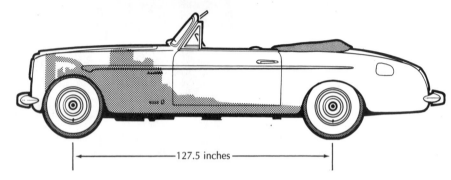

←— 59.19 inches —→

←——————— 127.5 inches ———————→

Packard Vignale

Base price	N/a
Equipment on dR car	Straight-eight engine with optional high-compression head, two-barrel carburetor, individual reclining front seats, leather upholstery, map pockets, electric turn signals, clock, white-wall tires

ENGINE

Type	Straight 8
Bore x stroke	3.25 inches x 4.25 inches
Displacement	282.1 cubic inches
Compression ratio	6.85:1
Horsepower @ rpm	120 @ 3,600
Torque @ rpm	221 lb. ft. @ 2,000 (est.)
Taxable horsepower	33.8
Valve gear	L-head
Valve lifters	Solid
Main bearings	5
Carburetor	1 Stromberg 2-bbl downdraft
Fuel system	AC mechanical pump
Lubrication system	Pressure with gear pump
Cooling system	Pressure with centrifugal pump
Exhaust system	2.25-inch single
Electrical system	6-volt

TRANSMISSION

Type	3-speed manual
Ratios: 1st	2.43:1
2nd	1.53:1
3rd	1.00:1
Reverse	3.16:1

CLUTCH

Type	Long semi-centrifugal, single dry disc
Diameter	10 inches

DIFFERENTIAL

Type	Hypoid
Ratio	4.36:1

STEERING

Type	Worm and roller
Turns lock-to-lock	4.25
Ratio	20.2:1
Turning diameter	43 feet

BRAKES

Type	Bendix 4-wheel hydraulic
Drum diameter	12 inches
Effective area	182 square inches
Parking brake	Mechanical, on rear service brakes

CHASSIS & BODY

Construction	Separate body and frame
Frame	Steel channel with I-beam X-member
Body	Hand-hammered aluminum with steel front fenders
Body style	4-seat convertible coupe

SUSPENSION

Front	Independent, lower lateral arms and leading torque arms, lever-type shock absorbers acting as upper control arms, coil springs, anti-roll bar
Rear	Live axle, semi-elliptic springs, stagger-mounted, lever-type shock absorbers, Panhard rod with its own third lever-type shock absorber, anti-roll bar.
Shock absorbers	Delco two-way
Tires	Denman Super-Safety 7.00 x 16 four-ply
Wheels	Motor Wheel 16-inch stamped steel

WEIGHTS AND MEASURES

Wheelbase	127.5 inches
Overall length	N/a
Overall width	N/a
Overall height	N/a
Front track	59.19 inches
Rear track	60 inches
Min. road clearance	N/a
Shipping weight	N/a

CAPACITIES

Crankcase	6 quarts (less filter)
Fuel tank	21 gallons
Transmission	2 pounds
Rear axle	6 pounds
Cooling system	16 quarts (with heater)

CALCULATED DATA

Horsepower per c.i.d.	0.42
Weight per hp	N/a
Weight per c.i.d.	N/a
P.S.I. (brakes)	N/a

This page: Door handles are beautifully crafted with tiny push-buttons. *Facing page, top:* Vignale's creative interpretation of Packard's traditional grille is modern and attractive. *Center:* Gas filler is well hidden away. *Bottom:* License plate frame/stoplamps look more like something from a Chrysler product than a Packard.

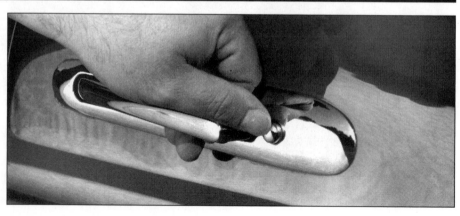

PACKARD

believable 19,000-some miles showing on its odometer. Still, Smith and Wolgin had the car completely restored by Scott Veasey of the Tom Sparks shop in Hollywood, trading its original blue-green metallic paint and maroon leather interior for an appropriate Ferrari red, complemented by tan hides. Veasey finished the car in just 11 weeks — in time for the 1990 Pebble Beach concours, where it won first prize for postwar European coachwork. Since then, it has garnered five more awards for continental coachwork, plus best-in-show honors at both the Fresno concours and at Packards International in Newport Beach.

Although it does somewhat resemble a Vignale Ferrari grown to Packard proportions, our driveReport car is really quite handsome up close and "in the metal." The Italian journal *Tuttosport* once wrote of Vignale that "his cars first surprise and then convince you," and that's certainly true in this case. The body-color side spear is a particularly clever touch, providing relief from the otherwise slab sides without the garishness of bright trim. Hammered right into the metal, rather than added on, it also no doubt enhances the stiffness of the panels. The body, incidentally, is formed from aluminum, except for the front fenders which are steel — presumably to protect them from careless mechanics while the engine is being serviced.

Inside, the Vignale Packard treads a

PACKARD

fine line between traditional American luxury and Italian *gran turismo.* You sit *on*, rather than *in*, the individual front seats, perched atop the puffy rolls of upholstery. A set of thumb screws down where the seats hinge for access to the rear compartment provides some adjustment for the backrest angle — a mechanically simple, but not particularly convenient arrangement. Front leg room would be tight for anyone over six

feet. The rear seat itself about equals the front for comfort, but there's even less leg room back there.

The top is heavy, but works so smoothly that two people can raise or lower it with very little effort. Clamped to the windshield header with three bail-type latches, it frankly looks a little too big for the car. It also reduces rearward visibility to just about none. But that extra bulk leaves plenty of head room inside, and its chrome-plated framework adds a pleasant, expensive look. Folded down, the top stows neatly beneath a padded tonneau cover.

The dashboard presents its own paradox: Its neat row of rectangular gauges looks like a standard US production design, but it isn't from any Packard we can recall. Further, while the temperature, fuel, oil, and ampere gauges are labeled in English, the speedometer reads in *kilometers* per hour. And the auxiliary controls are marked only with initials for words which we suspect are not English — "AVV" for the starter, for example, and "Q" for the cigarette lighter.

Punching the AVV button, however, brings an unmistakably Packard power plant to life — smooth, but with just enough growl to suggest real performance. Unfortunately, this particular Packard was suffering from an intermittent ignition problem on the day of our drive; so we weren't able to fairly evaluate its straight-line capability. Other One-Twenties that have appeared in *SIA* driveReports, however, have exhibited particularly good low-end torque and have cruised comfortably at modern highway speeds. We're sure this one would, too, were it running properly.

At least all of the major controls — clutch, brakes, gearshift, and steering — feel solid and smooth, even if they do require some effort. The column-mounted shifter, if anything, feels a little *too* tight, certainly not conducive to speed shifting.

The chair-high seats provide a commanding view down the road. The view up close isn't so bad, either, with gauges that read easily despite their fussy Deco detailing. And given the low cut of the windshield, surprisingly little buffeting disturbs the peace in the cockpit.

As one might expect, the stock Pack-

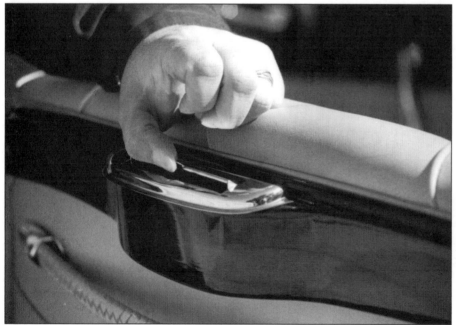

Top: *Packard corners with minimal body roll.* ***Above:*** *Chromed ashtray is fitted in highly polished wood trim on back of front seat.*

One-Twenty: Packard's Maligned Savior

Necessity has had many children, and regular *SIA* readers know by now that the Packard One-Twenty was one of them. From the banner year of 1928, when Packard built 49,698 automobiles and earned nearly $22 million, the company slipped quickly into the doldrums of the Depression, losing $6 million in 1932, on model-year sales of just 16,613 cars. Even then, Packard still enjoyed close to 40 percent of the market for cars costing more than $2,000; the problem was that the market itself was rapidly disappearing. And despite rosy predictions from Washington, no one was really sure that that market would ever return.

Packard President Alvan Macauley saw the future with admirable clarity: Cadillac, Lincoln, and the big Chryslers and Imperials would survive on the strength of Chevrolet, Ford, and Plymouth. The independent luxury car makers would have to find new markets or perish.

Actually, Packard had casually considered expanding into the more "popular" price range during the boom time of the twenties. The smart and stylish "Light Eight," with its 127.75-inch wheelbase, tentatively tested the lower-priced waters in 1932; it sold 6,750 units, accounting for more than one-third of Packard's production that year. But with prices in the $1,800-$1,950 range, the Light Eight clearly wasn't going to raise any sweat at Oldsmobile or Dodge agencies.

In March 1934, however, Macauley announced Packard's serious commitment to "marketing a wider range of products.... We started some time ago the development of this lower-priced car. The results are encouraging." Still, Packard had never truly mass-produced *anything;* this was totally new territory, and Macauley realized he needed new men who knew the terrain. To manage the whole operation, he called in master salesman Max Gilman, previously of Packard's New York office. To fill the position of assistant vice president for manufacturing and production manager for the new car line, Macauley hired George T. Christopher, who brought with him cost-cutting experience from Oldsmobile, Pontiac, and Buick. Also from Pontiac came Earl H. Smith and Edwin H. Johnson, to assist Packard veterans Jesse Vincent and Clyde Paton in keeping costs down. Erwin L. Bare, from Hupp, supervised engineering of the new bodies, while ex-Willys man E.A. Weiss oversaw the chassis.

Macauley even lured away Chevrolet sales manager Bill Packer to teach Packard dealers how to sell a mass-market product. Accustomed to leisure-class buyers who purchased new Packards with cash, the dealers had to learn how to promote installment loans, get the down-payment in hand, and close the deal fast.

At the same time, however, the old guard made sure the cost cutting didn't go *too* far. Colonel Vincent insisted on aluminum pistons. All body parts had to be painted as a set, to ensure a perfect color match. Closed cars would have wool upholstery; open cars, leather. Better, the Packard veterans argued, that the new car cost more than its competitors than to have it compromise the Packard name.

In all, Macauley committed $6.2 million to the effort. But the car that debuted in January 1935 was worth every nickel. Its wheelbase of 120 inches placed it squarely in Buick Series 50/Chrysler Airstream/ Oldsmobile Eight territory, while its massive X-braced frame assured Packard solidity. Its chassis featured independent front suspension and hydraulic brakes, neither of which would appear on the "senior" Packard Super Eight and Twelve until 1937.

Packard based the "Safe-T-fleX" suspension on the parallel-wishbone theory, but added a couple of clever twists. Delco lever shocks doubled as the upper wishbones, while the lower end of the steering upright was held by a single lateral link (which maintained the track) and a hefty, leading "torque arm" that met the frame in a ball of rubber beneath the cowl. The torque arm provided directional stability while at the same time transmitted road shocks to the strongest part of the frame and absorbed them there. The rear suspension, with its live axle and leaf springs, was somewhat more conventional. Even there, however, Packard engineered an innovation or two. Staggered lever shocks — the lever of the right-side unit projecting forward, the left side projecting back — helped control axle torque. An anti-roll bar linked the right-side shock absorber to the left side of the frame.

Vincent had briefly considered a V-8 for power, but the new car arrived with a 257-cubic-inch, L-head straight eight, developing 110 bhp at 3,850 rpm. Its fully counterbalanced crank, full floating aluminum pistons, austenitic exhaust valves, and aluminum head all typified Packard practice.

Packard named the new car after its wheelbase: the One-Twenty. Prices started at just $980 for the business coupe; the top-of-the-line touring sedan cost only $1,095. Sales positively exploded: Packard built 52,045 cars in 1935, handily shattering 1928's record.

1936 brought a three-eighths-inch longer stroke, raising displacement to 282 cubic inches and horsepower to 120. Packard now advertised "a horsepower for every inch." By August, Gilman announced a $5.1 million budget to double Packard's production capacity. The company closed the year with another new sales record of 83,226 automobiles and a profit of more than $7 million.

Packard reached even further downscale for 1937, introducing the $795 "Packard Six." This was essentially a One-Twenty minus five inches of wheelbase and two cylinders. At the opposite end of the junior-Packard scale, the company debuted a more lavishly trimmed "Deluxe" One-Twenty starting at $1,220; plus a seven-passenger One-Twenty sedan and limousine on a 138-inch wheelbase. Packard sales reached their all-time high of 109,518. Ninety percent of those were Sixes and One Twenties.

1938 brought revised styling: roomier, all-steel bodies — and a new nameplate. Having stretched the One-Twenty's wheelbase to 127.5 inches, Packard renamed it (temporarily) the "Packard Eight." A revised rear suspension featured extensive rubber isolation: Each spring leaf bore against its neighbor above through rubber pads, set into cups at its ends. A Panhard rod now limited axle sway. But a temporary worsening of the Depression dropped sales to a shade over 50,000 and brought a $1.6 million loss.

But 1939, the year our featured car's chassis left the factory, proved considerably kinder to Packard. As if to recapture the good fortune it had once brought, Packard revived the One-Twenty name for the 127.5-inch car; after all, the engine was still rated at 120 horsepower. Technical improvements included "Handishift" column-mounted gear-change and a third rear shock absorber acting directly on the Panhard rod. Gilman replaced Macauley as president, as Packard made some 75,000 cars and a modest $545,867.

With the One-Twenty and its six-cylinder companion, Packard had surely written *the* outstanding success story of the decade. Because of these cars alone, Packard quadrupled its sales and tripled its dealer network — all during the Depression years of 1932-39. Historians and enthusiasts who still blame the One-Twenty and the Six for sullying Packard's lofty status — and thereby ultimately killing the grand old marque — seem to have forgotten that, without the One-Twenty, Packard's demise would have certainly arrived at least 20 years sooner.

PACKARD

ard chassis rides smoothly, with a gentle but firm control of body motions. Yet its relatively quick steering ratio lends a sporty feel, and the big car corners with minimal body roll, despite audible complaints from the tires. The brakes require a firm foot but have little trouble bringing all that custom sheet metal to a swift and confident stop.

So despite its racy looks, the Vignale Packard doesn't drive like a sports car. But it does drive like a *Packard*. And had Vignale built more like it for a certain select clientele, that surely would have been enough. ❏

Acknowledgments and Bibliography
David Burgess-Wise, Ghia: Ford's Carrozzeria; *Fulvio Cinti*, "Fiat 1000 Record Sperimentale," Automobile Quarterly, *Volume 2, Number 3; Warren W. Fitzgerald*, "1952 Ferrari Type 340 Mexico Berlinetta," Road & Track, *May 1969; Beverly Rae Kimes (editor)*, Packard: A History of the Motorcar and the Company; *Beverly Rae Kimes and Henry Austin Clark, Jr.*, The Standard Catalog of American Cars 1805-1942; *Bob Mottar*, "Vignale di Torino," Sports Cars Illustrated, *December 1955; Ian Ward (editor)*, The World of Automobiles; *"Points on a Packard,"* The Autocar, *July 14, 1939; "Salon of Italian Coachwork,"* Road & Track, *March 1951.*
Thanks to David Burgess-Wise, Randy Ema, Kim M. Miller of the AACA Library and Research Center, Todd Wish, and special thanks to Mark Smith.

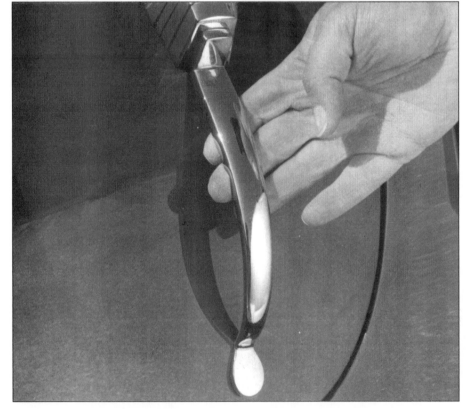

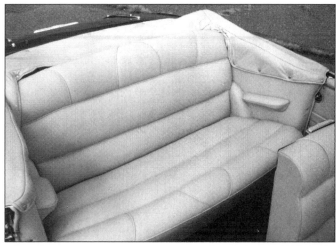

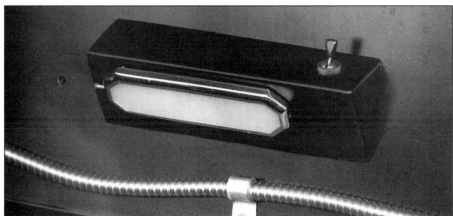

Facing page, top: L-head eight's rated at 120 bhp. **Center:** *More custom touches. Vignale badges accent handsome door pulls.* **Bottom:** *Elegantly shaped trunk handles incorporate separate locks.* **This page, above:** *Dash is disappointingly Spartan compared to the sumptuous swaths of leather in the seats.* **Left:** *Another Vignale addition, an underhood inspection light.* **Below:** *Packard's styling is most "continental"-looking in the back.*

Packard Model Year Production

Year	Production Totals		Year	Production Totals
1899	5		1931	15,450
1900	49		1932	16,613
1901	81		1933	4,800
1902-03	217		1934	8,000
1904	207		1935	31,956
1905	403		1936	61,027
1906	728		1937	87,243
1907	1,128		1938	55,718
1908	1,303		1939	46,405
1909	2,303		1940	98,000
1910	3,259		1941	72,855
1911	2,225		1942	33,776
1912	2,929		1946	30,793
1913	2,618		1947	51,086
1914	3,441		1948-49	145,441
1915	2,161		1949	59,390
1916	3,606		1950	46,650
1917	8,999		1951	**100,312***
1918-19	9,586		1952	62,601
1920-23	44,110		1953	89,730
1924	19,626		1954	28,205
1925-26	48,270		1955	55,517
1927	29,281		1956	28,835
1928	49,550		1957	4,809
1929	55,062		1958	2,622
1930	36,364			

* Packard's biggest year ever

Other Packard Books

The Coachbuilt Packard, Hugo Pfau

Fall of the Packard Motor Car Company, James A. Ward

Illustrated Packard Buyer's Guide, Richard Langworth

Packard, Dennis Adler

Packard, Richard Langworth

Packard, George H. Dammann and James Wren

The Packard Handbook, Robert B. Marvin

Packard Identification Guide Vol. 3, Robert Marvin

Packard Identification Manual, Packard International Motor Car Club

Packard Motor Car Vol. 1, Robert Marvin

Packard Motor Car Vol. 2, Robert Marvin

Packard Parts Interchange Manual Pt 1

Packard Parts Interchange Manual Pt 2

Packard Motor Cars 1935-1942 Photo Archive, Mark Patrick

Packard Motor Cars 1946-1958 Photo Archive, Mark Patrick

Packard 1946-1958 Gold Portfolio, R. M. Clarke

Packard at Speed, Robert Neal

Packard Engines, 1899-1958

Year	Cylinders	Displacement (cubic inches)	Bore x Stroke	Output
			Net horsepower ratings: 1899 to 1912	
1899	Horizontal-1	142.6	5.50 x 6.00 in.	9
1900	H-1	142.6	5.50 x 6.00 in.	9
1901	H-1	183.8	6.00 x 6.50 in.	12
1902	H-1	183.8	6.00 x 6.50 in.	12
1902	H-2	367.5	6.00 x 6.50 in.	24
1903	H-1	183.8	6.00 x 6.50 in.	12
1903	Inline-4	251.1	4.00 x 5.00 in.	24
1904	I-4	241.7	3.88 x 5.13 in.	22
1905	I-4	265.7	4.06 x 5.13 in.	28
1906	I-4	349.9	4.50 x 5.50 in.	24
1907	I-4	431.9	5.00 x 5.50 in.	30
1908	I-4	431.9	5.00 x 5.50 in.	30
1909	I-4	265.7	4.06 x 5.13 in.	18
1909	I-4	431.9	5.00 x 5.50 in.	30
1910	I-4	265.7	4.06 x 5.13 in.	18
1910	I-4	431.9	5.00 x 5.50 in.	30
1911	I-4	265.7	4.06 x 5.13 in.	18
1911	I-4	431.9	5.00 x 5.50 in.	30
1912	I-4	265.7	4.06 x 5.13 in.	18
1912	I-4	431.9	5.00 x 5.50 in.	30
1912	I-6	525	4.50 x 5.50 in.	48
			Gross Horsepower ratings: 1913 to 1958	
1913	I-6	415	4.00 x 5.50 in.	60
1913	I-6	525	4.50 x 5.50 in.	82
1914	I-6	415	4.00 x 5.50 in.	60
1914	I-6	525	4.50 x 5.50 in.	82
1915	I-6	415	4.00 x 5.50 in.	65
1915	I-6	525	4.50 x 5.50 in.	48
1916	V-12	424.1	3.00 x 5.00 in.	88
1917	V-12	424.1	3.00 x 5.00 in.	88
1918	V-12	424.1	3.00 x 5.00 in.	90
1919	V-12	424.1	3.00 x 5.00 in.	90
1920	V-12	424.1	3.00 x 5.00 in.	90
1921	I-6	241.5	3.38 x 4.50 in.	52
1921	V-12	424.1	3.00 x 5.00 in.	90
1922	I-6	268.4	3.38 x 5.00 in.	54
1922	V-12	424.1	3.00 x 5.00 in.	90
1923	I-6	268.4	3.38 x 5.00 in.	54

Packard Engines, 1899-1958

continued

Year	Cylinders	Displacement	Bore x Stroke	Output
1923	V-12	424.1	3.00 x 5.00 in.	90
1924	I-6	268.4	3.38 x 5.00 in.	54
1924	I-8	357.8	3.00 x 5.00 in.	85
1925	I-6	288.6	3.50 x 5.00 in.	60
1925	I-8	357.8	3.00 x 5.00 in.	85
1926	I-6	288.6	3.50 x 5.00 in.	60
1926	I-8	357.8	3.00 x 5.00 in.	85
1927	I-6	288.6	3.50 x 5.00 in.	82
1927	I-8	384.8	3.50 x 5.00 in.	109
1928	I-6	288.6	3.50 x 5.00 in.	82
1928	I-8	384.8	3.50 x 5.00 in.	109
1929	I-8	319.2	3.19 x 5.00 in.	90
1929	I-8	384.8	3.50 x 5.00 in.	105
1929	I-8	384.8	3.50 x 5.00 in.	130
1930	I-8	319.2	3.19 x 5.00 in.	90
1930	I-8	384.8	3.50 x 5.00 in.	106
1930	I-8	384.8	3.50 x 5.00 in.	125
1930	I-8	384.8	3.50 x 5.00 in.	145
1931	I-8	319.2	3.19 x 5.00 in.	100
1931	I-8	384.8	3.50 x 5.00 in.	120
1932	I-8	319.2	3.19 x 5.00 in.	110
1932	I-8	384.8	3.50 x 5.00 in.	135
1932	V-12	445.5	3.44 x 4.00 in.	160
1933	I-8	319.2	3.19 x 5.00 in.	120
1933	I-8	384.8	3.50 x 5.00 in.	145
1933	V-12	445.5	3.44 x 4.00 in.	160
1934	I-8	319.2	3.19 x 5.00 in.	120
1934	I-8	384.8	3.50 x 5.00 in.	145
1934	V-12	445.5	3.44 x 4.00 in.	160
1935	I-8	256.2	3.25 x 3.88 in.	110
1935	I-8	319.2	3.19 x 5.00 in.	130
1935	I-8	384.8	3.50 x 5.00 in.	150
1935	V-12	473.3	3.44 x 4.25 in.	175
1936	I-8	282	3.25 x 4.25 in.	120
1936	I-8	319.2	3.19 x 5.00 in.	130
1936	I-8	384.8	3.50 x 5.00 in.	150
1936	V-12	473.3	3.44 x 4.25 in.	175
1936	V-12	473.3	3.44 x 4.25 in.	180
1937	I-6	237	3.44 x 4.25 in.	100
1937	I-8	282	3.25 x 4.25 in.	120
1937	I-8	319.2	3.19 x 5.00 in.	135
1937	V-12	473.3	3.44 x 4.25 in.	175
1937	V-12	473.3	3.44 x 4.25 in.	180
1938	I-6	245	3.50 x 4.25 in.	100
1938	I-8	282	3.25 x 4.25 in.	120
1938	I-8	319.2	3.19 x 5.00 in.	130
1938	V-12	473.3	3.44 x 4.25 in.	175
1939	I-6	245	3.50 x 4.25 in.	100
1939	I-8	282	3.25 x 4.25 in.	120
1939	I-8	319.2	3.19 x 5.00 in.	130

Year	Cylinders	Displacement	Bore x Stroke	Output
1939	V-12	473.3	3.44 x 4.25 in.	175
1940	I-6	245	3.50 x 4.25 in.	100
1940	I-8	282	3.25 x 4.25 in.	120
1940	I-8	319.2	3.19 x 5.00 in.	130
1940	I-8	356	3.50 x 4.63 in.	160
1941	I-6	245	3.50 x 4.25 in.	100
1941	I-8	282	3.25 x 4.25 in.	120
1941	I-8	282	3.25 x 4.50 in.	125
1941	I-8	356	3.50 x 4.63 in.	160
1942	I-6	245	3.50 x 4.25 in.	105
1942	I-8	282	3.25 x 4.25 in.	125
1942	I-8	356	3.50 x 4.63 in.	165
1946	I-6	245	3.50 x 4.25 in.	105
1946	I-8	282	3.25 x 4.25 in.	125
1946	I-8	356	3.50 x 4.63 in.	165
1947	I-6	245	3.50 x 4.25 in.	105
1947	I-8	282	3.25 x 4.25 in.	125
1947	I-8	356	3.50 x 4.63 in.	165
1948	I-8	288	3.50 x 3.75 in.	125
1948	I-8	327	3.50 x 4.25 in.	145
1948	I-8	356	3.50 x 4.63 in.	160
1949	I-8	288	3.50 x 3.75 in.	130
1949	I-8	327	3.50 x 4.25 in.	145
1949	I-8	356	3.50 x 4.63 in.	160
1950	I-8	288	3.50 x 3.75 in.	135
1950	I-8	327	3.50 x 4.25 in.	150
1950	I-8	356	3.50 x 4.63 in.	165
1951	I-8	288	3.50 x 3.75 in.	135
1951	I-8	327	3.50 x 4.25 in.	150
1951	I-8	327	3.50 x 4.25 in.	155
1952	I-8	288	3.50 x 3.75 in.	135
1952	I-8	288	3.50 x 3.75 in.	138
1952	I-8	327	3.50 x 4.25 in.	150
1952	I-8	327	3.50 x 4.25 in.	155
1953	I-8	288	3.50 x 3.75 in.	150
1953	I-8	327	3.50 x 4.25 in.	160
1953	I-8	327	3.50 x 4.25 in.	180
1954	I-8	288	3.50 x 3.75 in.	150
1954	I-8	327	3.50 x 4.25 in.	165
1954	I-8	327	3.50 x 4.25 in.	185
1954	I-8	359	3.56 x 4.50 in.	212
1955	V-8	320	3.81 x 3.50 in.	225
1955	V-8	352	4.00 x 3.50 in.	245
1955	V-8	352	4.00 x 3.50 in.	260
1955	V-8	352	4.00 x 3.50 in.	275
1956	V-8	352	4.00 x 3.50 in.	240
1956	V-8	352	4.00 x 3.50 in.	275
1956	V-8	374	4.13 x 3.50 in.	290
1956	V-8	374	4.13 x 3.50 in.	310
1957	V-8	289	3.56 x 3.63 in.	275
1958	V-8	289	3.56 x 3.63 in.	225
1958	V-8	289	3.56 x 3.63 in.	275

Packard Clubs & Specialists

For a complete list of all regional Packard clubs and national clubs' chapters, visit **Car Club Central** at **www.hemmings.com**. With nearly 10,000 car clubs listed, it's the largest car club site in the world! Not wired? For the most up-to-date information, consult the latest issue of *Hemmings Motor News* and/or *Hemmings' Collector Car Almanac*. Call toll free, **1-800-CAR-HERE, Ext. 550**.

PACKARD CLUBS

1948-1950 Packard Convertible Roster
84 Hoy Ave.
Fords, NJ 08863
732-738-7859

602 Packard Register
902 Packard Register
317 E. Acacia Rd.
Milwaukee, WI 53217

Blue Ribbon Packard Club
4210 St. Thomas Ave.
Louisville, KY 40218
502-499-9956

The Eastern Packard Club
P.O. Box 1259
Stratford, CT 06615

Old Dominion Packard Club
P.O. Box Q
Bethany, WV 26032

Packard Automobile Classics Inc.
420 S. Ludlow St.
Dayton, OH 45402
972-709-6185

Packard International Motor Car Club
302 French St.
Santa Ana, CA 92701
714-541-8431
(7 regional chapters; 2 international chapters)

Packard Truck Organization
1196 Mountain Rd.
York Springs, PA 17372
717-528-4920

The Packard V-8 Roster
1948-50 Packard Convertible Roster
84 Hoy Ave.
Fords, NJ 08863
732-738-7859

Other Important Clubs

American Truck Historical Society
300 Office Park Dr.
Birmingham, AL 35223
205-870-0566
(70 regional chapters; 7 international chapters)

Antique Automobile Club of America
501 W. Governor Road
Hershey, PA 17033
717-534-1910
(311 regional chapters; 5 international chapters)

Antique Truck Club of America
PO Box 291
Hershey, PA 17033
717-533-9032
(17 regional chapters; 1 international chapter)

Classic Car Club of America
1645 Des Plaines River Road, Suite 7A
Des Plaines, IL 60018-2206
847-390-0443
(26 regional chapters)

Horseless Carriage Club of America
3311 Fairhaven Dr.
Orange, CA 92866-1357
661-326-1023
(91 regional chapters; 7 international chapters)

National Woodie Club
P.O. Box 6134
Lincoln, NE 68506
402-488-0990

Veteran Motor Car Club of America
4441 W. Altadena Ave.
Glendale, AZ 85304-3526
800-428-7327
(82 regional chapters)

PACKARD SPECIALISTS

Brinton's Antique Auto Parts
6826 SW McVey Ave.
Redmond, OR 97756
541-548-3483
Used parts, 1920-1958

Hibernia Auto Restorations
One Maple Terrace
Hibernia, NJ 07842
973-627-1882
Full restoration and service

Kanter Auto Products
76 Monroe St.
Boonton, NJ 07005
800-526-1096
Mechanical parts and accessories

Lincoln Highway Packards
Main St.
Schellsburg, PA 15559
814-733-4356
Packard restoration and repair

Packard Store
9 Hall Hill Road
Sterling, CT 06377
860-564-5345
Body and mechanical parts

Potomac Packard
3031 Hunt Rd.
Oakton, VA 22124
800-859-9532
Wiring harnesses & electrical parts

Al Prueitt & Sons
8 Winter Ave.
Glen Rock, PA 17327
717-428-1305
Complete restorations

White Post Restorations
P.O. Drawer D
White Post, VA 22663
540-837-1140
Showroom quality restorations